"In *Not Ashamed,* Ruth Tucker adds another engrossing chapter to the story of Christian missions—a contemporary chapter that is still being written. It's the story of how Moishe Rosen, a young American Jew, came to faith in Jesus as the promised Messiah of Israel. By winning to that faith a following of other young Jews, he spearheaded an evangelistic movement that through the years has been making an international impact.

"In *Not Ashamed* meet some of the unique and gifted individuals who have served with this cutting-edge organization. Learn about the unconventional methods of witnessing that have proved to be so effective and provoked such angry criticism. Be blessed as you read this account of how God's Spirit has been working as powerfully in our day as He did in the first century, bringing not only Gentiles but Jews to Himself."

VERNON C. GROUNDS
CHANCELLOR, DENVER SEMINARY

"Jesus is for Jews. *Not Ashamed: The Story of Jews for Jesus* is the story of a people dedicated to making that known. From beginning to end, this book tells about the tenacity and determination necessary to make Jesus known among 'His' people. This is a story dedicated to God."

DWIGHT GIBSON
NORTH AMERICAN DIRECTOR,
EVANGELICAL FELLOWSHIP

D0052813

# NOT ASHAMED

## The Story of Jews for Jesus

## Ruth A. Tucker

*forward by*

## J.I. Packer

Multnomah Publishers® *Sisters, Oregon*

NOT ASHAMED: The Story of Jews for Jesus
published by Multnomah Publishers, Inc.

© 1999 by Ruth A. Tucker
International Standard Book Number: 1-57673-700-4

Cover illustration by Henk Dawson

Designed by Kirk DouPonce

Scripture quotations are from:
*New American Standard Bible* (NASB) © 1960, 1977 by the Lockman Foundation

*Multnomah* is a trademark of Multnomah Publishers, Inc.,
and is registered in the U.S. Patent and Trademark Office.

Printed in the United States of America

For information:
MULTNOMAH PUBLISHERS, INC.
POST OFFICE BOX 1720
SISTERS, OREGON 97759

Library of Congress Cataloging–in–Publication Data:
Tucker, Ruth A.
Not Ashamed/by Ruth A. Tucker
o.cm.
ISBN 1-57673-602-4

00 01 02 03 04 05 — 10 9 8 7 6 5 4 3 2 1

# Table of Contents

# Foreword

Jews for Jesus is a worldwide Christian mission that was born against the background of California's Jesus movement and has grown steadily ever since. Holding that Jesus of Nazareth—God incarnate, crucified, risen, and now reigning—is the true Messiah foretold in the Old Testament and the true fulfillment of Jewish hopes, the mission exists to press his claims on Jewish people everywhere. It is based on two principles.

First, Jews who receive Jesus Christ as their Lord and Savior and who are "completed" and "fulfilled" thereby do not need to leave behind their Jewish identity or break with Jewish ways. As Judaizing was not a theological requirement for the first gentile Christians, so gentilizing is not a cultural requirement for today's Jewish believers. Though they belong in the Christian church, which has been mainly gentile—non-Jewish, that is—for most of its life, within the church they are free to be as Jewish as they like.

Second, up-front, in-your-face challenge, with as much humor, chutzpah, and goodwill as possible, is the way to approach Jews evangelistically.

Principle one has to be maintained against official Judaism, which (let us be clear) is a post- and anti-Christian mutation of the Jewish religion that Christ knew. Official Judaism routinely denies that a Jew who becomes a Christian is still a Jew. Principle two means moving beyond the cool, low-key evangelistic style that often sets Western Christians apart from, for instance, their more exuberant African and Latin American counterparts.

Paul's "to the Jew first" (Romans 1:16) remains a pointer to a permanent priority in Christian evangelism. For many centuries the church lost sight of it, and some moderns have argued that Jews need not be evangelized at all, but Jews for Jesus is what it sounds like—Jewish Christians sharing their faith with other Jews—and we should thank God that they are there doing that.

Evangelicals differ on whether the state of Israel, now celebrating its first half-century, is a fulfillment of Bible prophecy, just as they differ on other questions about prophecy and Christ's return. Jews for Jesus leaves these questions open for discussion and dogmatizes only on the principle that the spiritual future for Jewish people is in the Christian community.

Ruth Tucker was the ideal person to write the history of Jews for Jesus' first twenty-five years. She has done a fine job, particularly in her profiling of Moishe Rosen, the portly, near-genius who envisioned and shaped the mission from the start. As Moishe would be the first to insist, the story is centrally about God's grace, and God must have all the glory for it.

So may God continue to use Jews for Jesus in the twenty-first century as he has done in the twentieth, and to him be all the praise, first to last.

J. I. Packer

# Introduction

"Southern Baptists Face Firestorm of Criticism for Plan to Attract Jews." The headline grabbed my attention. The story went on to say that in the fifty years since the Holocaust, mainline Christian churches have stopped talking about converting Jews. However, aggressive evangelical groups such as the San Francisco.organization "Jews for Jesus" have continued the crusade.

"Since the Holocaust." I pondered those words. I was born in 1945 at the very end of World War II. I had no participation in that war, and if I had, it would have been as an American, helping to stop Hitler. Nevertheless, I am an American of German heritage—my maiden name is Stellrecht. My German relatives either insist that they opposed Hitler or that they did not know what he was up to regarding the Jewish people. Yet I suspect that if they did not know, it was because they did not want to know. That was true of the vast majority of people in Germany at the time.

Through the years as I have learned more and more about the Holocaust, I have taken on part of that collective guilt of the German people. I remember describing this sense of guilt to my African students at Moffat College of the Bible in Kenya years ago. They were truly awestruck that a woman of German heritage was in their classroom repenting for the Holocaust. I was sincere, and they knew it.

Yet I realize that my penitence is not true repentance because I know that I was in no way responsible for what happened. My experience brings to mind the great German pastor and theologian, Dietrich Bonhoeffer. He was a friend of the Jewish people and eventually was hanged for conspiring against Hitler. Bonhoeffer wrote and preached on "cheap grace." My particular disorder is not a matter of cheap grace, but of cheap guilt. It is guilt that does not cost a thing, but allows me to be a part of a collective psyche of repentance for something I did not do. The only price I pay—if it is a price at all—is my commitment never to do anything that would offend a Jewish person. I do not mean only those who suffered personally in the Holocaust, but people whose ancestors suffered and died—any people in fact, who are connected through culture and heritage to those who suffered and died.

There is some of Hitler and the German people in all societies. There have been, and in some case still are, terrible dictators in Russia, China, Africa, South America—and in North America. These may not be on the scale of Hitler. Nevertheless, they take advantage of impressionable followers in an effort to eradicate unwanted peoples. Pol Pot, the Cambodian leader who is blamed for the deaths of two million and who died recently, immediately comes to mind. And on the other end of history, the Old Testament tells of atrocities among the Jewish people that we might wish were not recorded in Scripture.

What, then, ought to be our response to the Holocaust? Of course, it ought to be one of great sorrow and sadness and repentance—repentance for our own sins, the ones for which we are responsible. It ought also to be one of remembering and vowing that it will never happen again; to that end, our response ought to include education and humanitarianism and love for fellow human beings.

Should this collective response include a consensus that since this evil was perpetrated on the Jewish people, all Jewish evangelism ought to stop? *If* evangelism is an evil and destructive endeavor, certainly it should cease with regard to Jewish people and everyone else. Contrarily, if evangelism is a good endeavor—whether it is focused on an African-American (whose ancestors suffered in slavery), a Cambodian, a Mormon, or an unconverted member of a Baptist church—then it would truly be an insult to disregard the Jewish people in the proclamation of Christ.

Hitler's legacy has confused many people. Christians who believe that Jesus brings joy, peace, and the only way of reconciliation to God cannot allow themselves to be deterred by the fact that many people find that conviction insulting or even demeaning. The idea is to present the good news the way Jesus himself might present it—with love and compassion—and let others decide whether they will be insulted or intrigued.

And this is what Jews for Jesus is all about.

## THE ROSEN PARTNERSHIP

The organization of Jews for Jesus is philosophically driven, as Moishe Rosen, its founder and longtime director, insists. Yet the organization also has been personality driven—as much as Moishe would challenge that view. Jews for Jesus is more than an organization or ministry. It is a phenomenon. Like other such ministries that have erupted on the scene throughout history—such as the Salvation Army in the nineteenth century, with William Booth at the helm, or the Quakers two centuries earlier, led by George Fox—a strong, colorful, and controversial individual rose up as the "prophet-founder." In Jews for Jesus, Moishe is that individual.

Moishe likes to tell this story about his early days of faith. When he announced his plans to go to Bible college in the East, his father feared he may have truly gone over the edge in his fervor for Jesus. He insisted that Moishe see a psychiatrist. Moishe was not offended because "I thought there was always the possibility that I might really be insane." After two sessions (at fifty dollars an hour), the doctor sent Moishe a letter: To whom it may concern: Martin Rosen...was examined psychiatrically by the undersigned on August 2 and 3, 1954. He was found to be psychiatrically normal. In summing it up Moishe says, "So no matter what anyone says about my mental stability these days, I at least have a letter to prove [my sanity]. Most people don't."[1]

A letter written more than forty years ago does not prove a thing. No doubt many still question Moishe's sanity. But today, unlike forty-five years ago, Moishe simply does not care. If any of his traits rises above others, perhaps it is his sense of security. He is who he is, and if people have problems with that, so be it.

That sense of security became quickly evident to me as I began working on this book. My first two encounters with Moishe did not go as I had hoped. Indeed, I found him downright unpleasant. He was under the impression that I had come to write a promotional book for the organization, and he was not eager to take part in that. I persisted and tried to make my case. He interrupted, insisting that it would be a waste of time to write a volume of glowing testimonies. To my every effort to defend my credentials as a writer and historian, he responded by putting the most unflattering face on Jews for Jesus, as only he could do. He kept insisting that if I were going to maintain my credibility as a historian, I would have to cover all the conflicts and scandals and internal dissension that had ever arisen. I argued back that my purpose was not to do an exposé of the movement—that task would be left to someone else. My goal was to provide a trustworthy history of the people and the organization.

In the end, I think I charmed him more than I convinced him. We proceeded with plans for interviews, but I will never forget my bewilderment over that first conversation. Before I agreed to write this book, I had asked, "How much interference will I get from Mr. Rosen?" I was concerned that he might want to put his own spin on my work and turn it into just another exaggerated Protestant hagiography. I quickly discovered that Moishe's intent was the exact opposite, and I never doubted for a moment that he was for real.

The story of Jews for Jesus cannot be grasped without an attempt to understand Moishe Rosen. He is a complex man, who becomes even more enigmatic when viewed in light of his half-century-long marriage to Ceil. To say they are opposites is an understatement. Ceil is as strong willed today as she was when she stood up to Moishe in the second year of their marriage and told him that her commitment to God came before her commitment to him. On the other hand, she is shy and reserved with strangers, and nothing in her youth or early adult years could have prepared her to be married to a zealot like Moishe, a self-described fanatic when it comes to promoting the gospel of Jesus.

The battles and controversies that raged around Jews for Jesus only seemed to energize Moishe, while the effect on Ceil was often the opposite. Ceil, however, never pretended to be something she was not. From the beginning, she did not participate in street preaching or "broadsiding"—handing out pamphlets on crowded city sidewalks. Once—and only once—she stood on a soapbox and gave her testimony on a New York street corner. A photo exists to prove it. On one other occasion—only once—she handed out broadsides. Moishe had told her, "For your own sake, you should try

these difficult things at least once, and then if you feel you can't do it, don't."
It was wise and loving counsel, and she followed it. When she decided that
those activities were not for her, she never did them again. She did not make
excuses for her absence; none was necessary. Ceil, more than anyone else,
has kept Moishe from acting more on his eccentricities than he might otherwise have done.

As I reflect on their many years of marriage and ministry, I am reminded
of A. W. Tozer's perceptive portrait of A. B. Simpson, founder of the Christian and Missionary Alliance, and his wife Margaret.

> The wife of a prophet has no easy road to travel. She cannot always
> see her husband's vision, yet as his wife she must go along with him
> wherever his vision takes him. She is compelled therefore to walk
> by faith a good deal of the time—and her husband's faith at that.
> Mrs. Simpson tried hard to understand, but if she sometimes lost
> patience with her devoted but impractical husband she is not for
> that cause to be too much censured....Mr. Simpson had heard the
> Voice ordering him out, and he went without fear. His wife had
> heard nothing, but she was compelled to go anyway. That she was
> a bit unsympathetic at times has been held against her by many.
> That she managed to keep within far sight of her absent-minded
> high soaring husband should be set down to her everlasting honor.
> It is no easy job being wife to such a man as A. B. Simpson was.[2]

## EAVESDROPPING ON A COUNCIL MEETING

Moishe is in many ways larger than life—physically, intellectually, and tem-
peramentally. Yet despite his overwhelming presence—and I mean presence—he cannot be equated with the movement or organization itself.
Philosophy and strategy drive Jews for Jesus, making it far bigger than the
person and personality of Moishe Rosen. That became very evident in the
1996 transfer of leadership from Moishe to David Brickner. Without Moishe
at the helm, the movement is not quite the same as it was. It is, some would

say, a more democratic organization with an emphasis on shared leadership. David is clearly the executive director, but doesn't have the *presence* that Moishe did. Consequently, the collective mindset is more evident. Indeed, it is fair to say that the organization itself has a personality. It is a collective personality that has inherited traits from its father Moishe, but like any child, it has a temperament of its own.

The organization is composed of many headstrong and opinionated individuals. This was apparent at a council meeting I attended in San Francisco. Leaders from the home office were present, as well as those who had flown in from across the country and around the world. I was immediately struck by how efficiently the meetings were run and how effectively a consensus was reached, often after intense and sometimes heated discussion. Some matters were tedious to me as an outsider—such as the issue of educational funding for staff children, though it did interest me that one of the strongest supporters was a single woman who personally had nothing to gain. Other matters grabbed my attention, particularly the issue relating to a charge of sexual harassment. The accused was a young man working for the organization; the accuser was a female volunteer. Compared with the 1998–99 White House scandals that made headlines, the charges were relatively mild and were not reported until almost two years after the fact. Nevertheless, the council took the issue very seriously and resolved it in a way that could serve as a model for other organizations dealing with such matters.

Another item on the council's agenda was a statement of core values. This brief document was the product of many long hours of work by a subcommittee, and the only business of the council was to approve, disapprove, or amend it. Again, whether it was the time of the afternoon or the subject matter, my interest was not riveted on the document. One part of the discussion, however, did grab my attention—a suggestion that the document be amended to include the core value of *fun* or *community* or *sense of humor.* There was an immediate reaction from several on the council that such things, while true of the organization, were not core values per se. Others thought such a statement necessary in order to reflect accurately the character of Jews for Jesus. I do not remember which argument won the day, and to me it does not really matter. What I found most interesting was the seemingly unanimous consensus in the group that this ministry did have a unique spirit of fun and humor and community. And this was not a group of "honeymooners." It takes many years of working up through the ranks to sit on the council.

This collective sense of humor and community was evident in several situations. Before I left San Francisco, I wanted to develop an outline of pivotal events. One evening I managed to get three of the "old-timers" together. Tuvya, Susan, and Jhan had been with the movement since the 1970s. While I typed on my laptop computer, they talked—often all at the same time. My goal was to record certain events and later go back to them, but getting those three off one event and on to the next was more of a challenge than I had expected. They argued and squabbled and contested one another's versions of the same account, and they laughed. I have rarely been in the midst of such laughter, as they recounted long-forgotten incidents. It was like a raucous family gathering when the intensity of raw emotion is suddenly interrupted by a chorus of laughter. That impromptu late-night meeting gave me a glimpse of the collective personality of Jews for Jesus.

## AN OUTSIDER'S PERSPECTIVE

One advantage in getting to know Jews for Jesus was that I had no preconceived ideas. Certainly I had been aware of the organization over the years. David Mishkin, a San Francisco-based missionary, had made a seder presentation at my home church the day before I received a phone call—out of the blue—asking me to consider this assignment. I was unaware of the controversies that had been so much a part of the movement in the early years; nor was I aware that many regarded this movement as extreme when it came to proper Christian behavior.

My training and background helped prepare me for this assignment. I am a historian, and years of research and analysis for my master's thesis and doctoral dissertation aided me in my inquiry. I have also done significant research in the area of cultic movements, which culminated in the book: *Another Gospel: Cults, Alternative Religions and the New Age Movement.* From that study, I can say without reservation that Jews for Jesus is not a cult (as it has been called on occasion), nor is it cultic in its practices or organizational structure. I have also worked closely with, and done research on, three other groups that have been deemed cultic or "on the fringe." These are the Worldwide Church of God (which has a cultic heritage), Jesus People USA, and University Bible Fellowship.

From these groups I have come to understand, at least to a small degree, how it feels to face opposition and rejection—sometimes from fellow Christians. I have been personally criticized for overlooking heresy and befriending those whom others view as dangerous or outside Christian orthodoxy. Controversy is not something I sought, but I was convinced in each case that I was doing what would most honor God.

And so it is with my relationship with Jews for Jesus. I was warned that taking on this project might jeopardize my reputation (whatever that is). However, again I was convinced that I could do an honest investigation that would shed light on a group that has often been unfairly maligned.

Even before I had signed on the dotted line, I was telling a friend about the project, and her response, like so many others, was that Jews for Jesus are not Jews; they are Christians and should not claim to be Jews. I reminded her that Jewish people come in many varieties: Orthodox and ultra-Orthodox, Conservative and Reform, nonreligious (atheistic and agnostic), political and cultural. She responded by insisting that accepting Jesus as Messiah makes one a Christian and that you cannot be a Christian and a Jew at the same time. If I had really wanted to marshal a defense for my argument, I might have cited America's most famous settler of disputes, Ann Landers, who weighed in on the subject in 1984: "A Jew who wishes to dissociate himself from Judaism and take up Catholicism, Christian Science or Confucianism, for example, is still a Jew by heritage. No amount of disavowing will transform him into a Gentile."[3]

As a historian, what I find most ironic—perhaps even amusing—in these charges and countercharges is that through the ages, it has been the denial of one's Jewish heritage that has caused bitterness in the Jewish community. Anyone born of a Jewish mother is a Jew, and the fact that some Jews choose to pass as non-Jews infuriates many people. A recent example of this involved Secretary of State Madeleine Albright, whom some accused of denying her Jewish heritage.

But in the case of Jews for Jesus, the situation is reversed. I do understand to some extent one Jewish person accusing another of not being a Jew. I grew up in fundamentalism, and identifying who was and was not a Christian was part of the framework of that upbringing. Even as a young adult, I was sure my friend Kit couldn't be a Christian because she was a Lutheran. I now know differently. Yet Christianity, unlike Judaism, is defined by doctrine and belief. There is no such thing as an *atheist Christian,* yet there are *atheist Jews*—because Jewish people are defined by so much more than religion.

As a student of religions, all this makes sense to me. Historic Christianity is self-defined by its three branches—Orthodox, Roman Catholic, and Protestant. They all believe that Jesus is the promised Messiah and truly God and that the Bible is the only Scripture given by God. Thus, while Mormons claim to be Christian, I would argue that they are not. They have three additional scriptures and many major doctrines that have no basis in the Bible or in historic Christian teachings. On the other hand, when a Jewish person claims to be a messianic Jew or a Christian—or when a Christian with at least one Jewish parent claims to be Jewish—I have no difficulty with that duality. Being Jewish, unlike being Christian, is not strictly defined by a single book or set of doctrines. Of course, the Torah is *the* book for religious Jews, but many nonreligious Jews ignore it altogether.

I find this controversy over who is a Jew fascinating. As part of my research for this project I watched a taped copy of a Sally Jesse Raphael show that featured two staff members of Jews for Jesus, Susan Perlman and Tuvya Zaretsky, an Episcopal priest, and a Jewish rabbi, who debated who is or is not a Jew. The rabbi was adamant that Susan and Tuvya were not Jewish, and a woman in the audience presented a pitiful scenario about how sad it was for the children of these professed messianic Jews to struggle with their identity and be confronted with so many different holidays. I listened with amusement. Having just spent time with Jews for Jesus in San Francisco, I found that they rather enjoyed celebrating a lot of holidays. And they—and I—have no doubt at all who they are. They look Jewish. They act Jewish. They are Jewish.

People have no problem identifying certain characteristics of people within their own culture. I was reminded of this at a recent meeting of the American Society of Missiology in Chicago. At lunch, one professor accused me in a lighthearted way of being too direct and asking too many pointed questions. She said that as an Asian (she identified with the Filipinos with whom she has worked), she was much more subtle and less direct. Then she made an interesting comment. Knowing I was working on this book, she laughingly suggested that I was taking on the ways of my Jewish friends, implying that Jews are more direct than Asians. Yes, Jewish people I have met tend to be forthright and direct. But so do I, and that way of relating has helped me on this project. I am simply not trained in the art of subtlety, and in my interviewing and research I have an advantage in dealing with people who are not especially subtle either.

Researching and writing this book has broadened me as a Christian and historian. I have come to appreciate the breadth that Jewish believers add to the Christian faith. As one who was schooled in dispensationalism, with a heavy focus on the writings of the apostle Paul, I have seen among messianic Jews a great appreciation for the Old Testament and the blending of the Old and the New. I have also come to know and appreciate Hebrew Christians through generations of church history, and my new interest in this move-ment will certainly find its way into the church history text I am in the process of writing.

Susan Perlman called me to propose this project at a most inopportune time as I was overwhelmed with other responsibilities. Yet I accepted the invitation to write the story of Jews for Jesus as the opportunity of a lifetime, and it has turned out to be just that.

This book is not a chronological catalogue of events, but a depiction of many of the people, ideas, and adventures that have comprised the move-ment and the mission known as Jews for Jesus. Nor is the book compre-hensive by any means; to try to describe everything that has made Jews for

Jesus would fill several volumes, and I was commissioned to write but one. I do hope that readers will find the book informative, but would refer them to the organization itself should they be interested in such matters as the group's doctrinal statement, mission statement, and core values.

The word *shalom* comes to mind as I reflect on the twenty-five-year history of Jews for Jesus. This word has deep meaning for me, and I do not use it lightly. I consider the word a gift from Jewish people to all people. It is like no other word in English or any other language—a word that means far more than *peace*. Shalom connotes contentment and serenity and even inner joy amid adversity. It means "All is well." It also carries the meaning of wholeness and completeness. For most of twenty years, I have used the word in signing my books as well as all my correspondence. A shalom plaque given me by dear friends hangs in my kitchen, and another hangs in the hallway upstairs.

There truly has been a sense of peace and contentment amid adversity in the ministry of Jews for Jesus. More important, there has been a certainty of completeness and wholeness—the wholeness that they as Jews have found in Jesus. That shalom has been part of the relationship I have had with this ministry over the past several months.

My life has been transformed—for the better—through this encounter with some of the most sensitive, devoted, and clear-thinking people I have ever met. To them, shalom. To them, I dedicate this book.

# CHAPTER ONE

# MOISHE ROSEN

## *The Man behind the Movement*

W riting biographical material about a living person is a dangerous pursuit. As a historian, I would much rather write about dead people. I like the sense of closure in researching a person from beginning to end. Having said that, I surely do not wish for the soon demise of Moishe Rosen, founder of Jews for Jesus. I would like to think of him as a friend—though I have only begun to get to know him. And even as I come to know him better, I wonder, "Can I grasp the essence of this man?"

If Moishe has one overriding attribute, I believe it is that he is ever changing and always adapting. Some of his ideas and opinions shift from day to day; consistency would not be his primary attribute (except regarding doctrines or principles—those he repeats quite firmly, without variation).

The freedom with which Moishe expressed his thoughts to me certainly did not seem calculated to impress. Some of our interviews seemed little more than a stream of consciousness on his part. I found myself wondering, "Why is he telling me this? I did not ask—and do I really want to know?" As I reflect back now, I am convinced that if there was any calculation behind his blatant honesty, it was to build trust. And that is what he has done over the years with his "followers" (a term that Moishe adamantly rejects).

During the early years of Jews for Jesus, Moishe appeared to be headstrong and patriarchal. Yet his authoritarian style (so noted by critics) served to protect and refine his young followers. I doubt that he received much power-based ego gratification since power, as an end in itself, appears to be the least of his needs.

Despite Moishe's insistence that those who join the staff are not "followers," as

*I see it, they certainly were in the early years—and arguably, still are today. He insists that he does not want followers and never did. All he wants is for people to follow the Lord. It is dangerous, he warns, for people to follow an individual with all his weaknesses and flaws—and he is not averse to divulging his own. Yet, I have found—as have thousands of others—that there is something compelling about this man. People gravitate toward him, not because he exudes a charismatic and charming personality. He does not. In fact, the opposite is true. His lure is his keen mind, his fascination with new ideas, and his very forthright openness and honesty—all conveyed through his often barely audible voice and his penetrating eyes. These traits draw people to him—strong-willed people who demand much of a leader. To them, a leader is exactly what he is. Moishe's own view of himself is simply that he is an ordinary person who has done some extraordinary things—a man who happened to be at the right place at the right time…with enough sense to take hold of a God-given opportunity.*

---

*I'm overweight, overbearing, and over forty. What am I doing leading a youth movement?* That statement summed up Moishe Rosen's thoughts in the early days of his ministry to the college-aged Jewish "hippies" and "Jesus freaks" of the late sixties and early seventies.

From the beginning, Moishe has been anything but politically correct. Indeed, Jews for Jesus evolved in a strange, albeit indirect, way from something of a faux pas. It was the spring of 1969, the height of the hippie movement in New York City. Moishe was the featured speaker for a group of Christian students at Columbia University. As was often the case, his biting humor offered comic relief during the course of a serious address. Typical of his store of wisecracks was a Ronald Reagan quip: "A hippie dresses like Tarzan, walks like Jane, and smells like Cheetah." The students loved it, but Bob Berk, a Jewish believer Moishe met that day, was less than amused. Later he asked Moishe if he had ever actually smelled a hippie. Moishe retorted that he had never gotten *close* enough to smell one. Bob rebuked him for his callousness and informed him that many of the very hippies he had ridiculed were spiritually hungry

Jewish youth—just the sort of people he *ought* to be meeting.[1]

That was a turning point in Moishe's ministry. He remembered the scorn and ridicule he had encountered as a child from an Orthodox Jewish home, and now he was guilty of scorning others from his own protected vantage point. He was a successful high-level executive in a Jewish mission, shielded by a receptionist, a secretary, and two assistants. He was part of a world of respectable achievers. He had presumed the hippies ambling the streets in ragged jeans and T-shirts were "losers." But his conscience was pricked: *Nobody sees me without making an appointment well in advance. I have become more concerned with administrative procedures than with people. How can I get to know the hippies?*[2]

Moishe found the answer to his question in Greenwich Village, a favorite hippie hangout. As he began spending time there regularly, the window of his world opened to a wider vision of ministry. But simply talking and listening to a few dozen young people was not enough. With the right set of tools, he could reach so many more.

Unable to find printed literature suitable for reaching this new generation, Moishe began writing his own crude tracts. The cover of the first one pictured a full-figured, square-bodied man with the caption "A Message from Squares." No typeset or clip art, just Moishe's own writing—scrawl, really—but the short, pithy, disconnected statements were attention grabbers: "Hey you, with the beard on your face!" "We think you are beautiful." "God likes beards, too." "He didn't want the Israelites to even trim their beards." "You're brave to do your own thing."[3] The tract went on to challenge the reader with a more poetic than cohesive message that ended with John 3:16: "For God so loved the world that he gave his one and only Son, that whoever believes in him shall not perish but have eternal life."

His next tract, titled "Peace Isn't Nothing," was a message to antiwar protesters. These tracts, which Moishe later dubbed "broadsides," worked. As he put it, "Soon there were wall-to-wall hippies in my office."[4] And many of them came to know Jesus as their Messiah.

Moishe had stepped out of his own comfortable world and into the youth movement that was flowering in the late 1960s. Within weeks he had begun offering a relevant message to the counterculture—and especially to the Jewish counterculture. No other ministries to Jews at that time seemed to be speaking the language of youth.

### EARLY YEARS: BEHIND EVERY GREAT MAN...

Born in Kansas City, Missouri, on April 12, 1932, Martin Meyer Rosen was officially brought under the covenant of Abraham and given the Hebrew name "Moishe" at his circumcision. His Orthodox grandfather lovingly called him "Moysheleh," the Yiddish diminuitive. His mother usually called him by the anglicized "Martin"—until she wanted to be stern. Then it was "Moisheh Meyer!..."

Religion was not a vital aspect of Moishe's early years. After his grandfather's death, his family switched from strict religious observance to a nominal Orthodoxy. His family still belonged to the Orthodox synagogue, but behind closed doors, his mother fried bacon for breakfast. Yet Moishe's Jewish identity and heritage were unmistakable and unshakable—particularly when it came to family.

At fourteen, Moishe began keeping company with Ceil, a shy but headstrong Jewish girl who had recently moved to his Denver neighborhood from Boston. Moishe immediately decided that this petite brunette was by far the prettiest girl in the neighborhood. He was charmed by her "exotic" accent and quiet ways.

Ceil, despite her initial reserve, found herself at ease with this tall, gangly admirer. Having never known anything but strictly kosher rules and regulations at home, she also found the more relaxed atmosphere of the Rosen household inviting. She had already begun to chafe against the strictness of Orthodox Judaism and was even entertaining thoughts of atheism as an option. When she was fifteen, Ceil's Jewish Orthodoxy and her rebellious venture into atheism were briefly challenged. The vehicle was music; the setting, her public high school:

> I remember participating when the girls' chorus in our high school gave a Christmas pageant. We dressed up as Israeli women, with long, flowing gowns. As we glided across the stage in slow, dance-like rhythm, singing, "O come, O come Immanuel/And ransom

captive Israel," something stirred within me. I suddenly realized that Jesus was Jewish and it made me wonder for just a moment if he could be for us after all.[5]

Ceil quickly set aside those thoughts, and under her parents' roof, she remained outwardly observant, while inwardly disenchanted with Orthodox Judaism. At eighteen, Ceil married Moishe, and totally discarded her Orthodox upbringing. "The freedom was exhilarating!" she remembered. "We would not have an Orthodox home; we would be modern American Jews without any hang-ups about religion. We were both proud of our heritage and knew certain ties and roots should be maintained. But the pressure to 'be religious' was off."[6]

No longer constrained to "be religious," Ceil found herself less resentful, and once again she began contemplating God. She even told God she was sorry she had said he was not real. She was ready to worship him in any way he would show her—even if it meant returning to the Orthodox Judaism she had rejected. Then something happened.

Christmas is not a season for Jewish people, but Ceil loved music and could not resist listening to Christmas carols, which she found very appealing. She was particularly captivated by "O Little Town of Bethlehem," which seemed to repeat over and again in her mind, even after the record player was turned off. One night as she looked into the starry sky, she contemplated the star of Bethlehem—and Jesus. Yet, she feared such thoughts. Jews simply did not believe in Jesus, for if they did, they were ostracized from their families and the whole Jewish community. But she could not control her curiosity and needed a means to satisfy it. That means came in the form of an inexpensive Bible she had discovered at a five and ten cent store.

Finally, I asked Cousin Dorothy to purchase the Bible for me—but I didn't show how eager I was to read it. As soon as she left, I opened to the beginning of the New Testament and began reading the Book of Matthew. Then I went on to read Mark, then Luke and John.[7]

Ceil quickly realized that Jesus was Jewish and that she was not "reading about some foreign religion." But more than that, Jesus was "so practical, down-to-earth…and at the same time, there was something unmistakably divine about him. He spoke with authority."[8] Ceil's sense of excitement far exceeded the exhilaration she had felt less than two years earlier when she had dropped the pretense of Orthodoxy. Now, as a wife and the mother of an infant daughter, she was grateful to God for his blessings. And her relationship with God had a new focus: Jesus, a Jewish man who had lived and died nearly two thousand years earlier. Yet Orthodox or not, her culture considered Jesus taboo. There were no family members, no friends with whom she could talk about it…so she prayed. She would trust God to meet her need—and he did.

The angel-messenger came in the form of a woman—Hannah Wago. Hannah visited Ceil at the request of a Christian family who had been praying faithfully for the Rosens. They were unaware of Ceil's Bible reading or of her prayer that God would send someone to her. That visit was the first of many meetings between the two women—meetings that focused on Bible study and doctrinal issues.

It was a relationship that Moishe did not welcome. The more Ceil learned, the more certain she became that Jesus is the Jewish Messiah. As she became more assured in her faith, she tried telling Moishe, who summarily dismissed all overtures regarding the gospel. So angry was he that he insisted that Ceil and Hannah stop seeing each other. One day, when he came home to find Ceil talking on the phone with Hannah, "he ripped the phone out of the wall!"[9]

When Moishe finally demanded that Ceil abandon her newfound faith, her response was unequivocal: "Please don't make me choose between you and God. If it were anything else, you know I would choose you. But if you give me an ultimatum about this, I'll have to choose God."[10]

It was Easter Sunday, 1953. Ceil went to church, an act that was an outward sign of a very momentous inward transformation, though she took care to be very discreet. She was not trying to make a statement or cause a commotion in the neighborhood. Indeed, she hid her hat under her coat as she walked to the waiting car. But once she was in church, the subterfuge was over. When the altar call was given at the end of the service, she made her way forward to make public confession of her faith. And she prayed fervently that her husband would believe in Jesus.

Those prayers were answered. Moishe's decision to follow Jesus came soon after—a result of his attempt to make a case against Christianity. He had vowed he would prove Ceil wrong. But the more he learned about Jesus and the New Testament, the more he realized that Ceil had found the truth. On Pentecost Sunday, 1953, Moishe went to church with Ceil, and as she had done earlier, made public profession of his faith. Then came a less public but more far-reaching profession to family and friends.

### ENDURING THE FALLOUT

For the Rosens, as is true with most Jews who believe Jesus is the Messiah, the price was high. Ceil's adoptive parents moved away, ostensibly to Israel. She never saw or heard from them again. Moishe's parents initially disowned him and refused to see him. However, they had not counted on not seeing their granddaughter, and she acted as a softening agent. Slowly, the fractured family ties were somewhat mended—as best they could be in such a situation.

God had answered Ceil's prayers, but in a sense she got more than she had bargained for. Moishe was not destined to become a "Sunday Christian" whose profession of faith was known only to fellow church members. "Once my husband committed his life to Y'shua (Jesus)," wrote Ceil, "he could not bear to stand idly by while the majority of our people went on believing that Jesus was only for Gentiles."[11] His first priority was to learn and experience as much as possible of his newfound faith. His zeal could not be contained. Moishe later wrote:

> The only spiritual authority I knew, outside of the Bible, was the church, so I took everything my new minister said very seriously. All he had to do was to drop a hint that the members of the congregation should do this or that, and I'd try. We went to Sunday school, church, the Baptist Training Union on Sunday afternoons, and the evening service. The pastor suggested that more people should be attending the Wednesday night prayer meetings, and I arranged my hours at the sporting goods store so that I could comply....[12]

## THE EARLY MINISTRY

Moishe Rosen is not the type to pepper his conversation with such phrases as "God told me this" or "God showed me that." But there was no doubt in his mind that God wanted him to devote his life to telling other Jewish people about Jesus.

While training at Northeastern Bible College in New Jersey, Moishe began working with the American Board of Missions to the Jews (ABMJ). He describes himself in those early days as a rather ineffective evangelist who preferred janitorial duties to street preaching. He was shy, and his communication skills were limited by a stammer. When he was assigned to street preach, he picked an isolated traffic island that almost no pedestrians used. After introductory testimonies by two other individuals, Moishe was on deck.

> I had written my speech on school notebook paper, and I read it as though I were delivering a proclamation. Nobody at all walked by in the forty-five minutes we were out there, and I was relieved when it was over. I thanked God for our lack of listeners and wondered if I could legitimately call myself a failure and turn the future street-corner assignments over to someone else who would do a better job.[13]

Despite his initial bumbling, Moishe continued the outdoor evangelism while completing his Bible college education. He studied other street preachers' styles and became skilled in the technique of holding a crowd—especially as he learned to relish rather than fear hecklers. "I usually found that the heckler helped to build up the crowd, and once the crowd got large enough, I started hitting them with my message."[14] He learned to understand his opponents and, above all, not to take their insults personally. "Jewish hecklers are like Jews in practically every other field of endeavor. They always want to be the best. Their heckling is not usually vicious. They do it for sport."[15]

After completing his Bible education, Moishe began full-time work with the ABMJ. His first assignment was to direct their work in Los Angeles.

Among numerous other tasks, he preached on street corners and in parks, where he had many unusual confrontations with people who opposed his message. One such encounter with a heckler, also named Moishe, developed into a friendship of sorts. Moishe the heckler was a frustrated opera singer hoping to make it big in Hollywood. He often showed up where Moishe was preaching and stopped the sermon by singing at the top of his lungs. Finally, after another frustrated sermon attempt, Moishe Rosen asked the other Moishe if he could have a word with him privately. He explained to the heckler that preaching was his livelihood and that his job would be in jeopardy if he were unable to perform his duty. Moishe the heckler understood and appreciated that line of reasoning. Moishe the preacher recalled that:

> Moishe not only agreed to let me preach, but he became a friend. He wasn't a believer, but he would meet me in the park and sing songs for me. Sometimes he would sing Jewish songs, other times he sang operatic arias....I brought him an Intervarsity hymnal and he began singing some of my kind of Christian songs, but since he had never heard them before we had some very unusual renditions. Afterwards, we'd go out and get some coffee together. He would never come to any of the meetings we conducted at the mission center, but he kept in touch....[16]

Moishe speaks as much about those who rejected his message as those who accepted it, but considering the difficulty of Jewish evangelism, he was highly successful in his ministry. His own records indicate that:

> It would be impossible to keep score of how many people I led to Christ, because much of the time the people to whom I had a ministry accepted Christ privately, outside my presence. I have always tried to avoid pressuring people. My journals show that in ten years of ministry in Los Angeles there were 265 Jewish people who accepted Christ in my presence or shortly after our encounter. During that same period there were about 1,100 Gentiles who made a similar commitment.[17]

In 1965, as a result of Moishe's successful evangelistic outreach in Los Angeles, Daniel Fuchs, director of the ABMJ, asked him to head the organization's training program for all new candidates. Two years later, that program and the Rosens themselves were transferred to New York. There, Moishe became consumed with training and administrative duties. He reviewed applications, consulted psychologists, taught classes, administered exams, preached weekly at the local congregation, traveled as a guest speaker representing the mission at various churches and conferences, and headed a major building program. All the while he continued weekly street preaching, but with no time for personal interaction. "The results," by his own account, "were almost disastrous." He had become a "self-satisfied religious bureaucrat." He was a credit to the conservative Christian establishment: He was clean-shaven and conventional. But amid all this ministry to reach Jewish people, his own Jewish identity began "subtly slipping away."[18]

Moishe's mother's death brought him to his senses. He deeply regretted that in many ways, his mother had lost her Jewish son—an unnecessary loss. Moreover, he realized that he could never be truly effective in reaching Jews for Jesus as long as he was a poster boy for the stereotypical Jewish convert who essentially abandoned his Jewishness.

It was about this time that Bob Berk challenged Moishe to reach out to the hippies in New York City. Moishe's subsequent appreciation of the "Jesus Revolution" and how it tied in with his own calling led him back to California—this time to San Francisco. He was convinced that God was calling him to reach hippies with the gospel, a conclusion some might have regarded as a cosmic joke, considering his image at the time.

"I weighed an all-time high of 327 pounds, was still an extremely conservative dresser, and had my crew cut shorn even shorter than usual," Moishe recalled. "But that wasn't all. I was thirty-eight years old and had no special experience or training in youth work. Yet I had no doubt that God was leading me from New York to San Francisco," Moishe states matter-of-factly. Then he quickly emphasizes that he rarely uses words like *leading* when speaking of God. In this case, he had a "literal vision"—not the first one he had experienced—but he is quick to add, "I never trusted them."[19]

(Not meaning that he paid them no heed, but that he always looked for corroborating evidence of God's direction.)

This vision, combined with his own experience and observations, persuaded Moishe that the whole Jewish mission endeavor was failing. Some Jewish people were coming to faith in Jesus, but he felt that this was usually *in spite* of mission practices, not *because* of them. Everyone in the field of Jewish missions, he concluded, was adrift. Most of the missions were continuing to do the things they had always done with minimal success and without realizing that programs once established to speak to a particular situation were hanging limply in place long after the situation had changed. There was a desperate need for a "vision"—and that was what Moishe got.

In the summer of 1970, as Moishe likes to tell it, he headed west to San Francisco with nine females: his wife; his two daughters; two sisters from Philadelphia who were believers in Jesus; one Jewish believer who had been part of the hippie scene in New York; two "kosher-hearted" gentile Christians who'd trained with him at the mission; and the family dog, also a female.

Thus the concept of "Rosen's project" developed. The project was a response to "the problem," and the problem, according to Moishe, was "how to communicate to people who did not want to hear our message and were sure that they already knew why anything we would tell them about Jesus couldn't be true."[20] "How to communicate" has been Moishe's vision ever since. For more than twenty-five years *communication* has been the driving force for Moishe—and for Jews for Jesus.

## A MAN OF AMBIGUITY AND PARADOX

Moishe and the ministry of Jews for Jesus are enigmatic in many respects.

By his own admission, Moishe is a radical, a fanatic. Those he trained are regarded by many as in-your-face zealots, always pushing the envelope in style, though not in substance. Yet he (and the majority of the staff) are not outgoing by nature.

Another seeming paradox brings together two images many would see as mutually exclusive: Moishe was born a Jew and says he will die a Jew, yet he is also a Baptist minister.

Nor is it simple to grasp the relationship with non-Jewish Christians.

Jews for Jesus welcomes non-Jews to the staff in an administrative capacity, but they are not frontline missionaries unless they have a Jewish spouse. Moishe explains that it is not a matter of prejudice, but of practical necessity to keep the title of the organization genuine. Yet Jews for Jesus has closer contact with Christian churches than other messianic Jewish ministries.

Another seeming paradox: Is this man truly a radical or a conservative? He would probably say both.

Moishe is widely regarded in the Jewish community as a thorn in the flesh, or worse, as an utterly despicable renegade. But among messianic Jews, he could be considered a conservative, and some of his opinions would probably surprise the mainstream Jewish community. This was evident in 1975, when the six-decade-old Hebrew Christian Alliance of America met at Messiah College, near Harrisburg, Pennsylvania. At that meeting the Alliance voted to change its name to the Messianic Jewish Alliance. Many messianic Jewish ministries were represented, with divergent points of view. Robert Coote, associate editor of *Eternity* magazine, offered an interesting portrait of Moishe:

> Also present at the conference was Moishe Rosen who displayed his engaging sense of humor and astute practicality as he affirmed the name change and other aspects of the Messianic Jewish movement. But he was equally clear in warning that the fundamental mission of the Alliance was not to discover its Jewishness but to proclaim Christ as the only Savior for Jews lost without Him. He also called for "a little humility" to balance the grand strategies and projections that currently characterize the movement....
>
> Several critics are particularly concerned by the use of the term "rabbi." Says Moishe Rosen, "The use of this term is like a diploma-mill doctorate, an undeserved honor, which they arrogate to themselves. It is designed to mislead people to think that there is more validity to the man's standing in the Jewish community than is true." Likewise the Jews for Jesus do not support the "fourth branch of Judaism" emphasis, but instead stress their relationship to the actual membership in local (Gentile) churches.
>
> Another concern is the fear of an incipient anti-Gentilism....

One group [that] is guarding against anti-Gentilism...is Jews for Jesus....[21]

## THE PERSONALITY BEHIND THE MISSION

You do not get to be founder and executive director of a high-powered organization without people forming all kinds of opinions regarding your personality. That certainly has been the case with Moishe.

Some have described Moishe as a humble man. And if humility means looking at one's abilities realistically, then yes, he is humble. He has a good sense of who he is and who he is not. This is evident in his shunning of titles:

I don't refer to myself as "reverend," though I am ordained, and I don't call myself "doctor".... The highest thing anyone can call us is a servant or slave of Jesus—so don't call me by my titles, call me "brother," call me "friend," or call me "Moishe." After all, Jesus invited us to call him by his first name. Was he a rabbi? Surely. Was he learned? Undoubtedly. Yet he never stood on ceremony or lorded it over people.

Leaders...need to be subject to what they themselves preach. They need to be submitted to others, to admonish people lovingly and to respect people's rights. They must not manipulate people. If you want to lead, demonstrate your leadership by being the best foot-washer in the congregation, by being the best servant. That is what qualifies people for leadership.[22]

Everyone in the organization knew Moishe's philosophy of titles. But that does not mean he was lax in the area of respect. He certainly expected the staff to respect his authority as executive director. No one bowed down to him as a cult leader. But there are those—some who have left and some still with the organization—who say that he has the ability to intimidate and that he used it, more so in the past than today. Through the years, they recall, his displeasure sometimes cut the air like a razor-sharp knife. If he felt people were not listening, he would yell. He would glower. And there was a time or two when, in a very deliberate display of disapproval, he threw something across the room. Though he never aimed at or intended to hurt anyone, these were nonetheless intimidating experiences. This is not top-secret information, disclosed behind closed doors. According to Moishe, he intended such scenes to provide shock value to drive home his point. (Perhaps, but sometimes those on the receiving end were too shocked to appreciate the value.)

Such displays frequently related to the matter of high expectations. Moishe in his own way was and still is a perfectionist. He would not tolerate the slipshod way of doing things that he felt characterized too many Christian organizations. In Moishe's mind, any undertaking carried out under the banner of Jews for Jesus had to be first rate. When it was not—and such was not infrequent—Moishe showed visible displeasure. He also expected missionaries and other staff to be fully prepared to present their ideas in staff meetings. Oh, there were brainstorming sessions where everyone was free to be creative and toss out ideas spontaneously. But for any kind of serious proposal, Moishe expected the staff to think things through clearly ahead of time and to know how much projects would cost in terms of time and other resources. Anyone who presented an idea had to be prepared to answer such questions, and if answers were not forthcoming, he or she could end up in the proverbial hot seat. As a result, some staff members have said they were too intimidated to speak up.

Some longtime staff have left the organization because of differences with Moishe and with the philosophical underpinnings of the organization. Severing ties with an organization is routine in both secular and Christian circles, but in the case of Jews for Jesus, the fracture is often more personal. Because of the fatherly role Moishe has played, Jews for Jesus—especially in the early days—was more like a family than an organization. Severing ties with family can be traumatic and painful, and there are many wounds that are not yet healed.

Regarding relationships in broader evangelical circles, Moishe is held in almost universal high esteem. He has managed to cross denominational lines easily from fundamentalist to Pentecostal to mainline Protestants. Yet within the narrower circles of messianic Jewish organizations and congregations, there is often a less-than-subtle rivalry and sometimes overt criticism. As the largest, most visible, and most controversial of these groups, Jews for Jesus has been an easy target. Some messianic Jewish groups have criticized Moishe for being too cozy with Christian churches and for failing to make Jews for Jesus what they would see as a more distinctively Jewish organization. After all, he is an ordained Baptist minister and a member of a Baptist church, not the leader or even a member of a messianic congregation. He has sought to stay above such criticism and to keep his feet firmly planted within both Christian and messianic Jewish circles.

As with titles, Moishe does not care much about labels:

> I don't care what you call me. Call me a "Hebrew Christian," a "Jewish Christian," or a "Messianic Jew." As long as you don't say that I am this and not that, because I am all three. We're talking about language, and I refuse to allow division to occur over the way in which people use words. I've heard people say, "Don't say Jesus, say *Yeshua*."
>
> I frequently use the name *"Yeshua"* interchangeably with Jesus, but when a rabbi wants to refer to the Nazarene, he doesn't call him *"Yeshua,"* he calls him "Jesus." I use the word which most effectively communicates to people what I am trying to say.[23]

Some reporters, when first encountering Moishe, describe him as little more than a buffoon. That was the experience of William Willoughby when he met him in the 1970s at a convention of American Baptist churches in Denver. Referring to him as "one zany person," Willoughby went on to say, "He was one who paraded around town in such a way as to draw attention to himself.... I thought he bordered (make that double-bordered) on being a publicity hound and egotist." But Willoughby went on to direct his comments personally to the man he calls, "my friend Moishe":

> Sorry about those first impressions, Moishe. I soon discovered what you were up to, and after some reflecting on the problems involved in getting the attention of the press for the cause you were espousing, I suppose your theatrics, while out of line, were in line as well.[24]

Today Moishe is regarded by many as the twentieth century's leading missiologist in the field of Jewish evangelism. His books are widely read, and he has been a frequent conference speaker. Vernon Grounds, former president of Denver Conservative Baptist Seminary, characterizes his ministry in colorful terms: "He is a dynamic and creative witness! When Moishe Rosen comes into a city there is either a revival or a riot."[25]

## REFLECTIONS ON A LIFE OF MINISTRY

Why did Moishe get involved in Jewish evangelism and go on to found Jews for Jesus? In part, it is his unbounded enthusiasm for anything or anyone he really likes. "I've always been the kind of person that if I found a really good restaurant, I'd tell everybody about it until it gets so crowded that I can no longer get a reservation." Why tell everybody about Jesus? For the same reason. "I just want to share my discovery."[26]

But there were other reasons, both divine and human, that Moishe became involved in Jewish evangelism—reasons he disclosed in a 1982 interview:

> First because of the call of God.
> The second reason. Pure arrogance. I felt the reason why Jews didn't believe in Jesus was because I wasn't there to tell them.
> Third, I saw the need for a ministry to Jews by Jews.[27]

## "RETIREMENT" MINISTRY

Even as he moves into his late sixties, Moishe Rosen is still as outspoken and outrageous as he was back in his forties—at least I cannot imagine him being any less so then than he is now! "Retirement" is in quotation marks because although he retired from the position of executive director in 1996, Moishe remains actively employed with Jews for Jesus. Was it difficult for the founding executive director to say it is time for someone else to take over? Perhaps not, because he believed it was the will of God. He said it was another of those rare instances when God specifically led him. But the reality of living with that decision day-to-day is difficult, and no doubt it is also frustrating to be without many of the duties and decisions that occupied the lion's share of his time and energy for so many years.

Yet there are definite benefits to this stage of ministry. In some respects, Moishe has come full circle, back to the early days of one-on-one evangelistic outreach. An in-house cartoon reveals his favorite evangelistic tool. In the first panel he is on the phone saying, "I had a terrific week. Monday I witnessed to someone in London." The second panel: "Tuesday I witnessed to someone in Australia and prayed with someone in New York...." The third panel: "Wednesday I was telling someone in Denver how to witness to her Jewish husband." The fourth panel: "Jet lag? Nah, I don't get jet lag." And the last panel: "But Ceil says if I spend any more time on the Internet, she'll send my *computer* flying!"[28]

The cartoon is somewhat exaggerated since Moishe does travel quite a bit, representing Jews for Jesus—and he does get jet lag—but when he is home, he is usually at his computer. So, a quarter century after he founded Jews for Jesus, Moishe, in pseudo retirement, sometimes spends up to several hours a day on-line.

> Now that I have more time to be a missionary instead of directing other missionaries, the chat room on America Online has become a regular witnessing medium for me. In vocal conversation I frequently stammer, and the cadence of my conversational speech is so irregular that people often interrupt me in mid-sentence. They begin responding without realizing that I haven't finished what I wanted to say. For me, "chatting" about spiritual matters by computer is ideal because it gives me time to collect my thoughts and express them without interruption.[29]

One of the highlights of Moishe's on-line journeys was the discovery of a Jews for Jesus chat room. He entered the room with several other people and found a "very good witness was in progress." He introduced himself as the founder of the movement, and after a friendly welcome from the others in the room, he answered some of their questions.

> Imagine my surprise to find that chat room! As the founder of Jews for Jesus, I thought I knew most of our activities, and I hadn't heard

of that one.... My inquiry at our headquarters office led me to the conclusion that no one in our organization had done it. Then, further investigation led me to a most delightful truth.[30]

That truth was that a fifteen-year-old Jewish girl and her mother had found their Messiah through a chat room—and it was the daughter who was in charge of this one, giving scriptural answers to the many inquiries. Moishe and she became friends. In fact, he writes, "I got in the habit of opening a Jews for Jesus chat room whenever my young friend didn't."[31]

For those who might think Moishe has served long enough to spend his last decades in the leisurely life of a retirement village, his response is that he is doing exactly what he ought to be doing. He has surrendered the reins of leadership but is maintaining a focus on the future—investing the remainder of his life in young people on the net.

# CHAPTER TWO

# A LEGACY OF FAITH

## A Look at Jewish Christianity

Jesus was a Jew. I have known that fact since my earliest years in Sunday school. Nevertheless, in the farming community where I lived in northern Wisconsin, there were no Jewish people, or if there were, I was unaware of them. The only Jewish people I knew were all those Old and New Testament personalities—heroes and villains—dressed in bathrobes and sandals. The fact that Sunday school depictions of these storybook characters reflected little, if any, authentic Jewishness escaped me entirely—not only then, but through most of my adult years. Then I took on this project.

Did Jesus look like any of the men I have come to know in Jews for Jesus? Was he, like many of them, a fast talker and quick to respond? Expressive in his gestures? Did he have a quick wit and a hearty laugh? Did he enjoy a lively social gathering? Who was Jesus—this Jewish man from Israel, whose very personhood has been entombed for centuries under layers of gentile Christianity? Until recently, I simply had no frame of reference in which to place the Jewish people. This has been an unfortunate legacy not only for me, but for most of the Christian church—the utter failure to know the people and the culture of Jesus, who was born and lived and died a Jew.

That failure may have contributed to a history of anti-Semitism cloaked in clerical robes. It is impossible to understand the challenges of Jewish evangelism apart from the distrust that "Christian" anti-Semitism has fostered within the Jewish community. Anyone who is interested in Jewish missions cannot avoid those tragic chapters of church history.

*As a historian, I felt I could not present Jews for Jesus without providing a historical overview of Jewish believers in Jesus and messianic missions since the time of Christ. The long heritage of reaching out to Jews with the Good News of Jesus began with the apostles themselves. The Jews for Jesus organization can be understood only in the light of this remarkable heritage.*

*I confess that I have not previously included messianic Jews in my subject matter. I have followed the course of earlier historians, who since the days of the apostolic church have been telling the story of the Christian church without giving as much as a sentence to Hebrew Christians.*

*I have been changed by this project, and that omission will not occur again— not in my teaching nor in my ongoing writing of a church history text. The followers of Jesus are one, and to omit any part is a loss to the whole.*

—m—

Moishe Rosen has taken a very direct approach in reminding people of the Jewish roots of Christianity, beginning with the name of the organization he founded. He insists that, "It's not an oxymoron that Jews should be for Jesus. Jesus was a Jew and his ministry was to Jews. If the Jews didn't need Jesus, why didn't he come by way of Norway or Ireland?" Indeed, Christianity was initially a Jewish religion made up of Jews who objected to the inclusion of Gentiles. "Those...pork eaters? Who wants them?" He reminds non-Jewish audiences of their non-Jewish heritage. "You are not the original Christians. We (Jews) are, but we welcome you..."[1] While the mainstream Jewish community disagrees that it is Jewish to believe that Jesus is the Messiah, there has been a movement to "reclaim" Jesus as a Jew.

The New Testament offers sparse information to the Gentile seeking to fully understand Jewish culture. Why? Because the Jewishness of Jesus was so obvious, such a given. The skeleton outline of his Jewishness is immediately evident to anyone reading the Gospel accounts. These include his circumcision, his attendance at festivals, his practice of everyday Jewish customs, and his synagogue worship. It is assumed that readers have some understanding of these activities, but often they do not.

Jesus the Jew frequently has been misinterpreted and therefore misrepresented by academics and clergy, as well as by lay people. We can never fully unravel the complexity of Jesus, but recent scholarship has corrected some of the most blatant distortions of him and the context of his culture. Ben Witherington III has contributed to a fuller understanding of Jesus in his book, *The Jesus Quest: The Third Search for the Jew of Nazareth:*

> The image of a gentle Jesus, meek and mild, going about Galilee offering entertaining stories called parables or engaging in abstract academic debates about various religious notions fails to convey the sensitive and sometimes hostile atmosphere in which Jesus operated and the *effect* his teaching would have had on those who lived in this environment. It was an atmosphere in which politics and religion were almost always mixed, and messianic claims, actions or ideas were normally viewed by those in power as threats to the political status quo.[2]

Witherington emphasizes Jesus' Jewishness: "Whatever else we might say, Jesus was certainly a devout Jew who was deeply aware of Jewish sensibilities." And the ministry and message of Jesus was distinctly Jewish as well: "It would be a mistake to see Jesus as inaugurating some sort of generic or universal religion denuded of all characteristically Jewish elements." He dealt with issues and questions that were the Jewish topics of the day: marriage and divorce, the law and ritual purity, resurrection, angels, and the afterlife. Indeed, as revolutionary as Jesus was in his teaching, he presented "a religious worldview thoroughly grounded in the Hebrew Scriptures." Most importantly, according to Witherington, "Jesus was not offering to Jews a non-Jewish alternative. He was offering to his audience some form of what I call a messianic, eschatological and sapiential Judaism."[3]

The history of Jewish missions actually began with Jesus, who sent his twelve Jewish disciples out to reach other Jews with the good news that he, Jesus, was the Jewish Messiah. Sometimes he and his disciples reached beyond their own culture. When they were passing through Samaria and stopped briefly in Sychar, Jesus identified himself to the Samaritan woman as the Messiah. She believed and so did others in Sychar. Jewish believers, however, were the mainstay of the early "cult of Jesus," as early Christianity was often called. After the Crucifixion, Ascension, and Pentecost, when Peter preached to great crowds of people in Jerusalem, many thousands of Jews believed in Jesus as Messiah (Acts 21:20). In his book *Famous Hebrew Christians,* Jacob Gartenhaus wrote, "Thus, and obviously, the church in Jerusalem was composed entirely of Jews. And Jews became, necessarily, the first missionaries of the Christian church by preaching among the Gentiles."[4]

Christian scholars have often overlooked the Jewishness of the early church. Many portray the Christian movement as though it were a non-Jewish faith from the outset. That was not the case, according to James D. G. Dunn, professor of divinity at the University of Durham in England. His research points out that the first believers were not starting a new religion, but rather bringing renewal to Judaism. They saw their faith in Jesus "as a fulfilled Judaism" and practiced a form of the faith that "we today would scarcely recognize—Jewish Christianity, or perhaps more precisely, a form of Jewish messianism." Like Jews for Jesus today, "Their belief in Jesus as the risen Messiah made sense to them only in the context of Judaism."[5]

These Jews, or Nazarenes as they were often called, had a newfound faith in Jesus, not a new culture nor a new heritage. They naturally expressed their faith in the Jewish Messiah from their own context—as Jews. The early church liturgy, for example, drew heavily from the synagogue liturgy. These new believers solved their social problems in a Jewish context as well: "There arose a murmuring of the Hellenists [Jews born outside of Israel] against the Hebrews [born in Israel], because their widows were neglected in the daily ministration" (Acts 6:1). The Jerusalem Nazarenes responded to this dispute by appointing seven deacons to administer the care of the needy. This action was taken in good Jewish fashion, and may actually have involved "the establishment of a Nazarene synagogue." Establishing a synagogue was not an extraordinary event. Any group of ten qualified Jewish men could do so, and in Jerusalem as elsewhere there were many synagogues that represented particular nationalities or trades. "It is not, therefore, unreasonable to suppose," writes Hugh J. Schonfield, "that those of the 'Way of Jesus' did, in fact, establish a synagogue of their own."6

How were these early Jews for Jesus perceived by the other religious Jews of their day? A religious Jew such as Saul of Tarsus?

N. T. Wright sums up the pre-Jesus agenda of this Pharisee of Pharisees:

> First, he was zealous for Israel's God and for the Torah. This was a matter of personal piety, no doubt, and of fervent prayer and study.... It was zeal to see God honoured which necessitated stamping out, by whatever means were necessary, all forms of disloyalty to the Torah among Jews.... Second, Saul intended that he and others should keep the Torah so wholeheartedly in the present that they would be marked out already as those who would be vindicated on the great coming day when YHWH finally acted to save and redeem his people. Third, he intended to hasten this day by forcing other Jews to keep the Torah in his way, using violence as and when necessary.7

Saul ardently awaited Israel's redemption. It would not have occurred to him that that redemption hinged upon an obscure Galilean carpenter turned miracle worker who dared to reinterpret the Torah. There was no place for a crucified messiah in Saul's hope for Israel—in his longing for God's promised intervention in history.

God did intervene, not only in the life of Israel, but in the life of Saul. And he did so in a way that was diametrically opposite of anything Saul could have expected. The account is recorded in the book of Acts:

> Now Saul, still breathing threats and murder against the disciples of the Lord, went to the high priest, and asked for letters from him to the synagogues at Damascus, so that if he found any belonging to the Way, both men and women, he might bring them bound to Jerusalem. And it came about that as he journeyed, he was approaching Damascus and suddenly a light from heaven flashed around him: and he fell to the ground, and heard a voice saying,

"Saul, Saul, why are your persecuting Me?" And he said, "Who art Thou, Lord?" And He said, "I am Jesus whom you are persecuting." (Acts 9:1–5, NAS)

Truly God had come barging into history. The resurrected Messiah appeared to Saul, and the world would never be the same. On the road to Damascus Saul "joined Jews for Jesus." In many ways, he epitomizes the transformation that occurs in Jews who follow Jesus; his is a story of Jews in every generation. N. T. Wright places him in his proper context:

Saul's vision on the road to Damascus thus equipped him with an entirely new perspective, though one which kept its roots firm and deep within his previous covenantal theology. Israel's destiny had been summed up and achieved in Jesus the Messiah. The Age to Come had been inaugurated. Saul himself was summoned to be its agent. He was to declare to the pagan world that YHWH, the God of Israel, was the one true God of the whole world....[8]

Saul of Tarsus depicts the most astonishing change of heart in the New Testament. His Damascus Road experience and subsequent fervent mission to see Gentiles saved shows just how radically Jesus impacted his brethren according to the flesh. However, Paul's dedication to bringing the gospel to Gentiles was not without problems. As Gentiles accepted the gospel, particularly through the mission outreach of Paul and Barnabas, a debate began to rage. Would Gentiles have to become Jews—through circumcision and obedience to the law of Moses—in order to be accepted into this messianic movement? Many of the new gentile converts had already been closely tied to a synagogue, attracted to the comparative simplicity of doctrine and the concern for personal piety. "To them," writes Schonfield, "the messianic message, which promised personal salvation and immediate reception into the fellowship of faith without circumcision and other restrictive rites, was doubly welcome."[9]

This new "gentile Christianity," however, presented a dilemma. How could there be a unified following of Jesus based on two groups of people living by two very distinct sets of rules and regulation? So significant was the issue that a council, the first of the church, was convened in Jerusalem. The council did nothing to infringe on Jewish traditions or culture, but it did rule essentially "that God was calling out from among the Gentiles a people for His Name, who, without becoming Jews, were to share with them all the privileges of the covenants of promise." The decision was stunning: "Believing Gentiles were admitted to an associate membership of the House of Israel, subject only to the Noahic laws."[10]

The conflict between Jew and Gentile did not end with the Jerusalem council; a greater one that developed before the end of the first century was between Jews who believed in Jesus and those who did not. Many of the Jewish believers fled Jerusalem at the time of the first Jewish revolt against Rome between A.D. 66 and 70, in accordance with Jesus' warning. They returned only after Titus had crushed the city and killed more than a million people. Initially, this fulfillment of Jesus' prophecy (Luke 21:20–21) enhanced the witness of the Jewish Christians. Many Jewish leaders, however, felt threatened by the Jesus movement and banned Jewish Christians from synagogues. Several decades later during the second Jewish revolt, Jewish Christians joined in, but that spirit of unity was short lived. "When Rabbi Akiba heralded the rebel leader Bar Cochba as the Messiah, the believers of necessity had to disassociate themselves. This ultimately led to their bitter ejection from the Jewish community."[11]

The widening chasm between the Jewish believers in Jesus and the mainstream Jewish community corresponded with the ever increasing ranks of non-Jews into the church. Ostracized by the members of their cultural community and outnumbered by members of an alien culture in their faith community, Jewish believers in Jesus became scarce. And the Jewishness of Christianity was gradually forgotten. It is interesting that early Christianity drew heavily from Jewish beliefs and practices on the one hand, while defining itself against Judaism on the other. Dunn sees an evolution of theological understanding in the early church and with that, a gradual change in terminology. As Gentiles became more prominent in the early church, there was a shift in focus from Jesus as Messiah to Jesus as Son of God. The latter term appears frequently in Paul's writing and is meaningful to both Jews and

Gentiles. The term "Messiah," on the other hand, had less significance to non-Jewish believers. Because of its association with Jewish nationalism, it might even have had negative connotations. Unfortunately, with the diminished emphasis on Jesus as Messiah, there occurred a parallel decline of Jewishness in general, and Christianity eventually became an almost non-Jewish faith.[12]

### JEWISH CHRISTIAN MARTYRDOM

Jewish Christians were among the first martyrs of the church. In the great classic, *Foxe's Christian Martyrs of the World,* there is a chapter entitled "The Lives, Sufferings, and Cruel Deaths of the Apostles and Evangelists." Stephen, the first martyr mentioned in the New Testament, was stoned following his fiery sermon before the Sanhedrin, with Saul—who was to become the great apostle Paul—"giving approval to his death" (Acts 8:1). The martyrdom of James the apostle, slain by Herod Agrippa, is also recorded in the New Testament. He was a dynamic leader among the Jerusalem Nazarenes, which is why the authorities, both civil and religious, wanted to be rid of him. Clement of Rome later recorded a powerful story connected with his death:

> The man who led him to the judgment seat, seeing him bearing his testimony to the faith, and moved by the fact, confessed himself a Christian. Both, therefore were led away to die. On their way, he entreated James to be forgiven of him, and James, considering a little, replied "Peace be with thee," and kissed him; and then both were beheaded at the same time.[13]

The martyrdom of the other apostles is handed down only through tradition, but Foxe tells the story of each one from Philip the evangelist to Matthew, Mark, Andrew, Peter, and Paul, the latter two suffering a cruel death at the orders of Emperor Nero.

Timothy, another Jewish Christian martyr, is known through Paul's letters. While Timothy's father was a Gentile, his mother was a Jewish follower of Jesus, as was his grandmother. Foxe describes his martyrdom in Ephesus while witnessing to Gentiles:

At this time the heathen were about to celebrate a feast, the principal ceremonies of which were that the people should carry wands in their hands, go masked, and bear about the streets the images of their gods. When Timothy met the procession, he reproved them for their idolatry, which so angered them that they fell upon him with their sticks, and beat him in so dreadful a manner that he died of the bruises two days after.[14]

### JEWISH LEADERSHIP IN THE EARLY CHURCH

Early church history depicts many Jews in leading roles. In fact, the great ecclesiastical historian Eusebius confirms that the bishops of Jerusalem were Jewish until well into the second century:

The chronology of the bishops of Jerusalem I nowhere found in writing, for tradition says that they were all short-lived. But I have learned this much from writing, that until the siege of the Jews, which took place under Adrian, there were fifteen bishops in succession there, all of whom were said to have been of Hebrew descent, and to have received the knowledge of Christ in purity.... For the whole Church consisted then of believing Hebrews who continued from the days of the apostles until the siege which took place at this time....[15]

Eusebius refers to these early Jewish leaders as bishops, but F. F. Bruce points out that "in their Jewish Christian community they would certainly have been called elders." And these were probably not a succession of men, as Eusebius would imply, but rather a body of leaders. James, the brother of Jesus, had led the Jerusalem church for most of two decades before the first Jewish revolt; and following the war, apparently, Simon the son of Clopas filled that role. These Jewish followers of Jesus were still part of the Jewish community. They were often viewed as heretics, and they had lively interaction with their fellow Jews, as F. F. Bruce has shown:

There is ample evidence in the rabbinical writings and elsewhere of the energy with which these Nazarenes and their fellow Jews engaged in theological debate. The destruction of the temple must have provided the Nazarenes with a powerful apologetic. They could refer to the prediction of Jesus—now so literally fulfilled— that one stone would not be left standing upon another of that magnificent building. They could appeal to the disappearance of the priestly order as proof that they had been right in recognizing Jesus as the Messiah, divinely commissioned to inaugurate the new order. And they freely invoked the prophetic scriptures, which both sides alike accepted as supremely authoritative, in support of their arguments.[16]

Jewish Christians were shunned by fellow Jews and fared little better in the Christian community in the early centuries. By the time of Constantine, Jewish Christians were clearly a minority, and the church itself had become deeply infected by worldliness. Uniformity was a priority for Constantine, and Jews who refused to convert to Christianity were persecuted.

Considering the exclusive Jewish nature of the first church council, the Council of Jerusalem, it was an unusual turn of events that Jewish Christians had virtually no role in subsequent councils. Philip Yancey comments on this omission:

In the church we affirmed Jesus as "the only-begotten Son of God, begotten of his Father before all worlds.... Very God of Very God." Those creedal statements, though, are light-years removed from the Gospels' account of Jesus growing up in a Jewish family in the agricultural town of Nazareth. I later learned that not even converted Jews—who might have rooted Jesus more solidly in Jewish soil— were invited to the Council of Chalcedon that composed the creed. We Gentiles face the constant danger of letting Jesus' Jewishness, and even his humanity, slip away.[17]

The Council of Nicea in 325 elevated anti-Judaism to official church policy. Close ties between Christians and Jews were forbidden, and Christians were not permitted to visit synagogues. Emperor Constantine banned

Christians from converting to Judaism, but, according to Rabbi Larry Gevirtz, certainly not the reverse:

> Yet if conversion to Judaism was forbidden, conversion to Christianity—especially by Jews—became a major goal. It was the one and only way for Jews to save their "tainted souls." Therefore, all methods of coercion became permissible in order to make Jews change their faith. Jews were forced to attend churches, where they had to listen to priests condemn their present status. Jewish leaders such as the *Ramban* (Nachmanides) were forced, even though they knew they would lose, to debate Christian spokesmen as part of an attempt to make the Jews see the "error" of their ways. Sometimes the choice was made painfully clear, either convert, or forfeit your place in society, your right to stay in the country, or at times your way of life.[18]

Yet a significant number of Jewish people continued to follow Jesus. Today's Jewish community almost universally accepts the notion that messianic Jews were solely a first-century phenomenon and that after the first century, Jews no longer looked to Jesus as Messiah. Research has shown that this was not the case. John Gager begins the introduction of his book, *The Origins of Anti-Semitism,* with an interesting scenario: Let us imagine a conversation involving a Jew, a Christian, and two Gentiles, one a Roman and the other a Greek from Alexandria. The time is A.D. 138, the Romans have just decisively crushed the final Jewish revolt in Palestine.

> "This Jesus whom you worship," says the Jew. "How can you expect us to take your claims about him seriously? Equal to God? A crucified messiah? Your own writings tell the truth about him—a man of dubious parentage, untutored in the traditions of the fathers...."
>
> "The Jews are a rebellious and stiff-necked people," the Christian retorts. "The Pharisees and Sadducees have led you away from the paths of righteousness. You killed the ancient prophets sent to you by God and now you have killed Jesus, whom God has made

Lord and Christ for all nations.... God has established a new covenant for a new people. We are the new Israel...."

The Greek now joins in. "What foolishness! All this nonsense about messiahs, divine covenants with the Jews, and Commandments! I say, a plague on all religious fanatics!..."

The Roman takes a different view.... "The Jews have really made quite an impression in Rome. Many of our people are attracted to their cult and choose to take up this or that Jewish custom...."

Up to this point, a fifth man has listened in silence. Now he is moved to speak. He identifies himself as both a Jew and a Christian, throwing the others into a state of confusion.... "Look here," he begins, "there's no doubt at all about who Jesus is. In addition to his miracles and resurrection, who can fail to be convinced by the extraordinary number of prophecies that have found their fulfillment in him?"[19]

Gager continues by explaining that these conversations, while fictional, typify the views expressed during the early centuries of the Christian era. Gager, unlike so many who deal with the relationship between Jews and Christians, acknowledges Jews who believe in Jesus—and even places them at the climax of his story. The failure of Christian as well as Jewish scholars to deal with the early Jewish Christians leaves an unfortunate omission in the study of religious history.

What history does show, and perhaps more Jewish people are aware of it than Christians, is that Christians "flirted" with Judaism and that early church fathers reacted with great venom. Notable church leaders—including Tertullian, Justin, and Origen—spoke loudly against "Judaizing," but John Chrysostom's words stand out as particularly inflammatory. Known as "golden mouthed" for his eloquent preaching, he is also remembered for his diatribes against women and Jews. His fear of Judaizing among Christians seems to indicate that it was real. Perhaps part of the reaction was to Jewish Christians who were still making their presence known in the church, insisting that Jewish holidays and rituals were not inconsistent with the Christian faith.

Chrysostom's series of eight sermons against Judaizing, delivered in 386 while he was serving as a presbyter in Antioch, indicates how seriously he thought the issue affected the church. "The timing of these sermons," according to John Gager, "is of interest in that they are addressed not to the Christian calendar but rather to the Jewish festivals (Rosh Hashanah, Yom Kippur, and Sukkoth) of the autumn season."[20] His sermons were an effort to dissuade the *many* Christians in Antioch from celebrating these festivals as they were accustomed to do. What were their crimes? They participated in the festivals and fasts and observed the Sabbath and circumcision rites—in addition to adopting superstitious practices relating to spells and charms.

The eloquent preacher was ruthless in his attacks. He compared the synagogue to a theater or brothel. He was utterly contemptuous of Jewish people. "The Jews have degenerated to the level of dogs," he wrote. "They are drunkards and gluttons. They beat their servants. They are ignorant of God. Their festivals are worthless.... [They are] the Christ killers."[21]

Gager concludes that Chrysostom's diatribes indicate a much more widespread Jewish influence within the church than most historians have believed or recorded:

> It would appear, then, that popular Christianity was not nearly as convinced as were its leaders that the beliefs and practices of Judaism had been rendered powerless by the appearance of Christianity. John Chrysostom's homilies against the Jews are revealing on this point.... For significant numbers of Christians in late antiquity, Judaism continued to represent a powerful and vigorous religious tradition. Unlike their ecclesiastical and theological superiors, they saw no need to define themselves in opposition to Judaism or to cut themselves off from this obvious source of power.[22]

Augustine of Hippo (A.D. 354–430), regarded as one of the greatest theologians in church history, also fueled the flames of anti-Semitism. His influence was felt for centuries as writings such as the following spread throughout the church:

> The Jews live under God's curse because they rejected Christ; as a result of this crime they are condemned to a life of abasement and

humiliation; living in a state of misery alongside Christians they will be a perpetual reminder of the results of rebellion against Christ.[23]

As anti-Semitism spread, it affected the church's attitude toward Jewish Christians as well as unbelieving Jews. "The name of Nazarene, formerly honoured by every follower of the Man of Nazareth," wrote Hugh Schonfield, "was now wholly discarded by the Catholic Church, and reserved exclusively for the 'heresy' of the faith which he had founded." From the era of Constantine on, the Jewish Christian community was identified as Jews who converted to Catholicism—Jews who had no ties to the Nazarenes.[24]

One of the most prominent of these "non-Jewish Jewish Christians" was Epiphanius, born in Israel around A.D. 303. As a young man, he inherited great wealth and property following the deaths of his wife and father-in-law. Soon after, while surveying his property, Epiphanius encountered a monk whose simplicity and charity so impressed him that he converted to Catholicism. He founded a monastery near his village. He was known for his entanglements in theological debate—especially concerning his strong disagreement with the school of Origen. At age sixty-five he was made Bishop of Constantia in Cyprus, and in the decades that followed, he was widely recognized for his scholarly learning. In A.D. 382, at the age of seventy-nine, the emperor called him to Rome to help settle a church dispute. At age ninety-one he was back in Jerusalem, where, according to Schonfield, "he betrayed something of his Jewish origin in denouncing the use of images which he found painted on a cloth in a Christian church."[25]

Epiphanius died at age one hundred, but not before returning to Constantinople, where he attended a synod and took a stand against John Chrysostom. He did not oppose Chrysostom's harsh words against Jews, but the fact that Chrysostom had sheltered disciples of Origen. Epiphanius's major legacy was his lengthy work *Panarion,* an encyclopedia of Jewish and Christian sectarian groups. That work stands today as a major source of information about early Judeo-Christian beliefs. In summing up his life and contributions, Schonfield wrote:

He was a sincere, though somewhat over-zealous and imprudent churchman, who followed the orthodoxy of his day with commendable loyalty. It is unfortunate that he was out of sympathy with his Nazarene brethren, but this was probably due to his early conversion and training in monastic circles. He never appears to have been in direct contact with either Nazarenes or Ebionites, whom he castigates unmercifully.[26]

Epiphanius's stance against Nazarenes and Jews was expected of any Jew who converted to Christianity. All Catechumen in Constantinople, for example, were required to recite a virtual creed of denunciation that illustrates the anti-Semitism of the church in the generations following the reign of Constantine:

> I renounce all customs, rites, legalisms, unleavened breads and sacrifice of lambs of the Hebrews, and all the other feasts of the Hebrews, sacrifices, prayers, aspersions, purifications...Sabbaths, and superstitions, and hymns and chants and observances and synagogues, and the food and drink of the Hebrews; in one word, I renounce absolutely everything Jewish, every law, rite and custom...and I join myself to the true Christ and God....[27]

This type of inflammatory rhetoric against Jews and Judaizing set the stage for the vicious anti-Semitism that marked the Middle Ages. By the fifth century, Jewish persecution was systematic and certain. Synagogues were destroyed. Jews were denied political and social rights and had to pay onerous taxes for no other reason than the fact that they were Jewish. According to V. Raymond Edman, "As medieval times wore on, the anti-Jewish feeling on the part of professing Christendom was on the increase, especially in Western Europe...despite the undeniable fact that 'the Jews were the great scientific, commercial, and philosophic intermediaries of the Middle Ages.'" This hatred of Jews arose in part because usury was forbidden among Christians, and thus Jews became the money-lenders—often charging high interest rates.[28]

Somehow, in spite of the widespread anti-Semitism, one Jewish convert rose to the highest position in the medieval Catholic Church. Pope Anacle-tus II was Jewish. In the minds of some medieval churchmen, however, such a turn of events was as great a scandal as was the reign of the female Pope Johanna, who wore "the triple crown" for two years during the mid-ninth century. However, Pope Johanna was a myth (widely believed until the fif-teenth century), while Pope Anacletus was not. Unfortunately, he can hardly be considered a good candidate for messianic Jews seeking historical role models. Born into a wealthy Christian Jewish banking family, he rose to power in the church through political connections. As with most popes in the twelfth century, he was not known for piety or scholarship. A majority of cardinals elected him, but there was already a pope in office, Innocent II, who had been elected by a minority of cardinals. With the support of Norman military forces, Anacletus took possession of Rome, and Innocent fled to France. But in the final analysis, the Catholic church listed Innocent II as pope during this period and Anacletus as antipope.[29]

Designations of pope or antipope relate less to facts and the majority vote than to the politics of power which determine winners and losers in his-tory. Innocent's reputation of superior learning and piety would not have been sufficient grounds for declaring him the legitimate pope, nor probably would Anacletus's Jewish background have been sufficient grounds for declaring him the antipope. It is, however, more than a minor footnote to this story that Bernard of Clairvaux, a supporter of Innocent, wrote in a letter that "to the shame of Christ a man of Jewish origin was come to occupy the chair of St. Peter."[30] That a man of Bernard's stature would fail to see how absurdly incongruous it was to suggest that a *Jew* should not represent Christ in the highest office of the church—or that a Jew should not follow in the succession of Peter—symbolizes the irrationality of Christian anti-Semitism through the ages. It is as though Christian leaders were totally oblivious to the fact that Peter, and indeed Jesus himself, were Jews.

Although institutional anti-Semitism was a fact of life, personal interac-tions between Jews and Christians were often friendly through the end of the twelfth century. However, by the thirteenth century widespread violent per-secution of Jews by church leaders was in full force, as churchmen fanned the flame of anti-Semitism.

The principle religious motive for the persecution of the Jews was to make life so miserable for them that they would seek relief in conversion to Christianity. Baptism was the *sine qua non* of the medieval church for admission to the fold. Baptism of the Jews was to be by choice, but if necessary, by compulsion, and either motivation made the rite effective. To achieve that end, "every expedient (in Spain) was tried—the seizure of all Jewish children, to be shut up in monasteries, or to be given to God-fearing Christians, the alternatives of expulsion or conversion....[31]

In 1215, at the Fourth Lateran Council, Pope Innocent III decreed that Jews would be required to wear a badge of identification on their outer garments. Henceforth, "the Jew was a marked man, a pariah, to be beaten, abused, reviled, scorned, and without being allowed to take offense at anything."[32] By this time most Jewish people had been confined to the ghetto, which further identified them as outcasts. The ghetto allowed Jews to be easy prey for the crusaders, whose terrorizing of Jews beginning with the first Crusade in 1095, is well documented. Led by Urban II and Peter the Hermit, the Crusade was not to massacre Jews, but that is what occurred along the way. German and French crusaders, using the excuse of avenging those who crucified Christ, began pillaging Jewish ghettos. The story has been passed down in Jewish tradition:

> In this horrible day men were seen to slay their own children to save them from the worse usage of these savages. Women, having deliberately tied stones round themselves that they might sink, plunged from the bridge, to save their honour and escape baptism. The husbands had rather send them to the bosom of Abraham than leave them to the mercy, or rather the lustful cruelties, of the Christians.[33]

## THE SPANISH INQUISITION

Fifteenth-century Spain was a dreadful time and place for Jewish people. Forced mass conversions gave an outward appearance that Judaism was not being practiced in the Spanish dominions. Nevertheless, underground Judaism was widespread, and those suspected "troublers of Israel" were hunted down by Dominicans and brought before the Inquisition. Thomas de Torquemada, a Dominican, was the inquisitor-general whose name has gone down in infamy as the personification of evil in the name of Christianity. In a single year, nearly three hundred Jews were burned at the stake in Seville alone, and more than seventeen thousand were sentenced to prison.[34] Atrocities against Jews during this time are too numerous to recount. These are well known in today's Jewish community. Next to the Holocaust, nothing has created more negative Jewish feelings towards Christians and Christianity than the Inquisition.

## REFORMATION PROTESTANTISM AND THE JEWS

Protestants who think that the Catholic church bears the entire burden of shameful behavior towards Jews are sadly mistaken. Unfortunately, the Protestant Reformation with its focus on the Bible and the apostolic church, failed to reverse the situation.

The greatest Jewish Christian to influence the Protestant Reformation was Nicholas of Lyra, a late medieval scholar, whom Martin Luther considered the best Bible commentator of the Middle Ages. His Jewish heritage has been challenged by some historians, but early sources suggest that this Oxford-educated Englishman was forced to leave England when Edward I banished Jews from his realm. Nicholas relocated in Paris, was baptized into the Catholic church, and joined the Franciscans. He earned a Doctor of Theology degree and became a teacher at the Sorbonne, gaining a reputation for his Biblical scholarship. "Well versed in Talmudical literature, he favoured the literal interpretation of Scripture after the method of the great Jewish commentator Rashi. For him the intention of the author was the most important canon of exegesis...."[35]

This serious study of the biblical text greatly influenced Martin Luther. Nicholas had written some eighty-five books covering the entire Bible and was proficient in Old Testament Hebrew. Reflecting on his method, Nicholas wrote: "I intend to insist upon the literal sense and sometimes to insert brief mystical expositions, though rarely."[36] So significant was his role in paving the way for straightforward biblical interpretation that a proverb was widely disseminated at the time of the Reformation:

Had Lyra not played his Lyre,
Luther would not have danced.

Martin Luther's anti-Semitism is well documented. Indeed, some would argue that the German anti-Semitism that gave birth to Hitler had its origins in Luther's pervasive religious influence over the German people. But Luther's most vociferous denunciations were reserved for the Roman Catholics. He gave mixed signals regarding Jewish people, arguing on one occasion that Jews of his day ought not be blamed for the sins of their fathers, nor be blamed for not converting to the corrupt Christianity of Rome:

> If I were a Jew, I would suffer the rack ten times before I would go over to the pope.
> The papists have so demeaned themselves that a good Christian would rather be a Jew than one of them, and a Jew would rather be a sow than a Christian.
> What good can we do the Jews when we constrain them, malign them, and hate them as dogs? When we deny them work and force them to usury, how can that help? We should use toward the Jews, not the pope's but Christ's law of love. If some are stiff-necked, what does that matter? We are not all good Christians.[37]

Eventually, Luther's ambivalent anti-Semitism manifested itself publicly, in the form of a tract he wrote much later in life. Roland Bainton writes: "One could wish that Luther had died before ever this tract was written." The tract was a response to rumors that Jews were seeking to convert Christians and to "the blasphemy of the rabbis" (and rabbinic writings) who defame the "dear Savior."[38] Blasphemy was a civil crime, and some would argue that Luther was a product of his times. Moreover, some of the rabbinical writings designed to keep Jewish people from considering Jesus would upset any Christian.

Yet, friends and enemies alike recognized the evil consequences of Luther's attacks. His closest friends pleaded with him to discontinue his anti-Jewish diatribes, but to no avail. One of his most often cited anti-Semitic writings proscribed an abominable program for Jews:

> Thus, Luther now proposed seven measures of "sharp mercy" that German princes could take against Jews: (1) burn their schools and synagogues; (2) transfer Jews to community settlements; (3) confiscate all Jewish literature, which was blasphemous; (4) prohibit rabbis to teach, on pain of death; (5) deny Jews safe-conduct, so as to prevent the spread of Judaism; (6) appropriate their wealth and use it to support converts and to prevent the Jews' practice of usury; (7) assign Jews to manual labor as a form of penance.[39]

Historian Eric Gritsch concludes that "Luther was not an anti-Semite in the racist sense. His arguments against Jews were theological, not biological."[40] But such a conclusion in no sense excuses Luther. The fiery rhetoric of that widely distributed treatise fulfilled its purpose. It set his Lutheran followers and German people against the Jews and served as a foundation for the worst anti-Semitic violence of human history.

In the centuries that followed the Reformation, anti-Semitism continued to infect both Protestant and Catholic churches. Equally significant is that few church leaders spoke out strongly against it.

## BOUND BY SUFFERING

Those who wonder how the church's history of persecuting Jews is relevant to Jewish missions today need to know that many powerful ties besides religious values bind Jewish families to a long tradition of Judaism. Those ties include stories of suffering. Indeed, Moishe Rosen's grandparents endured persecution in Russia simply for being Jews. On Good Friday, his grandfather would hide, a typical practice of many Jewish people who found they were targets of those seeking to "avenge" the death of Christ. "Often encouraged by inflammatory sermons from Orthodox priests and made brave by liquor, the people of the town would turn on their Jewish neighbors."[41]

"Christian" anti-Semitism was prevalent through the nineteenth century. This was true in North America, as well as elsewhere in the world. Yet some voices rang out against such prejudice, including one of America's most noted preachers of the last half of the nineteenth century, Henry Ward Beecher:

> The ignorance and superstition of medieval Europe may account for the prejudice of the Dark Age. But how a Christian nowadays can turn from a Jew, I cannot imagine. Christianity itself sucked at the bosom of Judaism. Our roots are in the Old Testament. We are Jews ourselves gone to blossom and fruit; Christianity is Judaism in evolution, and it would seem strange for the seed to turn against the stock on which it was grown.[42]

# CHAPTER THREE

# MESSIANIC JEWS AND MISSION OUTREACH

## Modern Missionary Efforts

I am convinced, as was Ralph Waldo Emerson, that there is "properly no history, only biography." Thus, this book has a biographical slant, as does this chapter in particular. Through biography we find role models—friends from the past (or dead friends, as I like to call them)—whose voices rise out of the grave to challenge us in how we live our lives in relation to God and others in the world around us.

Discovering messianic Jewish role models was new for me. With the exception of Solomon Ginsburg, a missionary to Brazil, I have never written about Jewish Christians. Ginsburg, born in 1867 in Poland, was the son of a rabbi. Not wanting to become a rabbi himself, he fled to London to live with an uncle—also an Orthodox Jew. The fifty-third chapter of Isaiah prompted him to study the Scriptures and to find Jesus as his Messiah.

As I have researched this book, I have become truly aware of the great Jewish Christians in generations past. And I am convinced that their stories are as important for Gentiles—maybe more important—as they are for Jews. Of course, Jewish people who follow Jesus need to be aware of their long heritage, but the gentile majority dare never forget those Jews who sacrificed much to profess publicly their faith in the Messiah. Even as I often remind my male students that they need to study the great contributions women have made in church history, so do non-Jews need to learn the stories of the great Jewish Christians.

*A very personal benefit that this research has given me is the discovery of a*
*great nineteenth-century Jewish Christian church historian. I have found a role*
*model in the person of August Neander. Indeed, my latest book acquisitions, from*
*the large collection in the basement of the Kregal bookstore about a mile from my*
*home, have been four volumes of his monumental history of the church, the oldest*
*published in 1850, the year of his death.*

—ɯ—

The nineteenth century saw a rise in the effectiveness of Protestant missions
whose outreach was specifically to Jews. At least the number of baptisms
would indicate so, according to the primary source of information on this
era, a book entitled *Jewish Baptisms in the Nineteenth Century.* The author, J.
F. de le Roi, was an ordained minister who served as a missionary with the
London Society for Promoting Christianity among the Jews. According to his
calculations, nearly a quarter million Jews were baptized during that hundred-
year period. *The Universal Jewish Encyclopedia,* however, took issue: "These
figures are manifestly too low.... Actually the number of converts during this
period must have been considerably higher."[1]

Jewish opposition to conversion was strong in the nineteenth century, as
it has been in every period of history. Jesus was the focus of antagonism and
was often portrayed as a scandalous figure in myth and history. In his book,
*A Century of Jewish Missions,* A. E. Thompson summarizes one of the more
preposterous fictions that circulated among Orthodox Jews:

> They are told that Jesus was able to perform miracles because He
> stole into the Holy of Holies, secured the sacred name of Jehovah
> and inserted it in a slit made in His heel. As He was flying through
> the air, on a certain day, a Rabbi, who had resorted to the same
> means of securing super-human power, flying above Him, struck
> Him to the earth; whereupon the women and children pelted Him
> with stones and rotten vegetables. Judas, crouching to kiss His feet,
> secured this charm, broke His spell and made possible His capture.[2]

Where Jewish people had closer contact with Christians, the opposition often focused on theological issues, but in any case, Jews were strongly warned against Jesus. Children were taught to spit at the sound of his name, and a Jewish person who converted to Christianity was regarded as dead. "Not infrequently," wrote Thompson, "a public funeral is solemnized, and the name of such an unworthy scion cut off."[3] The word *meshumad* (Hebrew for apostate) "carries a powerful load of rage," according to Rabbi Neil Gillman of Jewish Theological Seminary. Indeed, "many legends in Jewish folklore portray the apostate as a greater enemy to the Jewish people than the Gentile." So odious was the convert that, according to the *Encyclopedia Judaica,* "It was customary to spit three times on the ground when meeting an apostate."[4]

This response was not typical of Reform Judaism, which, according to Thompson, gave Jesus "a place of honor among the Hebrew prophets." Isadore Singer, writing in the late nineteenth century, represents this perspective:

> I regard Jesus of Nazareth as a Jew of the Jews, one whom all Jewish people are learning to love. His teaching has been an immense service to the world in bringing Israel's God to the knowledge of hundreds of millions of mankind. When I was a boy, had my father, who was a very pious man, heard the name of Jesus uttered from the pulpit of our synagogue, he and every other man in the congregation would have left the building, and the Rabbi would have been dismissed at once. Now it is not strange in many synagogues to hear sermons preached eulogistic of this Jesus, and nobody thinks of protesting—in fact we are glad to claim Jesus as one of our people.[5]

Most people who have written about the history of missions to the Jews have been sympathetic, but opponents of Jewish evangelism have recorded their reflections as well. Jean-Marc Heimerdinger wrote about what he saw as "the old Christian habit of rewriting Jewish history in the light of the advent of Christ...by leaving out whole periods of time or by using negative classificatory terms such as 'Late Judaism'...." Regarding missionary endeavors to the Jews, he wrote:

The Jewish experience of Christian mission has been a long experience of threat, bullying, suffering and death. Some nineteenth-century Christian missions to the Jews did modify this negative Christian attitude towards the Jews, affirming that "the Jews too were loved by God." Such organizations came to regard anti-Semitism as an evil. But to the Jews this apparent gain had an ominous counterpart which was brought into sharp relief in statements such as the one made by the Protestant Federation of France: "A clear distinction should be drawn between anti-Semitism and the anti-Judaism which is involved in every summons to conversion.... The aim of general conversion cannot be anything less than the spiritual destruction of Judaism."[6]

Rabbi Larry Gevirtz argues throughout history that children were often targets of conversion. His account—assuming it is true—would disgrace any concept of Christian missions:

As late as 1858, an ailing Jewish infant named Edgar Mortara was secretly baptized in Italy by his Christian nurse, who felt this was the only way to "save" him. When the boy recovered, he was forcibly removed from his parents' home by the Church, and subsequently raised under Church auspices. The horrified parents and their supporters appealed to the Pope for help, only to be turned down. The boy lived his entire life as a Christian.[7]

Anti-Semitism in the church has continued down through the twentieth century, but as prominent Jewish Christians identified themselves with their people, the force of church-sponsored discrimination diminished.

Jewish Christians also had their supporters. Here is a look at some of them.

### BENJAMIN DISRAELI

This nineteenth-century British prime minister probably did more than any other single individual in the nineteenth century to focus attention on the issue of Jewishness and its relationship to Christianity. Disraeli became a

Christian as a youth, but he always retained his Jewish heritage and his Jewish pride. In addition to his political prowess, he became known for his diplomacy and for several works of fiction. In each of these endeavors, he championed the cause of Jews—enough so that his critics charged him with favoritism.

Disraeli, according to Hillel Halkin, "is one of those fascinatingly uncategorizable Jews that Jews themselves have never known how to think about." He was "not only inwardly preoccupied with his Jewishness, he publicly flaunted it," and he "was never so Jewish as when pushing the Tory claim to be the party of English and Anglican tradition." More importantly, Disraeli "genuinely convinced himself that Judaism and Christianity were essentially the same religion—or that, as stated by his character Tancred, the hero of the 1847 novel of the same name, 'Christianity is Judaism for the multitude, but still it is Judaism.'"[8]

Disraeli's Jewish pride was evident in his work "Lord George Bentinck." There he wrote that while "the other degraded races wear out and disappear, the Jew remains, as determined, as expert, as persevering, as full of resource and resolution as ever." Why was Disraeli so loyal to his Jewishness? Disraeli's recent biographer, Paul Smith, suggests that:

> Disraeli's "vaunting of the Jewish race" was less the product of an articulated theory than of "the necessary compensation for the devaluation of the Jewish [that was] rendered unavoidable by his Christianity. Disraeli, in other words, felt intensely Jewish without being able to anchor these feelings in Jewish religious practice or thought; and casting about for a rationalization of them, he came to believe, first, that they were "in his blood," and second, that this blood was superior.[9]

Perhaps modern-day critics could claim the same about Jews for Jesus. Yet those who interpret Jewish believers' desire to maintain their heritage as a demonstration of feelings of superiority, probably would not be inclined to view their own determination to maintain their non-Jewish cultural heritage in quite the same way.

Although some people have questioned the sincerity of Disraeli's Christian commitment, he argued well for the faith, believing that Christianity flowed very naturally from Old Testament Judaism. His defense of the faith and his challenge to the institutionalized church is as fresh today as it was more than a hundred years ago when he wrote it:

> In all church discussions we are apt to forget the second Testament is avowedly only a supplement. Jesus came to complete the "law and the prophets." Christianity is completed Judaism or it is nothing. Christianity is incomprehensible without Judaism, as Judaism is incomplete without Christianity.
>
> The law was not thundered forth from the Capitolian mount; the divine atonement was not fulfilled upon Mons Sacer. No; the order of our priesthood comes directly from the God of Israel; and the forms and ceremonies of the church are the regulations of His supreme intelligence. Rome indeed boasts that the authenticity of the second Testament depends upon the recognition of her infallibility. The authenticity of the second Testament depends upon the congruity with the first....
>
> When Omnipotence deigned to be incarnate, the Infallible Word did not select a Roman, but a Jewish frame. The prophets were not Romans but Jews; she who was blessed above all women, I never heard she was a Roman maiden. No, I should look to a land more distant than Italy, to a city more sacred even than Rome.
>
> The first preachers of the gospel were Jews, and none else; the historians of the gospel were Jews and none else. No one has ever been permitted to write under the inspiration of the Holy Spirit, except a Jew. For nearly a century no one believed in the good tidings except Jews. They nursed the sacred flame of which they were the consecrated and hereditary depositories.
>
> And when the time was ripe to diffuse the truth among the nations, it was not a senator of Rome or a philosopher of Athens who was personally appointed by our Lord for that office, but a Jew of Tarsus.

And the greater church, great even amidst its terrible corruptions, that has avenged the victory of Titus, and has changed every one of the Olympian temples into altars of the God of Sinai and of Calvary, was founded by another Jew, a Jew of Galilee.[10]

## MICHAEL SOLOMON ALEXANDER

Michael Solomon Alexander, one of the great Jewish Christian church leaders of the nineteenth century, served as Anglican bishop of Jerusalem prior to his death in 1845.

Alexander was born in 1799 into an Orthodox Jewish family living in a small town in Prussia. As a young adult he read the New Testament and was surprised to find that the Jesus he encountered there was very different from the one he had learned about as a child. He began to wonder if the rabbis had purposefully concealed the truth about Jesus. Putting aside such questions, he accepted an appointment as a rabbi, a profession that flowed naturally from his expertise in Hebrew and his gifts as a teacher. He gave Hebrew classes to interested Anglican clergymen, who challenged him further regarding the role of Jesus as Messiah. Through their influence and his personal study, he was slowly becoming convinced—a transformation he chose not to disguise. Accordingly, he was dismissed from his rabbinical duties, which allowed him to explore more fully the teaching of Jesus and the apostles.[11]

In 1825 Alexander publicly confessed his faith in Jesus as Messiah and was baptized. His wife did the same several months later. In 1827 after theological study, he was ordained a deacon in the Anglican Church. He later became a priest, serving as a missionary in Poland. After that, he returned to London, where he became a professor of Hebrew and Rabbinical Literature at King's College. In 1841 he was consecrated as the first bishop of Jerusalem, with the mission of bringing equal privilege and renewal to the Protestant church in the Holy Land. His presence there almost immediately stimulated the struggling church, as was evident in a letter home only months after he arrived: "There never have been such large congregations of Protestants as have been assembled since my arrival here. On Sunday last our chapel was literally crowded, and never did I wish more that our church was built."[12]

Alexander, however, was soon the center of controversy. While his assignment was to serve the Protestant church, he was a missionary at heart, and he continued to evangelize as a gifted teacher and an apologist for Jesus the Messiah. This mission work was expanded in 1843, when Alexander opened the doors of a training school for Hebrew Christian missionaries. The project quickly grew into a complex that offered new converts housing and training in various trades, while instructing them in the Christian faith. The "Bible Depot" was added in 1844, offering translations of the Bible in Hebrew, Greek, Arabic, French, German, and Italian, as well as tracts in Hebrew. The response of rabbis was one of anger and alarm, and Jews who accepted the literature or became involved in any way with the ministry were threatened with excommunication. Despite the opposition, the work went forward, and later that year a hospital was opened for Jews who could not otherwise afford medical care.[13]

Alexander's days of ministry were all too brief. In late November of 1845, while traveling through the desert to visit those under his care in Egypt (part of the Jerusalem diocese), he died unexpectedly of a heart condition. His wife later wrote a letter telling about the journey and the work:

> On setting out through the desert each day my beloved husband and myself rode our own horses; we generally were in advance of the caravan, and we used regularly to chant some of our Hebrew chants, and sang...hymns. Never did his warm and tender heart overflow so fully as when he spoke of Israel's future restoration.[14]

The news of his death brought great sorrow and a terrible sense of loss among the Protestants in Israel—but even more so among his Jewish converts. Thirty-one of them signed a letter commending his work and his sacrificial love:

> We feel collectively and individually that we have lost not only a true father in Christ, but also a loving brother and a most kind friend.... The affectionate love he bore to Israel, which peculiarly characterized him, could not fail to render him beloved by every

one who had the privilege of being acquainted with him.... He was
a burning and shining light; and when he was raised to the highest
dignity in the church, he conferred the most conspicuous honor on
our whole nation, but especially on the little band of Jewish believers With him captive, Judah's brightest earthly star has set, and the
top stone has been taken away from the rising Hebrew Church.[15]

## AUGUST NEANDER

Church historians seeking role models would do well to study the life and
writings of August Neander. He was one of the great church historians of the
nineteenth century, as is evident in his *magnum opus*, *A General History of the
Christian Religion and Church*. But he was far more than a scholar and professor. He was a deeply pious Christian—a true servant of Jesus, his Messiah—"one of the most outstanding believers and among the greatest
Hebrew Christians of all time."[16]

Born in Germany as David Mendel in 1789, he took the name Neander
("new man") when he was baptized at age seventeen. His conversion was a
result of deep spiritual conviction, influenced by Christian teachers. To the
pastor who baptized him, he wrote:

My reception into the Holy Covenant of the higher life is to me the
greatest thing for which I have to thank you, and I can only prove
my gratitude by striving to let the outward sign of baptism into a
new life become, indeed, the mark of the new life, proclaiming the
reality of the new birth.... [17]

Intending to enter the ministry, Neander studied theology at Halle. One
of his teachers there was the famed philosopher Friedrich Schleiermacher,
whose teaching and writing became foundational for many liberal theologians into the twentieth century. They later taught together at the University
of Berlin. Of this twist of fate, Neander's biographer writes:

It was a sad and singular sight to behold his former teacher,
Schleiermacher, a Christian by birth, inculcating in one lecture

room, with all the power of his mighty genius, those doctrines which led to the denial of the evangelical attributes of Jesus Christ, whilst in another room his pupil Neander, by birth a Jew, preached and taught salvation through faith in Christ the Son of God alone.[18]

Although Neander had intended to study for the ministry, he was never ordained; his *ministry* was that of a professor and church historian. He preached Christian truth, not from the pulpit, but from the lectern. He remained single throughout his life, residing with his sister. This allowed him to invest his life in his students, who became, as it were, his surrogate family. They "looked upon him as a father in God, and as a counselor" and often spent time in his home. He was also known for his humanitarian concerns:

> No needy person ever appealed to him in vain for aid. His charity and generosity were unbounded. His own wants were few and modest, and he gave the bulk of his income to others. The proceeds from the sale of his numerous works were devoted to philanthropic and missionary purposes. If he were short of money at any time, he would take a valuable book and pawn it, so that he might have something to give to any needy person who appealed to him.[19]

Church history was Neander's passion. His was a living history, not merely a rendition of the deeds of the dead, replete with creeds and councils and appropriate dates.

Neander's focus on individuals gave his works a biographical flavor, and he always sought to bring practical insight and application to the narrative. We see this in his brief reflection on the seventh-century monk Maximus:

> He was…distinguished for his zeal in endeavoring to promote a vital, practical Christianity, flowing out of the disposition of the heart, in opposition to a dead faith and outward works…. Christianity, as it seemed to him, forms the exact mean betwixt the too narrow apprehension of the idea of God in Judaism, and the too broad one of the deification of nature in paganism; and this mean is

expressed by the doctrine of the Trinity. The highest end of the whole creation he supposed to be the intimate union into which God entered it through Christ....[20]

Neander died at age sixty-two. His massive church history ended with Wycliffe and Hus. In fact, an editor worked from Neander's notes to complete those two sections. Neander's death left a void among his colleagues and students as well as among those who awaited future volumes on church history. His funeral was attended by government leaders and university officials as well as ordinary folks. The two-mile route between his home and the cemetery was lined by mourners—some who knew him, and many who did not. A contemporary periodical summed up his life:

> In the death of Neander, Germany has lost one of her greatest teachers, and the Christian world one of its greatest ornaments. A purer and nobler character has seldom adorned any church—one in which the loftiest powers of nature and the lowliest graces of the Gospel were finely blended, and which more fixed, therefore, at once the love and the admiration of all who came in contact with it.[21]

## JOSEPH RABINOWITZ

Joseph Rabinowitz, a little-known Russian Jew, paved the way for messianic Jews of the twentieth century. He was a self-educated lawyer who dreamed of a Jewish homeland where his people could be free from persecution. But more than that, he led a remarkable messianic movement in southern Russia and set forth issues that have been debated inside and outside messianic circles since his death in 1899.

Rabinowitz was born in 1837 and raised in fervent Chassidism. During his teen years, however, he was greatly influenced by the Enlightenment and moved away from his Jewish fundamentalism. Liberal thought served him well in his young adult life and for a time he was convinced that Enlightenment thought turned to action would bring an end to the terrible persecution of Jews. That hope faded, however, as he realized it was hollow and bereft of a spiritual compass.

Rabinowitz's transformation from a humanist to a follower of Jesus did not occur until he was in his forties, though accounts of his conversion vary. His own version revolves around the spiritual experience he had on the Mount of Olives in 1882. He had gone to Israel (then called Palestine) hoping to establish a Jewish colony, but was disappointed to find conditions unsuitable for settlement at that time. He had brought with him a New Testament, primarily to use as a geographical guide, but it proved to be more than that. Before leaving the country, he spent a solitary time near the Garden of Gethsemane, where he sat down and reflected on the dismal state of the Jewish people.

> Suddenly a word from the New Testament, a word he had read 15 years before without heeding it, penetrated his heart like a flash of lightning: "If the Son therefore shall make you free, ye shall be free indeed" (John 8:36). From that moment the truth that Jesus is the King, the Messiah, who alone can save Israel, gained power over his soul. Deeply moved, he immediately returned to his lodging, seized the New Testament, and while reading John's Gospel, was struck by these words: "Without me ye can do nothing" (John 15:5). In that way, by the providence of Almighty God, it came about that he was enlightened by the light of the Gospel. "Yeshua Achinu" (Jesus our brother) was from then on his watchword—the message he took back to Russia.[22]

Joseph Rabinowitz's conversion has been much debated. Some say that he went to Palestine as a seeker, New Testament in tow, and that the Mount of Olives experience was only one aspect of his long conversion process. Others say that it was not until two or more years after he returned to Russia that he actually professed a relationship with Jesus. However, no one disputes that within three years of his trip, Rabinowitz had founded a movement that was called the "Israelites of the New Covenant." He utilized many Jewish traditions that were absent from Christian churches, and, despite overtures from Christian groups, he insisted that his movement remain independent of any Christian denomination.

His preaching was illustrated with parables, the most famous of which was the parable of The Lost Wheel:

Two foolish people were traveling in a four-wheeled wagon. Noticing that the wagon moved heavily, they examined it, and found that a wheel was missing. One of the foolish people sprang out, and ran forward along the road, saying to every one he met, "We have lost a wheel. Have you seen one? At last a wise man said to him, "You are looking in the wrong direction! You should seek your wheel behind the wagon, not in front of it."

This is the mistake which the Jews have been making all these centuries. They have been looking forward instead of backward. It may be said that the four wheels of Hebrew history are Abraham, Moses, David, and Jesus. The Jews have been looking into the future when they should have been looking into the past. This is why they have not found their fourth wheel.

But God be thanked that the sons of the New Covenant (Jeremiah 31:31; Hebrews 8:8) have found Jesus, that most important wheel of all. Abraham, Moses, and David are, after all, only types and forerunners of Jesus. Thank God, we have found our brother Jesus, our all in all, who is made unto us wisdom and righteousness, and sanctification and redemption (1 Corinthians 1:30); in whom alone we have found light and life, liberty and love, both for the great present and for the still greater hereafter. And now we look with longing eyes and joyful hearts towards the brightness of His appearing.[23]

The Rabinowitz Movement, as it was called, quickly caught the attention of Christian observers outside Russia. A mission publication in Norway reported: "Throughout Christendom, wherever the cause of Israel is a heartfelt concern, our eyes have now been turning toward this remarkable movement. It evokes memories of the days of the early church." From Basel, Switzerland, a cleric wrote: "He is a preacher sent by God; it is said that since the time of the Apostle Paul, no one has understood how to preach so mightily to the Jewish people as Rabinowitz." From St. Petersburg, a Christian scholar observed: "In Rabinowitz the Lord has sent us an Apostle Paul and a Jewish Luther."[24]

Today, a century after his death, Rabinowitz is no longer remembered alongside the apostle Paul or Martin Luther, but he is remembered in the messianic movement for relentlessly insisting "that a Jew who comes to faith in Jesus as Messiah does not need to give up his Jewish identity."[25] His movement never numbered more than in the hundreds. Significantly, however, it sparked interest throughout the Christian world—particularly from his travels through Europe and America—and brought acceptance to the concept of a truly messianic Jewish movement.

## LEOPOLD COHN

Leopold Cohn was born in Hungary and raised as a traditional Jew. At the age of seven, he lost both of his parents and learned early to depend on the God of Abraham. He excelled at his studies, became a district rabbi, and served as a magistrate for his community. But his rabbinical training was not enough to satisfy his curiosity about the Messiah. As he earnestly studied the Scriptures for himself, he became convinced that Jesus was the Promised One. The year was 1892. Outraged by this seeming betrayal, the Jewish community forced Cohn to flee Hungary, leaving his wife, Rose, and their children behind.

Cohn escaped to Edinburgh, where he studied at the divinity school and became a Fellow at the University, tutoring Hebrew. He was reunited with his family, and together they emigrated to the United States. Within two years, Cohn had started his own ministry. Scraping up the rent money from here and there, he simply opened a storefront in the Brownsville neighborhood of Brooklyn. Then he went out and preached on the street corners, inviting people to come to his storefront for Saturday meetings. Seven Jewish people came to the first meeting, sixteen to the second, and within weeks the room was filled to capacity. On weekdays, the space doubled as a reading room and classroom. There Cohn spent his evenings providing free English lessons to his fellow immigrant Jews—using the New Testament as a text. His priority was evangelism, but he also wanted to help meet the needs of other Jewish people who had come to begin a new life in America.

Cohn was high-minded and noble, but he had not planned to found a mission. He had not thought of himself as an evangelist—certainly not a mission director. Instead, his plan had been to stir interest in the New Testament and the Messiah and let others conduct the serious evangelism and teaching. To his surprise, his feeble efforts resulted in a "Jews for Jesus" movement that required his full-time attention. Several Baptist ministers offered to help financially through the Home Baptist Board. For some years, Cohn was under their umbrella, though he insisted on independence in his ministry endeavors. The budget was small, but the programs continued to expand.

After more than a decade of partnership with the Baptist Home Board, Cohn severed his ties with that organization and established the mission as an independent entity. A well-to-do supporter promised a substantial donation if Cohn would use it as a down payment on a building. When the Baptist Home Board insisted the check be signed over to them, Cohn refused, and a physical altercation ensued.

Soon after, Cohn expanded his outreach to Williamsburg, the most populous Jewish section of New York at that time. Cohn had a responsive spirit; when he saw needs and opportunities, he rallied to meet them. Once again, Jewish people came to his storefront meetings, though they endured persecution from their community leaders in doing so. Cohn's outreach involved children's ministries, which always required permission from the parents. But even more, Cohn recognized that the Industrial Revolution had provided a great opportunity to reach the untrained Jewish immigrants who lived in the Jewish tenements. He learned how to use a double needle sewing machine and opened a sewing school, drawing as many as two hundred girls, many of whose parents heard Cohn's message of the Messiah and believed. In the days before there were rescue missions, Cohn established a kosher food kitchen, founded a medical clinic, and delivered free coal to the Jewish poor. He did not consider his generous provisions handouts, but openings to proclaim the Messiah. To each person he helped he said, "Receive this in the name of Jesus."

Leopold Cohn died in 1936 and was succeeded by his son, Joseph Hoffman Cohn. The American Board of Missions to the Jews, now known as "Chosen People Ministries," was one of the most successful of the evangelical ministries to Jews in North America. By the mid-1950s the mission supported a staff of more than sixty people—one of whom was Moishe Rosen.

# CHAPTER FOUR

# AN UNLIKELY GENESIS

## *Jews for Jesus Gets Its Start*

The so-called "hippie movement" of the 1960s and 1970s entirely passed me by. I was attending a very conservative college where political dissent was not a part of campus life. So, unlike many of the early Jews for Jesus, I have no personal experience with the protests of that era. My reflection on that period has come primarily through my research of cultic groups that arose at that time.

Along with drugs, marches, and protests, the counterculture of the 1960s and 1970s gave rise to spiritual quests, religious and otherwise. A preponderance of gurus sprang up, claiming special knowledge of spiritual truth— usually spin-offs of Christianity or Eastern religions. Many used dubious means of recruiting and keeping followers, and their practices gave a new connotation to the word cult. Whereas any sect or group of people devoted to a common interest or belief can properly be termed a cult, the word took on a new and even sinister connotation, implying mind control and other abuses perpetrated by cult leaders. The high profile of such religious cults in the sixties and seventies sheds light on issues confronting the Jews for Jesus ministry in its earliest years.

The most pressing concern that leaders of the religious counterculture faced (cult leaders or not) was how to restrain the troops and how to control the recruits, the volunteers. Many leaders simply enforced authority from the top down, often through communal living and tight controls on lifestyle. Some such groups survived the turbulent sixties and seventies to come of age in the 1980s—though still under authoritarian control of the leader at the top.

In 1984 I embarked on what I called a "Cult Tour," traveling with my family to Massachusettes, Pennsylvania, Oregon, California, and Utah, and many places *in between. We visited "the Moonies" at their area headquarters in the New Yorker Hotel as well as at their Forty-second Street storefront. The atmosphere in both places was one of tight control as it had been some time earlier when I visited their Tarrytown, New York seminary. It did not take great sophistication to discern the carbon copy mindset of the cult members. The same was true of the Hare Krishnas in Philadelphia and in Limestone, West Virginia. It was also evident at the Rajneesh commune in Antelope, Oregon, which we visited two weeks later. And it certainly seemed true of Scientology, though I can scarcely lay claim to have visited that group. We were in their compound in Clearwater, Florida, briefly, but were unable to get past the front door of the headquarters in Los Angeles. This same level of secrecy and control was also evident with the Children of God and The Way International, cults that grew out of American Evangelicalism.*

*Thus, when I was reading newspaper files preparatory to writing this book, I was amazed to see Jews for Jesus named alongside those cultic movements time and time again.*

—⧟—

The origin of the Jews for Jesus organization goes back to a movement of Jews for Jesus in the mid-1960s in the notorious Haight-Ashbury section of San Francisco. There, drugs, free sex, and protests combined to make headlines out of hippies, 30 percent of whom, according to *Time* magazine, were Jewish. The Jesus Movement bloomed alongside "flower power," and many who later turned away from drugs and sex and turned on to Jesus were Jewish. By 1973, Moishe estimated that some 20 percent of the Jesus People in the Bay Area were Jewish.[1]

### "THE RANCH"

Although Jews for Jesus was officially born in 1973 in the San Francisco Bay area, a Christian couple in the backwoods of Oregon played a key role in the movement's origins. Jack and Liz Dunn (names changed to protect privacy) owned a house, known as "the ranch." The Dunns believed that God had told them to open their home to troubled young adults who wandered through the area. The ranch became a haven for hippies seeking spiritual answers and an incubator for several new Jewish believers in Jesus—Jewish believers who later formed the nucleus of the fledgling Jews for Jesus.

Efraim (Efi) Goldstein, who was then known as Freddy, was one of those hippies. He and his older brother, Baruch, then known as Bruce, had grown up in the Bronx. Efi says of himself, "I was a good Jewish boy. When we said the Shema ['Hear, O Israel, the Lord is our God, the Lord is One.'], I believed it."[2] Efraim went to Hebrew school and learned the basics of Judaism, but he also figured out that he was being taught to live according to tradition, not faith. That tradition eventually lost its importance to him as more exciting diversions drew his attention. The last time he remembers attending synagogue as a boy was after he accidentally burned down the family tent. From then on, he ventured into a new world where good Jewish boys from the Bronx were not supposed to go. First there was marijuana, then cocaine. But when some friends began using heroin, Efraim realized that he had come to a critical point in his life. He knew he could not go down that road and live.

Soon after his decision to turn away from hard drugs, Efraim met an old friend who had just come from Oregon with the news: "I've found Jesus." Stunned by her announcement, Efi nevertheless recognized a ring of truth to what she was saying. As she described the peace, joy, and meaning that she had discovered, he longed to find the same for himself. So he trekked to Oregon and spent time with the Dunns in their wooded retreat. While chopping wood there one day, Efi realized that he was free—he too had found forgiveness and new life in Jesus. He shared the news with his brother Bruce (who later took his Hebrew name as Efraim had done).

Bruce had been wounded in Vietnam and was living on disability, doing drugs, and disowning his Jewish heritage. He seemed to typify the "turn on, tune in, drop out" hippie philosophy. When Efraim started telling him about Jesus, Bruce figured that as the older brother it was his job to straighten Efraim out. But in order to do that, he had to understand what Efraim believed—and in the process, it was Bruce who got straightened out. He later wrote:

> My younger brother became a believer in Jesus, and as a result of his testimony and the testimony of some other Jewish people, I started examining the Scriptures....

You see, I never read the New Testament. Good Jewish boys and girls were not supposed to read the New Testament. Upon reading it, I was very much surprised to find a very Jewish Jesus, to find the disciples were Jewish, to find that the teachings of Jesus were ethical Jewish teachings. I came to the conclusion that if Jesus was not the messiah to Israel, then he could not be the savior for the Gentiles, either. He couldn't be one and not the other.

I became a believer, a follower of Jesus, for one reason and one reason only, and that was because I found it to be true, and I couldn't turn my back on the truth.[3]

Baruch's life changed radically. Soon afterwards he hooked up with Moishe Rosen and became one of the early band of enthusiasts who worked tirelessly. Eventually he became one of the ministry's top leaders.

Jhan Moskowitz, a good friend of Baruch's, was another of "the ranch crowd" who joined the ministry in the early years. Jhan's story was laced with anger and bitterness:

My father and mother were in a Nazi concentration camp, and my dad still has the number stamped on his arm. My people had suffered because of their Jewishness and I knew from an early age just how serious a thing it was to be a Jew. It was always *them* and *us*. *Them* included the Nazis and Christians."[4]

At seventeen, Jhan became a reserve member of the Israeli army and lived on a kibbutz, but was soon disillusioned and returned home to New York City, where he completed his university education. From New York, Jhan moved to California, met Baruch, and became part of the hippie subculture. But Jhan was restless. Florida was his next sojourn, and then he moved to Jamaica, where he was briefly associated with the Rastifarians. Back in California in 1971, Jhan was suddenly confronted with the issue of Jesus. Baruch had become a follower of Christ. Mitch Glaser, another old hippie friend, had also joined the Jesus revolution and was attending a Bible study taught by Moishe Rosen. Mitch and Baruch had a decided influence, but Jhan says the decisive moment came when God intervened to let him know for certain what was true. Jhan seized that moment and along with Moishe, Baruch, and Mitch became part of the nucleus of the Jews for Jesus movement.

In some respects, the earliest group of Jews for Jesus was not so different from the first-century motley crew who surrounded Jesus. Moishe was surely no messiah, but the former-hippies who followed him—the Goldstein brothers and their friends—were a "fringe" element, just as Jesus' first followers had been. And these young Jews for Jesus were as determined to follow Jesus as Peter, James, John, and the others had been.

In the early days, Moishe kept a close spiritual watch over his young associates. The small group was characterized by a sense of family that was especially welcome to those whose commitment to Christ had resulted in estrangement from their parents.

Moishe was keenly aware of the significance of what was happening, and he sought to explain it in biblical as well as sociological terms. In *The Tribal Concept*, an unpublished paper written in 1972, he argued that "Man, if indeed he is an animal, is a social animal and needs other men in order to be able to function as a man." Not surprisingly, he drew his premier illustration from his own Jewish heritage:

> One of the strengths of the Jewish people has always been that they've never gotten away from tribal social concepts.... In the tribe, every person is known to every other person and his relationships are secure and established. There are ways of gaining status according to function and conduct. There are certain tribal attitudes of consciousness which become the basis of sharing.

The tribal concept that Moishe was describing was taking shape in the summer and fall of 1972, while Moishe was still under the auspices of the ABMJ. As the budding movement took shape, a growing focus on Jewish ethnic identity, aggressive evangelism, and strong efforts to attract media attention combined to make this tightly knit tribe a force to be reckoned with.

### THE BUILDING OF AN ORGANIZATION

Moishe was building an organization even before he realized it. He was clearly the head of this group, but he was determined to build leadership in others. That determination along with his democratic inclinations set this religious movement apart from many of the other high-commitment movements of the 1970s—which often were dictatorships with virtually no decision making from the ranks. Not so with Moishe. He attracted people who were strong minded and creative, and he expected them to think and to take initiative. He once said of his position:

> My role is that of tribal leader. I preside over our weekly staff meetings and act as primary spokesman for the press and in major public debates. I'm usually the primary strategist in demonstrations and other confrontations, and I handle the overall coordination for our activities. But I am by no means a dictator.... On the contrary, I am frequently challenged or overridden on ideas I may propose to the group....[5]

Moishe's leadership style was due in large part to a very influential pastor who said toward the end of his ministry that if he had an opportunity to do it all over again, he would find ten men to disciple. Moishe recalls: "I made such a switch in my ministry in 1970. Before that time I had been a missionary 'to the Jews.' I decided to work with a few of the young Jews who had come to Christ.... I still continue to work with the same handful of people, except now they are evangelizing and discipling others." He also confessed that "the biggest problem in helping these young people find maturity is the fact that there are some areas of my own life where I am immature." Through his intense discipling relationships he discovered his own flaws and deficiencies.[6]

One of Moishe's strengths was recognizing what other people could do and helping them apply their gifts to the work of evangelism. That was the case with Steffi Geiser, an illustrator and designer for a New York advertising firm before she joined the group. In the early days, Moishe wrote:

My right-hand man is a woman, Steffi Geiser. As my prime adviser, she can usually pick out the flaws in a given plan of action or a piece of literature we propose. Her ability to estimate the potential effect on young people is phenomenal. She has been my co-strategist and expediter in dealing with creative communication.

Steffi and I are very different as individuals. We are both intense perfectionists, but I tend to be shy, quiet and contemplative, while Steffi is gregarious, winsome, and always making jokes.[7]

Steffi had come to California in 1971 while on vacation from the University of Buffalo. A Christian friend who was attending one of Moishe's Bible studies decided the two should meet. "When I first saw Moishe," Steffi later recalled, "he was heavier than he is now, and he looked very hokey to me. I thought that whole Bible-study thing was absurd.... The entire experience was bizarre." But two days later on Sunday, she was ready to make a faith commitment. Her friend and the others she was visiting were ecstatic, and they encouraged her to call Moishe. She did.

I called Moishe and said, "Mr. Rosen, I accepted Christ." He said, "Are you sure?" I said, "Uh, yeah." Then he replied, "That's nice, but we have some people here for dinner. I'll call you on Tuesday." Frankly, I was expecting him to jump up and down and appear immediately, but he was pretty cool about it. I know now that's his style, and I think it's probably wise because some young people jump into a Christian commitment without thinking through all the implications.[8]

The numbers of Jews for Jesus continued to increase, despite the fact that Moishe was brutally truthful about the circumstances the new recruits would find when they joined the staff. When Amy Rabinowitz, former vice president of a B'nai B'rith chapter, inquired about work as an office manager, he did not mince words: "I told her the hours were long, the pay was minuscule, I was eccentric, and the office was a madhouse." But she was not intimidated, and she joined the staff.[9]

The third in the trio of strong women to join Moishe in those early years was Susan Perlman, who today serves in the San Francisco headquarters as first assistant to David Brickner. She joined the movement in 1972, having come from New York, where she had worked in advertising. One of her most significant contributions to the work in the early years was her ability to communicate effectively with news organizations and reporters. Susan was usually the one to arrange an interview or get the media's attention when it was most advantageous for the ministry.

But all was not well in the bureaucratic Christian community. While Moishe and his crew did not back down from controversy, the ABMJ was not pleased with all aspects of "Rosen's experiment." The mission was concerned about its image and feared that the hippie subculture of the northern California group would alienate their supporting churches. Part of their concern stemmed from the tremendous backlash of disapproval in the Jewish community and how that would look to their Christian supporters. It is not that the Jewish community approved of the ABMJ, but that they had taken little notice of the mission, which at the time had a relatively low profile.

Articles about missionaries snatching Jewish souls became common in Jewish newspapers, and scathing quotes from community leaders appeared as counterpoint quotes in even the most positive articles in mainstream newspapers. Moishe maintained that most of the young Jews with whom he came in contact were not religious, but rather agnostics or atheists. Thus he claimed that the Jewish establishment—not Christian evangelists—was responsible for Jews turning elsewhere to find God. Even *religious* Jews, Moishe pointed out, had lost their faith in the supernatural, and "We're the ones believing in Isaiah, believing that God handed down the Ten Commandments. All of Judaism was founded on the basis of supernatural revelation. If it isn't true, let's drop the whole business."[10]

Nevertheless, the ABMJ did not appreciate the notoriety generated by Moishe and the early Jews for Jesus. Despite their concerns, Moishe persisted in doing what he thought was right. The parent organization finally took action and abruptly terminated Moishe's position. The group had covenanted to stay together for a year and a half, but Moishe had no idea how seriously the group would take that commitment now that ABMJ had fired him.

Moishe recalls his initial response to the unexpected news:

When I got fired, at first I felt so rejected. I expected the group to fragment and fall apart. I was thinking about what I would do to support my family. What I know best is being a salesman—I could have gotten a job selling almost anything and make as much money as I had been making before. And I figured I would keep witnessing in my spare time along with anyone else who wanted to stay. But then Amy Rabinowitz said, 'We'll all just raise our own support.' And she was so enthusiastic and seemed so sure it could be done that I got caught up in her enthusiasm. I sent out a letter to about 200 people on my Christmas list and was amazed at the response. The $5000 settlement I got from the ABMJ went into the "Hineni" album [the first recording of The Liberated Wailing Wall]—the singing group that was part of the movement.[11]

It was a time of uncertainty and tension. At issue was the survival of Jews for Jesus. In the end, eleven staff members who had been paid through the parent organization, including the members of The Liberated Wailing Wall, resigned and followed Moishe—in good tribal fashion. With that action in August of 1973, Jews for Jesus officially burst onto the scene as an organization in its own right.

With the help of a young friend, Byron Spradlin, then youth pastor of First Baptist Church of Richmond, California, Moishe pursued official legal status for the newly independent ministry. One September day, Byron and Moishe hammered out the articles of incorporation and bylaws at the Rosens' dining room table in Terra Linda, California. Byron became president of the board of directors and has continued in that capacity.

From its earliest days, the group had been known as "Jews for Jesus." Those words appeared on their T-shirts, denim jackets, posters, and literature as a slogan that identified who they were and what they were about. Nevertheless, for purposes of incorporation, Moishe had originally chosen the title "Hineni Ministries," first suggested by Tuvya Zaretsky as a good theme idea. The word also expressed the heart desire of the band of evangelists as it echoed the prophet Isaiah's response to God's call, recorded in Isaiah 6:8. There the Lord asks, "Whom shall I send, and who will go for us?" and Isaiah replies: "Hineni, [here am I] send me." Hineni became the theme of at least two original Jews for Jesus songs as well as the first album they produced. The two names, Hineni and Jews for Jesus, were used interchangeably at first. But early on, a Jewish not-for-Jesus ministry with a similar title challenged the incorporated name Hineni. While not one to back away from a confrontation, Moishe recognized the value of the less dignified but more readily understandable "Jews for Jesus." The group reverted entirely to the name that had coexisted both as a title and as a slogan from the start.

The methods and ideology that Moishe had used with the movement of Jews for Jesus, particularly the spirit of teamwork, carried over and made possible the shift from a movement into an organization. Moishe never considered himself very creative, but felt his strong point was in recognizing and encouraging creativity in others. He also knew that rejection is inherent in Jewish evangelism and that it is a lot easier (as well as biblical) to face that rejection as part of a tightly knit community. The Jews for Jesus could go out and risk ridicule with their street drama and their music because they did it in teams. They did it with people they knew and trusted, and they performed material that they had written together.

## THE LIBERATED WAILING WALL

One of the earliest Jews for Jesus teams combined music, drama, and a colorful sense of humor to proclaim the gospel well before the organization was officially incorporated. In fact, the team was, in a sense, the reason why the ministry became a corporation.

Much of the talent for the team came from Stuart Dauermann, whom Moishe met while still with the ABMJ in New York. Moishe recalls:

I met Stuart Dauermann when he was a student at Manhattan School of Music, working his way towards his Master's degree in music education. He wrote two original melodies for passages of Scripture: one was to the text of the 23rd Psalm and the other was to the Lord's Prayer. His talent was impressive. After I moved to San

Francisco, I wrote and told Stuart what we were doing and how we needed evangelistic music that could be sung on the streets. He came out in 1972 in a ragged old van with his piano in the back. He was a prolific songwriter and many were evangelistic in nature. Some had Jewish sounding melodies while others did not.[12]

Dauermann, whom Moishe regards as one of the most talented and gifted individuals ever to be associated with Jews for Jesus, wrote much of the music that the team recorded in the early years.

The Liberated Wailing Wall actually existed as an organization before Jews for Jesus. In the summer of 1973 Moishe arranged a church tour throughout the country. The group and the music were well received. The tour would not have been possible without Miriam Sleichter (later Miriam Nadler), a team member who bought with her own funds the van in which the team traveled. Again, Moishe recalls:

I knew that The Liberated Wailing Wall should continue after I was no longer with the ABMJ, so we incorporated under the name Hineni. Byron Spradlin, who was the team's trainer and coach, became the chairman and Board of Directors and I became the Vice President but we never expected much of that corporation. However, that corporation, Hineni ministries, was the shell that eventually contained Jew for Jesus.[13]

The Liberated Wailing Wall had a major role, not only in the incorporation of Jews for Jesus, but in helping to carry their message.

"Today, some of the very prettiest of religious music is coming from the Jews for Jesus movement," wrote William Willoughby. "I have to say that I find much of it so much more rewarding to the ear—and to the heart—than I do some of the rather banal stuff coming out of pop Christian groups." He points out, however, that the sound of The Liberated Wailing Wall has influenced—in a positive way—other forms of contemporary Christian music.[14]

The Liberated Wailing Wall was not always so "rewarding to the ear." The very earliest team was comprised of pretty much anyone who was willing to go out on the streets and sing about Jesus—Jewish style of course. They also performed skits at Simpson College, a local Bible school that Moishe had encouraged several of the early Jews for Jesus to attend. But before long the team was honed into a fairly tight group of musician-evangelists who made the first impression that many people received of Jews for Jesus. Their good humor and observable professionalism opened many doors for the ministry.

In fact, The Liberated Wailing Wall has been the most enduring (and often endearing) public representation of Jews for Jesus throughout the years. The group still ministers in churches and in open-air evangelism. The Jewish sound and high quality of the music have combined to bring this music team wide recognition in the Christian world—and even in the Jewish community. In reviewing their performance in Rochester, New York, in the spring of 1984, Rabbi Shamai Kanter confessed in a Jewish publication the dilemma he faced.

"Indeed, one of my problems here is in providing an accurate description of the performance while avoiding sentences that might be quoted by the Jews for Jesus as a "rave" review by *Moment* or by me."[15]

He did not offer a "rave" review. In fact much of the article was very critical. Yet despite his best efforts, the rabbi was unable to disguise the fact that he was impressed with the quality of the music and the entertainment value of the program. He wrote, "They began to play; and for a second, I felt right at home." Again he wrote: "The music lessons some dutiful Jewish parents had provided years ago had certainly borne fruit.... The professionalism of staging and choreography was apparent."[16]

Onstage, the performers came across as friendly, good-natured, eager. They made good use of techniques they, or their director, had learned at Jewish folk concerts and Shabbatonim: "Now I'm going to teach you some Hebrew so that you can sing along with us. Ready? La-la-la-la-la-la... I bet you didn't realize you knew some Hebrew already!"

The Assemblies of God audience responded favorably to the concert. There is a "degree of warmth and approval from Christian audiences that more than compensates for the hostility of other Jews," according to Rabbi Kanter. "And paradoxically, the more 'Jewishly' they present themselves in this context, the more approval they receive."[17]

Regarding the testimonies of the group, the rabbi conceded that they challenged the Jewish community. He summed up their conversion stories and added his own analysis: "I learned that God is real, that He is close to us, and that He cares about us."[18] No strongly Christological affirmation, no insight into the sinfulness of humanity requiring a divine sacrifice for redemption. His simple religious affirmation stands as a remarkable indictment of the general inhibition of contemporary Jews in speaking about personal religious faith.

While the rabbi missed the team's gospel message, hundreds of Jewish people who have come to their concerts over the years have not only heard the message, but embraced it.

In reflecting on their style of music, the group's press release says:

It is hard to describe the songs because they're more than just melody plus lyrics. Some songs reflect the poignant longing that has been a part of our synagogue worship throughout the ages. Others are bursting with the same joyful exuberance you expect to find at a Jewish wedding.

In the early 1980s, David Brickner joined The Liberated Wailing Wall and then became leader of the group, traveling and singing around the world to diverse audiences in Israel and South Africa. In an Idaho interview, he explained the style of music to a reporter:

We wanted a way to bring a little of our Jewishness to bear in gospel music. It's the kind of music King David might have felt comfortable with, contemporary yet ancient.

It's an expression of my heritage so I appreciate it more than contemporary Christian music. I think most churches are thrilled to experience a little Jewishness because it's part of their heritage, too.[19]

The Liberated Wailing Wall continues to exist as an ever-changing group of musicians who are first and foremost Jews for Jesus staff members. They commit to eighteen months of ministry with the team, though some sign up for a second tour of duty. They are primarily known for their concert tours, but along the way they are often out on the street corners distributing broadsides and sometimes singing. Most of the year they travel across North America in a forty-foot bus that takes them to churches and college campuses. Overseas tours are also part of their regular ministry.

## THE NEW JERUSALEM PLAYERS

The New Jerusalem Players also had its origins in the early 1970s. In 1977 Susan Perlman, one of the founding team members, described the group in a Christian magazine article. She likened this "Jewish gospel street theatre" to the drama of the Old Testament prophets:

> Dressed in colorful costumes and wearing face makeup, they present dramatic sketches dealing with issues that concern people today: alienation, disintegrating marriages, drugs, corruption. Their striking appearance and relevant material have compelled crowds of people to stop and listen. As many as 700 people have gathered on a street corner and 1000 on a campus to watch these dramas.[20]

Another of the founding members, Lyn Bond, Moishe's older daughter, gives her perspective:

> "I finished my B.A. in February of 1973 and came to live with my parents in San Francisco. Each of the previous two summers I had attended classes at San Francisco State University's Summer School. So I already was acquainted with the people who had gathered around my dad as part of the group that would become known as Jews for Jesus. I even tried singing with The Liberated Wailing Wall but when I went back to college in the Fall of '72 no one missed my voice.
>
> Several of us who were not quite so musically inclined had a vision and a burden to use our dramatic talent to spread the good news. At the time, none of us were employed by Jews for Jesus. Jhan

Moskowitz, the self-appointed leader of our "troop" was a student at Simpson Bible College and he was in the employ of the Christian and Missionary Alliance. Susan Perlman was working as a waitress in her "spare time" to put food on the table and a roof over her head. Tuvya Zaretsky was doing social work in a group home for boys and I earned my living teaching Nursery school. What we had in common was a desire to use our talents for the Lord even if it meant that we had to work at secular jobs in order to finance life's necessities.

We needed a name and at one of our frequent "brain storming sessions" we decided on New Jerusalem Players. We liked it because it alluded to the second coming of Christ.[21]

As early as 1973, the New Jerusalem Players were invited to make their presentations in some of the more progressive churches. Like The Liberated Wailing Wall, the team wanted to use their talents to help gentile brothers and sisters learn about the Hebrew Scripture and the Jewishness of Jesus. They hoped that, in turn, the local church would catch their vision for bringing the gospel back to the Jewish people.

The Jewish gospel drama team ministered effectively for several years as a changing troupe of evangelists who signed up for eighteen months at a time. Eventually they, too, toured in a forty-foot bus like their sister team. However, it was difficult for the ministry to maintain both teams, so the New Jerusalem Players were retired.

The New Jerusalem Players have not had the enduring legacy that record albums, cassette tapes, and compact discs have afforded The Liberated Wailing Wall. Yet, this lively street theatre team drew spontaneous crowds in a way that music teams could not have done and their scheduled presentations opened the doors to churches and college campuses that might otherwise have been closed.

## ADMINISTRATIVE CHANGES

Moishe's personal ministry changed following the separation from the American Board of Missions to the Jews. Evangelism had been his top priority. As pressing duties crowded in, he often found himself seeing to administrative matters while the others were out on the street distributing literature. Once again, not by choice, he was an "organization man." Fund-raising became a necessity if he wanted to maintain a full-time staff. One of the most significant changes related to the relationship between the organization and the church at large.

According to anthropologist Juliene Lipson, "Jews for Jesus broadened its approach to what it labeled 'Jewishizing the church'—teaching through drama, song, and testimonials about what it means to be Jewish." This focus paralleled the "Jewishizing" of Jews for Jesus, as the organization developed a very conscious "Hebrew Christian ethnic identity" and began restricting non-Jews to behind-the-scenes or minor roles.[22] Through the years, some people have criticized this as disparaging to gentile workers. The comeback response of Jews for Jesus has been that "It's a matter of maintaining authenticity. The very name Jews for Jesus dictates that our up-front missionaries be Jewish. We are ethnic Jews for Jesus. That doesn't mean that we don't welcome or appreciate our gentile brothers and sisters as full partners in this work. However they serve as administrative or volunteer workers."

What began with Moishe and a small group of followers in San Francisco in 1973 quickly gained momentum. The messianic movement was far broader than this budding organization, but this small group of former-hippies was making some noise. And as a result of their attention-getting tactics, they became a target of widespread opposition from the Jewish community.

# CHAPTER FIVE

# IN THE PRESENCE
# OF MY ENEMIES

## *Thriving in the Face of Hostility*

I n my study of cultic groups, I have come across many accounts of opposition and deprogramming. Some accounts tell of family members who organize support groups. The single common denominator in such families seems to be the experience of having had a child in a cult.

In the case of Jews for Jesus—which is not a cult—an entire community has mounted organized opposition. In fact, I have never read of as much organized opposition as confronts this group. This intense opposition sets Jews for Jesus apart from all the other groups I have researched. Add to that the fact that it is not just any community, but one that is scarred by its own history of being unjustly persecuted and that has resources to take on individuals or organizations it perceives as the enemy.

As an outsider, I found the opposition to Jews for Jesus strange and perplexing. Here are Jewish people—as Jewish as can be—who are not only ostracized by the Jewish community but obliterated as Jews. They are shunned by the very people who know so much about being shunned and are told that they cannot be Jews. Their heritage and very existence are denied. In extreme cases their property is vandalized and they are physically attacked. Does this not bring reminders of the ugly anti-Semitism that Jews have endured throughout history?

One hears that it is common for the persecuted to turn into the persecutors. As an outsider, I have not been privy to anti-Semitism. In the circles where I grew up, I never heard Jewish people referred to as "Christ killers." That notion was not

*remotely hinted at in my evangelical church upbringing or my training in Bible col-*
*lege. Nor has it ever come up in any of the Christian schools at which I have taught.*
*To the contrary, we regarded Jews as God's chosen people and recognized that Jesus*
*our Lord was a Jew. If we had a stereotyped idea of modern day Jews, it was that*
*they were honorable, intelligent, successful people.*

*But this writing project has broadened my understanding and made me more*
*aware of anti-Semitism from a personal perspective. It is real and it is painful. And*
*it confronts Jewish people in their everyday lives—not just as it has been recorded*
*historically and in contemporary newspaper accounts and television documen-*
*taries. It reveals in all its ugliness the depth of animosity that many people who call*
*themselves "Christian" have for Jews—an animosity that has been passed down*
*through the generations. One person crudely remarked to a staff member: "First*
*you killed him; now you believe in him?"*

*Expressions of contempt, however, are certainly not limited in their focus to*
*Jews, or more specifically to Jews for Jesus. Virtually all people who are involved in*
*street evangelism encounter slander and snide remarks. I have encountered*
*ridicule myself—especially in my college days when I was active in tract distribu-*
*tion. But Jews for Jesus are particularly vulnerable for no other reason than their*
*Jewishness. Their very vocal and visible witness almost invites opposition, and in*
*some cases this comes from those who cannot disguise their anti-Semitism.*

*Nevertheless, most of the hostility vented against Jews for Jesus comes from*
*other Jewish people—and perhaps with good reason. Most Jewish people are very*
*sensitive to anti-Semitism and are more than a little suspicious of that which*
*appears to fly in the face of "traditional" Jewish understanding. Thus when they*
*encounter the overt witness of Jews for Jesus they view it as just one more attack*
*on their heritage, their culture, their people—and they are determined that this*
*time the attack will not go unanswered.*

—ɯ—

Their harshest critics contend that Jews for Jesus purposely seek hostility and
persecution. Stanley Rosenbaum, a professor of Jewish Studies, does not mince
words: "I see now that many JFJs [initials commonly used by Jewish opponents in order to avoid the name of Jesus] are a species of mental masochist;

they expect and even want insult, something their callowness is almost bound to produce." Rosenbaum goes beyond what one might consider a spontaneous judgment and makes accusations that no trained critic would offer without a psychological profile of the movement to substantiate his claims.

> Jews for Jesus, in my experience, exhibit a high degree of sociopathology along with their sincerity. Many see themselves as misfits. It's a toss-up as to whether they would be better addressed by Jewish theologians or psychologists.... The "disease" they guard themselves most zealously against is independent thought.... Many come from unhappy homes in which they received too little attention.[1]

Such criticism has not stopped the organization from doing what it does best—challenging people to consider the claims of Jesus. Indeed, Jews for Jesus would argue that it is the Jewish community that guards "zealously against independent thought" on the issue of Jesus.

During the early 1970s, developments in Jewish-Christian relations seemed to prove that very point. The tension between Jewish people who do not believe in Jesus and those who do drew national attention in 1972. A Massachusetts rabbinical court decreed that any Jew who becomes a Christian has "betrayed his people" and "may not claim his right to be married to a member of the Jewish faith, the right of membership in a Jewish congregation, or the right of burial in a Jewish cemetery."[2]

It was all part of an attempt to prevent more Jewish people from considering Jesus. This is understandable if you realize that Jews who do not believe in Jesus view their disbelief as a crucial part of their Jewish identity. Therefore they cannot comprehend the claims that believing in him makes a Jew more Jewish, and they must see those claims and those who make them as threats.

## THE "THREAT" OF KEY 73

The Jewish community was especially up in arms regarding Key 73. This vast interdenominational evangelistic effort held in 1973 was "to share with every person in North America more fully and forcefully the claims and message of the Gospel of Jesus Christ."[3]

Nothing in recent history has alarmed the nation's Jewish community as much as Key 73 and its year-long goal of "calling our continent to Christ." The project embraced almost 150 denominations, dioceses, and independent groups, from Pentecostals to Roman Catholics.[4]

Many Jewish leaders saw Key 73 as an about-face for American Christianity. Liberal churches had assured Jewish leaders of their understanding that Jews do not need Jesus, and that all attempts by Christians to convert Jews should be discontinued. The Jewish community had taken these assurances as proof of a mainline Protestant consensus. This "calling to Christ" went directly against the implied agreement. Obviously, messianic Jewish groups, including Jews for Jesus, never signed on to that philosophy; if they did not think Jewish people needed Jesus in order to be saved, they would not have accepted him for themselves. But several non-Jewish Christian groups also held firmly to their commitment that Jesus is, as he claimed to be, the only way to the Father. Some of them issued a joint memo, publicly committing themselves to evangelism that would not exclude Jews.

Rabbi Solomon S. Bernard charged that Key 73 fostered "a stifling, suppressive" climate that infringed on the privacy of Jews and facilitated their "quick liquidation and extinction." Rabbi Marc Tanenbaum, a spokesman for the American Jewish Committee, portrayed Key 73 as "an assault on the honor, dignity and truth of Judaism." He challenged Christians to "cultivate your own garden before undermining a garden cultivated by others."[5]

In reflecting on Key 73 and the charges of anti-Semitism from rabbis and other Jewish leaders, Carl F. H. Henry, a leading evangelical theologian, offered a response in a *Christianity Today* editorial:

> Reference to evangelicals in the same context with Hitler and anti-Semitism so shocked numbers of evangelical leaders that Jewish-evangelical understanding may have been impaired. Many evangelicals felt that a wolf-cry of anti-Semitism was being sounded forth in an effort to disarm and discredit legitimate evangelism....
>
> But the issues were not that simple. Although evangelicals were

disconcerted by propagandistic attacks they feared would not be quickly undone, many were grateful that Tanenbaum had made evangelical interest in Jewry a national issue.... Many young Jews have become believers because they find no element of promise in Judaism apart from Messiah, and see the current emphasis on Jewish identity and uniqueness as a program of cultural renewal that eclipses central spiritual concerns....

The charge by Jewish rabbis that conversions are destructive of Jewish heritage and culture (Messianic Jews are called *meshumeds* or traitors) prompts two comments. While it is true that some Jewish believers write off their own heritage and forsake the marks of Hebrew culture, including observance of Jewish holidays, most Jews who have found Messiah have also come to a new awareness of their own heritage.[6]

Jews for Jesus always has and probably always will face opposition, and while they do not seek it, they have learned to measure their success in part by the opposition they encounter. "The fact that they oppose us means they are hearing our message," Moishe explains. Mission outreach to the Jews always has been viewed with hostility. How much more so would Jews for Jesus—a highly successful ministry, founded by a Jewish man and staffed by bright young Jews who are proud of their Jewish heritage and culture— engender opposition? The Jews for Jesus staff respond to accusations, pseudopsychoanalysis, and opposition in general without rancor. They figure, probably rightly so, that the only reason they face organized opposition is the fact that they are making a difference.

## LEVELS OF ORGANIZED JEWISH OPPOSITION

Moishe Rosen has delineated three levels of Jewish opposition that the Jews for Jesus ministry faces:

The first level of opposition is what Moishe calls the "establishment approach." He says, "The leading Jewish organizations won't talk to us. Instead they mount campaigns urging Christian groups with whom they often work closely not to support our efforts. This is usually ineffective because the Jewish community deals primarily with liberal Christian denominations who don't support us anyway. The Christian groups who do support our efforts usually do so out of strong conviction. They believe in what we're doing, not merely out of loyalty to us, but loyalty to the gospel. They won't be dissuaded by Jewish organizations or anyone else. It's an exercise in futility."

The second level of Jewish opposition to Jews for Jesus is a meeting of Jewish people speaking to their own community. These meetings usually take place in the local synagogue and are led by an "expert" on countering Jewish evangelism. Such opposition is not effective, according to Moishe, because "they talk to those people in the community who come to any announced meeting," and they do not draw the people who would most likely be attracted to Jews for Jesus. Some speakers have actually hurt their own cause by using arguments that rang hollow in the ears of spiritually astute Jewish hearers. Sometimes the opposition's warnings have even made people curious enough about Jews for Jesus to make their own inquiries.

The third level of opposition is the direct verbal—and sometimes physical—response. This response is also ineffective, according to Moishe, because "It makes us the underdogs and evokes sympathy. Most Jewish people feel compassion for us when they see us being persecuted and bullied." In a staff memo, Moishe instructed missionaries to keep this in mind. He pointed out that "Every time someone spits at us, shouts at us or strikes us, it serves God's purpose all the more. Nothing seems to impress our prospective inquirers more than the brutal way in which some elements of the Jewish community have been dealing with us."

Is there any form of opposition that works? According to Moishe, one Jewish countereffort was effective in slowing down the missionary outreach. It involved a group from New York who engaged members of Jews for Jesus in conversations while they were trying to hand out literature, thus keeping them from doing their jobs. The conversations were usually fruitless, although Moishe Rosen and other members of Jews for Jesus conceded that it was a clever tactic. Since then, instructions have gone out to field workers to avoid long conversations while distributing the broadsides; rather, to get a name and address and contact the person later.[7]

While some of the opposition to Jews for Jesus is well planned, some of it is spontaneous and at times it has turned violent.

## SPONTANEOUS OPPOSITION: THE "CAF RIOT"

Much of the opposition that confronts Jews for Jesus happens with little forethought. A passerby spits on, pushes, or punches the field worker, or simply grabs a stack of broadsides and throws them on the ground or into a trash can. Most common is verbal abuse, which is an everyday occurrence for the street evangelist. Sometimes an attack by one person incites others, as with the "Caf Riot" at Queens College in Flushing, New York, in 1980. The student newspaper told the story:

> Disturbances broke out in front of the Caf last Tuesday and Thursday when several students tried to prevent members of the Jews for Jesus from handing out literature on campus.
>
> Charges stemming from last Tuesday's incident have been filed with the Dean of Student's office by the Queens Christian Fellowship, the campus organization that sponsors the Jews for Jesus....
>
> In a related incident last Thursday, a near riot erupted when students offended by the Jews for Jesus tried to stop them from handing out pamphlets. Police were called to the scene.... Presidential Assistant and lawyer Dave Fields explained that..."contrary to popular belief, no City University by-laws prevent proselytizing on campus. Leafleting is protected by the Constitution as freedom of speech."
>
> After Thursday's incident, the student who struck the Jews for Jesus member explained his anger, commenting: "They are making a mockery of both Christianity and Judaism," adding that he couldn't contain himself....[8]

## ANTI-SEMITIC VANDALISM?

For David Baker, who headed the Los Angeles branch of Jews for Jesus in the early 1980s, violent anti-Semitism was the last thing he expected. "It was part of my mother and father's generation, but not mine," he told a reporter.

"It's kind of new to me." The violence erupted suddenly and unexpectedly at a time when anti-Semitic vandalism was occurring at a nearby cemetery and at a center for Holocaust studies. In David's case, he endured slashed tires, rocks thrown through his living room window, threatening late-night phone calls, and spray-painted signs on his garage door that read "Jews for Jesus get out of town or else—death."9

Was this actually anti-Semitism? Such was the characterization made by the Los Angeles *Herald Examiner* in its headline and in the article itself. Some would argue that those involved were more likely members of a Jewish fringe group who were taking an opportunity to harass Jews for Jesus. On the other hand, such fringe groups do all they can to insist that Jews for Jesus are not Jews. To mount attacks that would make them appear victims of anti-Semitism would only have the opposite effect.

### THE JEWISH DEFENSE LEAGUE

In the early days of the ministry, the strongest opposition to Jews for Jesus came from the Jewish Defense League, an organization known for its physical and often criminal attacks against anyone or anything it perceives to be anti-Jewish. One JDL member outlined the strategy:

> The Jewish Defense League is going to hassle the Jews for Jesus until they quit. No Jew should be subjected to the personal affront of having contact with these people. It's an insult. We are trying to show all Jews that they don't have to put up with this obnoxious phenomenon. When we go to a demonstration, we kick some shins, we hassle them, rough them up some, take away their literature. It's a bit juvenile, I admit, but the message to Jews is, "Stand up for yourselves, fight back, don't turn the other cheek."10

At one point Moishe was informed that the JDL had a price on his head—that he was targeted for assassination. He insists he did not become paranoid, but he took the threat seriously. The FBI warned him not to travel by a prearranged schedule, not to follow the same daily route when driving to and from work, and if possible not to travel alone. Did he hire a bodyguard? "No, the JDL can't shoot straight—though they did shoot holes through our office window on one occasion."[11]

## A CONSENSUS RESPONSE TO VIOLENCE

Jews for Jesus staffers are quick to point out that neither violence nor a mob mentality is typical of Jewish people, no matter how much anger is directed at Jews for Jesus. However, they know that there is always the possibility that they will face violent opposition from a fringe element.

During the early days of the ministry, Moishe and his young volunteers did not take lightly their decision to stand firm in the face of possible violence.

During their first New York City witnessing campaign, there were instances of extreme hostility. This was particularly true in the Diamond District, where large numbers of Chasidic Jews have traditionally worked. "Nine of us were surrounded by two or three hundred angry Chasidim," remembered missionary Mitch Glaser. "I actually feared that we would not walk away from the situation unharmed." When police arrived, however, the angry mob was disbanded, and the team of campaigners was escorted to safety.

When the team returned to its New York headquarters, Moishe put the issue of violence before the group. He warned them that there would be more threats of violence and that they should expect these threats to be carried out. He asked them if they were willing to go on, despite the risks, then distributed blank cards to each of the team members. They were to write yes or no, indicating whether or not they wished to continue a style of ministry that might elicit a violent response. Mitch Glaser later reflected on the moments that followed:

> As I sat there, fingering my blank card, it seemed like hours instead of minutes. I glanced around the room at my fellow workers, and a sense of our all being in it together, and the knowledge that we could depend on one another gave me the courage to vote "yes." The "yes" vote was unanimous, and we all felt strengthened and encouraged by our unity of purpose in the Lord.[12]

In addition to hostile, sometimes violent, opposition, the Jews for Jesus staff also faces opposition in the form of what they call "countermissionaries."

## COUNTERMISSIONARIES

A number of organizations have been founded for the explicit purpose of counteracting the work of the messianic movement—and specifically that of Jews for Jesus. One of the best known of these is Jews for Judaism, "a counter-missionary resource center" founded by Larry Levey in 1984. Levey, who for a time professed faith in Jesus, "came back to Judaism" after a rabbi intro-duced him to Torah Judaism, which he insists is "real" Judaism.

The organization is self-described as a group of "Torah-observant Jews who are experts in dealing with Jews for Jesus and other deceptive Christian missionary groups." Levey had only blistering words for Jews for Jesus and other such groups, whom he accuses of dishonesty: "When I look at the mis-sionary pamphlets, generally the emphasis is, 'Jesus is the Messiah predicted by the Jewish prophets.' Almost never do I see the statement, 'Jesus is God.' This is done on purpose."[13]

Some might suggest that Levey and his organization are themselves less than honest in their countermissionary activity. For example, one of the tracts they distributed quotes two well-known figures whom they identify as church fathers: Martin Luther and Adolf Hitler.[14]

One of Levey's most persistent tactics was his effort to persuade church leaders to turn their backs on messianic ministries.

The Jewish Community Relations Council (JCRC) is another group that seeks to counter missionary activity. This coalition of some fifty organizations includes the Task Force on Missionaries and Cults. Founded in the mid-1970s, the task force investigates—and sometimes infiltrates—groups it feels pose a threat to the Jewish people. They also seek to "deprogram" Jews who have become part of messianic groups. As part of this effort, the group cosponsors the Cult Hotline and Clinic in New York.[15]

The primary aim of the organization is to win Jews back to Judaism, and as part of this effort it sends letters every two weeks to about three hundred messianic Jews. It also has a speakers' bureau that sends rabbis and other Jewish leaders to college campuses and local synagogues to warn of the danger posed by messianic missionaries.[16]

Antimissionary groups are not limited to North America. Some groups that originated in the United States have branched out to other parts of the world, while others are native to various countries. In England, Rabbi Shmuel Arkush heads "Operation Judaism," which he claims is fighting missionaries nationwide. *Yad L'Achim* was founded in Israel in 1950, long before Jews for Jesus came on the scene, by Rabbi Shalom Ber Lifshitz. He wanted to preserve the "Old World" ways of Jewish immigrants who were faithful to the Torah and their traditions and, equally important, shield Jews from the influences of the missionaries.

The most common opposition confronting Jews for Jesus comes from individuals, freelancers, who write articles and books denouncing missionary activity. In many cases the writer is known only in Jewish circles. Some, however, are well known and widely respected. The bitter words of Elie Wiesel provide an example:

> "Come with us," the soul-hunters tell them, "be one of us. After all, we are Jews like you. Better still, only by becoming Jewish Christians or Christian Jews will you be truly Jewish...."
>
> I feel less revulsion for Christian missionaries than for their Jewish accomplices. The missionaries are at least honest. They proclaim openly that their aim is to absorb as many Jews as possible into their church. They aim to kill their victims' Jewishness by assimilating it. They give each individual Jew the choice between Judaism and Christianity—always doing their best to influence that choice.
>
> Their Jewish colleagues, however, the "Jews for Jesus," for example, are dishonest. They are hypocrites. They do not even have the courage to declare frankly that they have decided to repudiate their people and its memories.
>
> In telling their victim that he can be Jewish and Christian at the same time—as if the history of Christianity did not give them the lie—they are laying a trap of trickery and lies. Even more detestable, they play on their victim's vulnerabilities. They always

exploit weaknesses, ignorance, and unhappiness. They offer the victim a new "family" to replace his own, the "comradeship" he lacks, and at the outset, a "no obligation" religious atmosphere. Later, it is too late to turn back. "Operation Enticement" has been successful.[17]

In addition to the open hostility Jews for Jesus faces and in addition to the work of "countermissionaries," the group also has to deal with charges that it is deceptive in how it presents its message to Jews.

## THE CHARGE OF DECEPTIVENESS

Elie Wiesel's charge of deceptiveness is the most common accusation against Jews for Jesus and messianic Jews in general. This charge relates very closely to the issue of identity. Indeed, the fact that Jewish Christians in the past quarter century have maintained their Jewish heritage and identity is what angers many Jewish leaders the most. "Never in the past have people tried to have it both ways," argues Rabbi Michael Gold. "There have always been apostates. But these are people who use a lot of Hebrew to attract Jews." Gold, like many other rabbis, insists that Judaism and Christianity do not mix, and he asserts that any effort to mix them is inevitably an exercise in deception.

The claim that messianic Jews are deceptive is less than convincing—especially in the case of Jews for Jesus. Jews for Jesus staff wear the name of the organization on their T-shirts and jackets, and the name is every-where in their advertising. Since most other messianic groups are also very open about their identity, stories of so-called deception are manifestly self-contradictory.

Much like the "cult" label, the accusation that Jews for Jesus are deceptive simply is not supported by objective evidence. These widely stated charges are accepted and repeated in language that seems to take on private nuances. Thus, their adversaries interpret a difference of beliefs as an intent to deceive, and rather than simply insisting that Jews for Jesus are mistaken or wrong or even stupid for believing in Jesus, they label them dishonest. Opponents of Jews for Jesus do not find it enough to disagree with them;

they find it necessary to vilify them. That adds emotional valence where the weight of evidence is lacking.

## SHUNNING

Shunning is a tactic that has been employed by religious groups from time immemorial—by Muslims, Mormons, Jehovah's Witnesses, Jews…the list goes on. Shunning is generally reserved for those who convert to another religion.

This is particularly true of Jewish people, most of whom do not shun those who practice no religion at all or subscribe to agnosticism. There are even some hybrid religions (combinations of Judaism and Buddhism for example) which are deemed acceptable in many Jewish circles. Yet anyone who would "convert to Christianity" is regarded as being outside the Jewish community and is, for all practical purposes, shunned. In many instances, even family members shun the convert. This is not a matter of organized opposition; it is more of a response that is not so much planned as inherent in the Jewish culture.

Every member of Jews for Jesus has a story of how hurtful shunning has been, but the pain affects people besides those who are committed to full-time Jewish evangelism. Rachelle Birnbaum is a case in point. She grew up a "cultural" Jew, but found Christianity more spiritually satisfying than Judaism: "I wrestled with the spiritual side of myself and emerged in the Episcopal Church. I didn't give up the Jewish faith because I never had it." But her spiritual pilgrimage has made her an outcast: "One of the saddest things in my life is that it's been very difficult to have contact with the Jewish community. I'm not accepted by my own tradition." Not because she herself had turned away from her tradition in favor of another, she insists, because "The longer I'm in the church, the more Jewish I feel."[18]

But this is not how it ought to be, according to Ruth Mason, writing in *Reform Judaism:*

Actually, the tradition does accept her, even if individual Jews do not. According to *halachah* (Jewish religious law), a Jew who con-verts remains a Jew. Rabbi Neil Gillman, a theology professor at

Jewish Theological Seminary, says it is a case of sophisticated religion being more liberal than popular religion.[19]

Another woman who has had a similar experience is Donna Myers Ambrogi, a retired California attorney. She converted to Catholicism while a student at the University of Chicago and calls herself a "Jewish Christian." Like many converts, Ambrogi read and learned a lot more about Judaism after joining another religion. She says there had been no spiritual dimension to the Jewish heritage of her home.

I was never drawn to explore Judaism, never saw anything that engaged me spiritually or intellectually.... I can understand the feeling of betrayal among Jews, but I don't feel I betrayed anything. I was not rejecting a religious vision. I didn't have that as a Jew. I've never stopped being Jewish.... I continue to be very concerned about anti-Semitism. In no way have I rejected my involvement with the Jewish people. But it's very difficult for Jews to accept me."[20]

## THE BENEFITS OF OPPOSITION

Moishe Rosen has always tried to focus on the benefits of opposition. He points out that Jesus warned his followers that they would be forsaken by family and friends. The shunning and other forms of rejection do cause pain as intended, yet God's faithfulness in enabling the Jews for Jesus to endure it has served as a testimony to Christians and non-Christians alike.

While Moishe would readily admit that he would rather be liked and admired than ridiculed and rejected, he has always been careful to teach the staff that opposition reminds them of who they are. It helps the group to identify with Jesus and with the biblical call for Christians to bear the reproach of Christ "outside the camp" (Hebrews 13:13).

Moishe also points out that the opposition has helped the organization hold to high standards. "There are plenty of people who would love to call us on any mistakes. Of course that's not the only reason to do things right, but it hasn't hurt us to keep our opposition in mind."[21] The yearly audits and paper trails have disappointed some who apparently hope for some interesting dirt to dig. One well-known investigative television program considered doing a piece on Jews for Jesus, but after poking around their headquarters, apparently they did not find anything sensational enough to invite further investigation or reporting.

Perhaps the greatest value Jews for Jesus has found in opposition can be summed up in the oft-repeated aphorism Moishe has taught the staff: "Every knock is a boost." It is an application of sorts of Joseph's statement to his brothers: "What you intended for evil, God intended for good" (Genesis 50:20).

## OPPOSITION: HELPING TO MAKE JEWS FOR JESUS

Moishe believes that Jews for Jesus would not have gotten off the ground if it had not been for opposition of the Anti-Defamation League and the newspaper, the *Jewish Press*. The organization was unknown and underfunded in August of 1974; then word got out that Moishe had been invited to speak at a Jesus rally in Madison Square Garden. He was one of many and was scheduled to speak for twelve minutes at the end of a lengthy program. This was hardly a newsworthy event. Yet, for reasons Moishe has never understood, the *Jewish Press* published the headline "All Jewish organizations forbid members from attending Jesus Joy Festival to hear Moishe Rosen."

Moishe and his young staff quickly took advantage of this unexpected opportunity and sent copies of the article to the national news media. Support from Christians around the country began pouring in, and people were talking about Moishe Rosen.

> I was nobody, doing nothing until the ADL and the *Jewish Press* made me. By the time that the rally was held on Labor Day, because of the notoriety created by the ADL and the *Jewish Press*, I was the keynote speaker.... The ADL sent a very inept briefing sheet to the NYC police department which was designed to acquaint them on who we were. Instead of throwing us into the slammer as was anticipated, it was because of the ADL that we were assigned police for our protection and we received more welcome publicity.[22]

Moishe has always believed that "if the Jews for Jesus had the right kind of enemies, they didn't need many friends." The "right kind of enemies" ridicule the message—yet they proclaim that message while ridiculing it. Moishe insists that neither he nor the organization has ever done anything to provoke opposition; it comes as a response to the bold gospel message.

While the people with Jews for Jesus expect opposition from some sectors of the Jewish community, they have also received it from an unexpected source.

## THE UNEXPECTED: CHRISTIAN OPPOSITION

The most difficult opposition for messianic Jews to understand and endure comes from an unexpected quarter: the Christian community. In recent years much of the criticism of Jews for Jesus has come from leaders within Christian denominations and groups—primarily mainline Protestant and Roman Catholic. Most evangelicals support evangelism in general—and Jewish evangelism in particular. However, there have been some notable exceptions, including Billy Graham. An article in a Jewish magazine condemned Jewish evangelism and offered Graham as a sympathetic voice:

> While a few, more centrist, evangelicals like Billy Graham have criticized missionary activity focused solely on Jews, most Christian criticism of Messianic Judaism comes from Catholic and mainline liberal Protestant denominations, which have, in the post-Holocaust, post-Vatican II era largely abandoned Jewish missionizing.[23]

Catholics have not only abandoned their missionary outreach to Jews, but strongly condemn others who continue those endeavors. An editorial written in 1987 by Monseigneur George G. Higgins, offers a Roman Catholic perspective:

> When Jews for Jesus and messianic Jews first surfaced several years ago, Paulist Father John Sherrin—my dear friend and colleague— and I took them on in our respective columns. From a Catholic point of view, we tried to point out the theological pitfalls and essen-

tial unfairness of these types of aggressive and deceptive proselytizing tactics....

It was one thing for St. Paul, writing as a Jew to the first generation of Christians long before the Gospels themselves were set down to state: "Unto the Jews I become a Jew, that I might gain the Jews." It is quite another, after two millennia of development of church tradition to jettison that tradition and pretend it never happened.

Jews for Jesus represents a dangerous movement to its targets and practitioners. It is deceptive, reductionist and syncretistic.[24]

Many ecumenical groups have also publicly denounced evangelistic outreach to Jews, using labels and making statements that they do not substantiate. Such statements seem to be either assumed or taken from unchecked sources and repeated. An example of this was a statement on proselytism issued by the Interfaith Conference of Metropolitan Washington, D.C., in 1987. This conference of churches represents Catholics, Baptists, and a wide range of mainline denominations.

We condemn proselytizing efforts which delegitimize the faith tradition of the person whose conversion is being sought. Such tactics go beyond the bounds of appropriate and ethically based religious outreach. Examples of such practices are those that are common among groups that have adopted the label of Hebrew Christianity, messianic Judaism or Jews for Jesus. These groups specifically target Jews for conversion to their version of Christianity.... By celebrating Jewish festivals, worshipping on the Jewish Sabbath, appropriating Jewish symbols, rituals and prayers in their churches, and sometimes even calling their leaders "rabbi," they seek to win over, often by deception, many Jews who are sincerely looking for a path back to their ancient heritage.... These proselytizing techniques are tantamount to coerced conversions and should be condemned.[25]

To suggest that the effective evangelism of Jews for Jesus results in "coerced conversions" is an insult to Jewish people—who are presumably believed incapable of figuring out that a messianic congregation or an organization named *Jews for Jesus* really does believe Jesus is the Messiah. This is an issue that is rarely discussed among those who oppose Jewish evangelism. It is one thing to disagree with the beliefs of such groups and quite another to insult the intelligence of those who accept those beliefs.

An even stronger statement than that of the Interfaith Conference was issued in 1987 by the Episcopal bishops of Maryland. It was specifically directed at Jews for Jesus:

> [Their] message is one of hatred, anti-Semitism in its worst form and depends largely on deception and manipulation for its effect. It claims to be Jewish to the public but in fact sees itself as an evangelical fundamentalist group committed to the elimination of Judaism.[26]

The interfaith assemblies that denounce messianic Jews also deny them a part in interfaith dialogue. Jewish Christians, or messianic Jews, have been a people with an identity since New Testament times. To insist that a Jew who believes in Jesus give up his Jewish identity and behave and worship as a Gentile would be comparable to suggesting that a Native American who believes in Jesus must worship in the same manner as a suburban accountant who attends Willow Creek Church.

Dr. Walter Riggans, who has taught in the field of Jewish studies, wrote an article titled "Messianic Judaism: A Case of Identity Denied." In it he pointed out the faulty logic and utter inconsistency of denying messianic Jews a voice in interfaith dialogue:

> A truism of contemporary interreligious dialogue is that representatives of the various faith communities must accept and in fact welcome religious diversity and religio-cultural pluralism. If dialogue is to have integrity, each participant must be allowed to speak for and to be himself or herself. In no other sector has this point been more emphasized and modeled than in the Jewish-Christian dialogue. All are agreed that bridges need to be built between the Jewish and Christian communities to provide a better perspective on theologi-

cal issues, to foster cooperation at socio-ethical levels, and to bring about Christian repentance of anti-Semitic attitudes and actions, all hopefully leading to reconciliation and mutual respect.[27]

He goes on to write that the one religious group that might best be able to bridge the gap between Christians and Jews are messianic Jews, who are part of both religious traditions. Yet instead of being included in the dialogue, they are rejected by both sides.

They are disqualified altogether from participation in the dialogue, let alone from any sort of leading contribution. Participants in the dialogue nevertheless do not refrain from speaking about Jewish Christians in a prejudicial way. Even as the right of self-definition is denied to Messianic Jews, both Jewish and Christians dialogue participants impose their own definitions upon them.[28]

Jews for Jesus has a standard response to all such criticism—particularly that leveled by Jewish leaders. Challenged by critics to focus on the *real* issue, Moishe answered, "The real issue isn't whether or not we are nice, authentic or sincere people, it is whether or not Jesus is the Messiah."[29]

# CHAPTER SIX

# ANOTHER KIND OF OPPOSITION

## *Attempts at Religious "Deprogramming"*

B efore I began my research on Jews for Jesus, a friend insisted that I read the story of Ellen Kamentsky; in fact, she passed along a copy of Kamentsky's book to me. She was concerned that it was inflammatory material that could not be ignored and that Jews for Jesus might object to including such a story. Although I quickly learned that Jews for Jesus did not expect me to avoid "inflammatory" material, I found no bombshells in Ellen's book. She implies that she endured forms of mind control and "brainwashing," yet her book provides no substantiating evidence. To the contrary, for someone like myself who has read many accounts of cults that have used mind control techniques, the tactics of Jews for Jesus simply meet no such standard.

I did, however, find substantial evidence for mind control in a book that tells the story of another Jewish believer in Jesus, Ken Levitt. Ken's experience had all the marks of cultic brainwashing, perpetrated not by Jews for Jesus, but by professional "deprogrammers." The professionals were hired by family members, who apparently could not accept the fact that Ken chose to follow Jesus of his own free will. I seriously doubt that most Jewish people would condone deprogramming. However, experiences like Ken's demonstrate that responses to a controversial group can be far more threatening than any perceived threat from the group itself.

Side-by-side excerpts from Ellen's and Ken's books illustrate the range of emotional reactions young Jewish adults have when they make the decision to follow

*Jesus and the difficulty of continuing on in that faith in the face of intense opposi-tion from their families.*

—∿—

On January 26, 1983, the  headline in the *New York Post* read "Crowd Sees Woman's Kidnap Terror." Twenty-two-year-old Sandy Zimmerman, "an ardent member of Jews for Jesus," had been abducted in broad daylight, just before noon, as she walked past a theater in Greenwich Village. Police said her abductors were Jewish Defense League members on a deprogramming mission. It was a terrifying moment as she was pushed into a van by six men. Her companion tried to help her, but was shoved away while more than twenty people looked on in horror. One man was arrested at the scene. His rationale for the kidnapping was without apology: "The members of Jews for Jesus are thieves of the human soul. If our people decided to steal the body back it was an equal act that we warmly applaud."

Onlookers got the license plate number of the van and the abduction was short lived. Just after midnight police spotted the van parked in a Palisades Park, New Jersey, neighborhood. Sandy, physically unharmed, was being held by two Jewish deprogrammers, Galen and Elizabeth Kelly, her mother, and another man. They were arrested, charged with criminal restraint, and released on their own recognizance—except for Galen Kelly, who was retained at the Bergen County Jail.[1]

The story not only grabbed the attention of New Yorkers, it was printed in newspapers around the country. As it turned out, the young woman who had been abducted had no direct connection with Jews for Jesus. Yet the name association and resultant publicity brought Jews for Jesus into the story.

Regardless of what Sandy Zimmerman believed, her family was so upset with her decision that they had her abducted. Her story, while definitely not typical, is not unique, either. It illustrates the potential dangers a Jewish young person faced from misguided people who assume that a Jewish person who comes to Christ is either defective or has been coerced and needs to be rescued.

## ACCUSATIONS OF MANIPULATION

From the beginning, the Jews for Jesus doctrine always reflected historic Christian orthodoxy, and the lifestyle of staff and volunteers was fairly free and easygoing, even with the high level of commitment expected of them. Clearly, this is not the earmark of a religious cult.

One of the most troubling aspects of cultic groups is their insistence on separation from family. This was true of members of the Heaven's Gate cult, whose mass suicide made headlines in 1997. Unlike that group, the Unification Church, or other cults, Jews for Jesus has always encouraged those who came to faith in Christ to maintain close ties with family members.

Yet as Jews for Jesus reached more and more Jewish youths for Jesus, the opposition of the Jewish community increased. Some tried to marginalize Jewish converts, insisting they only believed because they were more needy, less intelligent, or otherwise emotionally impaired by broken homes or involvement in drugs. Others could not deny the fact that many of these new Jews for Jesus were bright, articulate, creative people. They *needed* to believe that such people would never fall for this Christian stuff unless they were being cleverly manipulated.

It seems as though some opponents of Jews for Jesus labeled them a cult not because there were classic earmarks of cult activity or leadership, but because it was the only acceptable explanation for why Jewish youth were turning to Jesus. It also provided the rationale to isolate Jews for Jesus from the rest of the Jewish community, or in some cases, to retaliate for what they saw as manipulation and deceit.

Many Jewish parents were incensed by what they considered deplorable proselytizing tactics that led to their sons' and daughters' faith in Christ. It was particularly difficult for parents to see their adult children volunteer for, or even join the staff of, Jews for Jesus. (The term "adult children" reflects the fact that Jews for Jesus do not maintain contact with people under the age of eighteen without parental permission.) They believed their children had been duped, and in response some parents employed expert "deprogrammers" to get their children out of what they saw as the control of a religious cult.

## THE PROCESS OF DEPROGRAMMING

Deprogramming is a very controversial method of "counterbrainwashing" that was frequently utilized in the 1970s. It since has been discredited, not only because of the legal problems surrounding the practice, but because it simply does not work. Most people who separate from cults or other religious groups are not influenced to do so by others. They just become disenchanted and leave.

Two books chronicle incidents of deprogramming Jews who came to Jesus. The first is by Ken Levitt with Ceil Rosen, *Kidnapped for My Faith* (1978). It graphically details the brutal but unsuccessful attempt to deprogram a Jewish man who was in his early twenties. The other book, by Ellen Kamentsky, is called *Hawking God: A Young Jewish Woman's Ordeal in Jews for Jesus* (1992). The latter gives a very different slant on deprogramming—or exit counseling, as it is sometimes called. Contrary to Ken's case, the tactics seemed to work in Ellen's story—at least to the extent that she left Jews for Jesus.

## TWO DISSIMILAR STORIES

Ken's story of attempted deprogramming is shocking. He was kidnapped—wrestled to the floor by two big men, handcuffed, blindfolded, and driven against his will to an undisclosed location where he was imprisoned in an attic. He was transferred to a second location in a matter of days. Of his situation there he wrote:

> For days I saw nothing but the walls of my basement prison. They still blindfolded me to go to the bathroom, and someone was always guarding me. Those four white walls with their sparse, ugly furnishings were my only world, my only reality, those hostile angry people my only human contact.[2]

Ellen's situation was entirely different from Ken's. She was a full-time staff member of Jews for Jesus, and her feelings about her life were somewhat ambivalent prior to the deprogramming. For one thing, Ellen was homesick. Her family lived on the East Coast, and she was in California. Complicating her loneliness was the birth of her first nephew three thousand miles away. Soon after his birth, she scheduled a flight to Boston, with no apparent objections from Jews for Jesus. Once there, her outlook on the life she had made for herself in California began to change. She later described feelings of doom along with fears that she would miss seeing her new nephew grow up.

In her book Ellen emphasizes her homesickness and unhappiness, especially as she focused on her infant nephew. While this sad story of an aunt not seeing her nephew take his first steps might be regarded as an unfortunate family circumstance, it was an unusual backdrop for a deprogramming episode.

Ellen writes that despite her unhappiness she was determined to return to California—until her mother persuaded her to meet with an "exit counselor" whose services had already been arranged. Ellen recalls meeting David Clark, then listening to his two-hour monologue, in which he told her about the years he had spent in a "destructive Christian group." He also told her that the organization had ruined his life and driven a friend to suicide.

Ken's and Ellen's deprogramming experiences are two very different stories. With regard to Jews for Jesus, neither describes abuse or cultic mind control. Both tell of high expectations and long hours of work, but no more so than one would find among ambitious young adults caught up in the fast pace of any modern business.

Both Ken and Ellen were raised in Jewish families. Ken's upbringing was Orthodox and the tight structure of his Jewish home offered him very little latitude.

> From the time I was old enough to read, my parents sent me to an orthodox Jewish Hebrew school.... My mother kept a kosher house. That meant we observed all the dietary restrictions prescribed in the Law of Moses. We ate no pork or shellfish, and didn't mix meat with dairy products. My parents also observed the Sabbath to the best of their ability, by doing no work, kindling no fire, riding in no vehicle, handling no money, from sunset Friday night until sunset Saturday night.[3]

Ellen's family was more relaxed about such things, but Jewish culture infused every aspect of her family life as she was growing up:

> Before I joined Jews for Jesus, my life was typical for a young, Jewish woman.... Judaism was not just a religion. Judaism infused our lives like ivy wrapping its way about an ancient structure. I was weaned on chicken soup and named in synagogue.... Many of my fondest memories are of the Jewish holidays.... I started Hebrew school in second grade.... My interest in Judaism blossomed as I studied for my Bat Mitzvah.[4]

After graduating from high school, Ken went on to Boston University, where he lacked motivation and finally "flunked out." At the same time, he became disillusioned about his Jewish faith and any belief in God at all.[5]

After high school Ellen enrolled at the University of Pennsylvania, and after college she worked briefly in retailing in New York City before returning to Boston disillusioned.

## STORIES OF CONVERSION

As young adults, both Ken and Ellen had come to a point in their lives where they were open to challenge in the area of religious faith. Ellen's challenge came from a male friend who introduced her to two new topics: prayer and Jesus Christ. Her meeting with her friend left her thinking about Christ, and she bought a Bible and continued to consider Jesus.

Ken's first serious thoughts about God arose as he was enjoying the beauty of creation on a camping trip with his friend Steve. Steve brought up the subject of God and told Ken about another Jewish friend who believed Jesus was the Messiah. The idea so intrigued Ken that after he returned home, he began to search for the truth reading the Old Testament prophecies that Steve had suggested. "When I came to the fifty-third chapter of Isaiah," he writes, "I was thunderstruck":

> He was despised and rejected of men; a man of sorrows, and acquainted with grief: and as one from whom men hid their face he

was despised, and we esteemed him not.

Surely he hath borne our griefs inflicted by us, and suffered sorrows we have caused: yet we did esteem him stricken, smitten of God, and afflicted. But he was wounded through our transgressions, bruised through our iniquities: the chastisement of our peace was upon him, and with his wounds we were healed.[6]

After studying other Old Testament passages and receiving a number of unusual signs Ken believed to be from God, he met with Ron, who was affiliated with Jews for Jesus. At that time, Ken finalized his decision to accept Jesus as Messiah.

Ellen's first serious encounter with a Christian was on a Greyhound bus on her way to Cape Cod to visit her sister. Maxine struck up a conversation with her, shared her faith, and offered to exchange phone numbers. Soon Ellen and Maxine were having Bible studies together, and through their friendship, Ellen met Jews for Jesus. She was quickly befriended by them and says that as a result she made a decision—one that she later came to regret:

I made a commitment that took three years of my life, alienated me from the non-Christian world and devastated my family. I didn't even realize that I was converting.... In a moment I prayed to receive Jesus. I became a Christian.[7]

## MEETING THE OPPOSITION

Both Ken and Ellen were involved in Jews for Jesus—Ken in 1976 and Ellen a decade later in 1986. The family opposition that Ken encountered was more severe than what Ellen faced. Perhaps it was because Ken's parents were more rigorous in their Jewish faith, or perhaps it was because the "cult scare" was at its height during the mid-1970s. By the 1980s, that fear was dying down. Either way, the most significant factor in Ken's situation was the fact that within a year after his decision to follow Jesus, he was making plans to marry Christine, a gentile Christian. He was kidnapped a few days before the wedding was to take place.

After many days of deprogramming, Ken was taken to a camp in the country, where he confessed that he was beginning to doubt his newly found faith. He was also beginning to doubt his decision to marry Christine yet felt guilty about the thought of breaking off the relationship. Despite his doubts, he knew he had to escape. Finally, one night he was able to slip away from the camp and call the police.

Ken filed charges against the kidnappers and was reunited with Christine. He also met with local staff from Jews for Jesus, then he flew with Christine to San Francisco. After rest and some counsel with Moishe, Ken and Christine drove to Reno and were married—almost two weeks after their original wedding date. Two weeks later, their friends in San Francisco gave them a wedding reception with traditional Jewish customs. Moishe presided.

The couple's happiness was marred by Ken's plans to testify in court against his parents—especially his father—who had been present at the time of the kidnapping. Ken dreaded the day but felt compelled to testify, particularly since his father was denying the abduction ever happened and was claiming that his son was emotionally unstable. The night before the trial was to start, however, Ken's father agreed to sign a sworn statement attesting to the kidnapping. The following morning Ken withdrew the charges.

Ellen's situation was not so spectacular. Her book does not focus on her departure from Jews for Jesus, but on her three years with the organization. When she was officially accepted on the staff of Jews for Jesus, she was ecstatic. She could not wait to tell her friends the news. Later, though, she described her missionary training as though it were a brainwashing. For those who have grown up in the evangelical community, her story is not particularly shocking.

> Thoughts of prayer, fellowship and Christian Scripture seeped into my brain like chloroform. My view of reality was colored by Fundamentalist values…[and] "Evangelism": the zealous preaching and dissemination of the Gospel….I took to the activity like a chocoholic takes to Godiva.[8]

To those familiar with cult mind control (a term that is rightly challenged by many), the strangest aspect of Ellen's book is that she offers no evidence of any form of brainwashing. In fact, she presents herself as remarkably free throughout her three years with Jews for Jesus. In addition to describing long hours of work and high expectations, she tells of personal vacations and of time spent with her family back in Boston. Her mentor, whom she characterizes as "permissive and playful," advised her not to visit her mother at the Cape, fearing she might seek to "rescue" her. Ellen "disregarded his advice." And as busy as she was with the ministry, she had time for quilting, which she described in detail in the book.

After her description of that creative endeavor, Ellen gives a rather contradictory account of herself as a helpless victim: "Already brainwashed...I had lost my capacity for reflective thought and critical thinking.... I was particularly vulnerable to mind control because I desperately wanted to please my supervisors." The evidence she offers for such mind control is The Worker's Covenant, a document that each Jews for Jesus staff member signs, agreeing to abide by the stated rules.[9]

In a chapter entitled "Souls or Stats?" Ellen takes Jews for Jesus to task for their focus on number of contacts and converts. Here her criticism is well taken but it is a charge that could rightly be made against almost any evangelistic organization. Moishe himself would admit that he had to fight this problem during his tenure as executive director, and it is still an issue today. It is all too easy to measure success by numbers and neglect the individual.

The next chapter in Ellen's book is entitled "Jock for Jesus." Here again, Ellen's story is not a typical version of cultic mind control. Her commitment to evangelism is evident, but in many ways she was enjoying a very typical California lifestyle:

Working out was a way of life in L.A. I decided to join the trend. I bought a trial membership at the Sports Connection. The club had two dance studios, free weights, Nautilus, massage, a snack bar, a sauna, and dozens of UJs [unbelieving Jews].... People felt more comfortable relating to me in the gym. I guess I looked more normal straining under a barbell than standing on a street corner. Sweat was a great equalizer.[10]

Ellen's membership in the Sports Connection, according to her supervisor, was a personal matter: She paid for the membership herself and enjoyed using the club in her free time. Any contacts that she might have made in that setting would have been viewed as volunteer activity that she engaged in during nonworking hours.

## COMPARISONS AND CONTRASTS

There are similarities between Ken's story and Ellen's. They both hailed from Boston, and both were raised to value their Jewish heritage. As young adults, both became disillusioned with their religion and began searching for a more meaningful relationship with God. Neither was accosted by an aggressive evangelist or taken to a retreat to be surrounded by zealous cultists. On the contrary, both made inquiries on their own and were introduced to Jews for Jesus only after they had raised questions. Neither indicate that Jews for Jesus pressured them to become affiliated with the organization. Ellen clearly implies that she had to jump through some hoops in order to be accepted on staff.

There are also significant differences between Ken's and Ellen's stories. Ken was not on staff with Jews for Jesus, but his impending marriage to a gentile Christian certainly demonstrated to his parents that his faith in Jesus was not merely a passing fad. Ellen was a paid staff member. She makes no claim that she carried out her activities with Jews for Jesus against her will; she simply did what was expected of all full-time staff.

The deprogramming efforts and results were also very different. Ken was forcibly kidnapped, while Ellen was invited to talk with an "exit counselor." Ken, while beginning to doubt his faith in Christ, resisted to the end. Ellen, on the other hand, essentially caved in. Ken's is the dramatic story. Ellen's story contains little, if any, drama. She was homesick; she was three thousand miles away from her newborn nephew; she was burned out; her mother requested that she talk with an exit counselor; and she freely decided to do so.

Ellen's story could have had any number of endings. She might have decided to leave Jews for Jesus after simply talking to her mother, or after an argument with her supervisor, or after an earthquake rocked Los Angeles. People quit their jobs all the time and move on to other things for any number of reasons. That is essentially what Ellen did, though in the process she renounced her faith in Jesus. It might even be argued that Ellen's deprogramming experience provided an excuse for her to continue a readjustment of priorities that had already begun shifting.

Ellen was not the first worker to leave an evangelistic organization and abandon her faith, nor will she be the last. Ken was not the first to face fierce opposition and a brutal assault for standing by his faith, nor will he be the last. Their stories were foretold in Scripture and have been told down through the ages. Some people withstand opposition; others do not.

The stories of Ken and Ellen offer insights into the destructive nature of deprogramming. In both their situations, professionals were hired to rescue them from a group that had never given evidence of using mind control. Both Ken and Ellen could have simply walked away from Jews for Jesus at any time, though in Ellen's case one might question whether it would have been ethical, given the fact that she had made a commitment (as is not uncommon) to work with the organization for eighteen months. On the other hand, the organization would not have been likely to hold her to that commitment if her faith was faltering.

It may be difficult to dissociate with a job, an organization, colleagues, or friends, but such decisions are common. They are made by people in all walks of life as a matter of course, and no one attributes the reason for them to mind control or the intervention of deprogrammers.

Moishe speaks with his usual bluntness on the issue of deprogramming: "If you've got enough money, you can 'deprogram' anyone from anything." What he meant was that there are people out there who know how to manipulate, intimidate, and coerce others for a living. But once the manipulation, intimidation, and coercion let up, the person is free once again to make his or her own decisions.

Moishe also says, "Deprogramming presumes that there is no such thing as free will, that all choices are conditioned choices. As Christians, we believe

God gives man a choice to trust him or to defy him.... A Christian honors a person's right to decide for himself. You always let them walk away when they want to walk away."[11]

# CHAPTER SEVEN

# THE LEGACY OF
# THE HOLOCAUST

## *A Barrier between Christ and Jews*

The story of Jews for Jews is entwined with Jewish immigration to North America and with the Holocaust—a fact that is powerfully illustrated by the legacies of two families, the Wertheims and the Bernds.

As I reflect on the German heritage of the Wertheim family, I am reminded of my own heritage, and I ponder the similarities and differences of our two immigrant families. Neither family could ever claim to be on the "winning" side of history. As historians look back, they see both Germans and Jews as losers. One family looks back with a sense of shame and denial, and another looks back with sorrow and outrage. My family settled in northern Wisconsin, in an area west of the small town of Spoone, where the name Stellrecht is more common than the name Smith. The Wertheim family found itself in a tight community amid the teeming millions of what was then the world's largest city, New York. But both families shared the common heritage of Germany.

I am in Germany as I write these reflections—my first visit to the land of my ancestors. I have come to get a feel for the work of Jews for Jesus among the Russians who have immigrated to Germany in recent years. But I am quickly reminded of the legacy of this beautiful land. I am staying at a rustic old mill that has been turned into a Christian retreat. A stream runs hard by one side; a meandering river, complete with stately white swans, on the other. The lush greenery all around includes overgrown gardens, desperately in need of pruning. This area is the Bible belt of Germany, where, I am told, there was more resistance to Nazis than elsewhere. Yet, even this serene pastoral setting, with its rocks along the river and the arching willow trees along the stream, holds secrets of Germany's terrible

*past. Indeed, if the rocks do not cry out against these past atrocities, voices do—*
*voices of Jewish people whose ancestry goes back to this land even as mine does.*

*One of these voices is that of Jonathan Bernd, who serves as the leader of Jews*
*for Jesus in London. During our casual conversation from the airport in Stuttgart*
*to the Old Mill retreat, I asked about his background. His English accent had*
*deceived me. Germany, I quickly learned, is the land of his heritage, too, but it is a*
*very different heritage than mine. Jonathan's father was escorted out of the coun-*
*try—fortunately for him—as a little boy of ten in 1939. He received two Red Cross*
*post cards from his mother and father before they were deported in 1939 to*
*Auschwitz, where they were killed before the end of the War.*

—m—

It may seem surprising that Jewish people with ties to Germany and the
Holocaust would become followers of Jesus. Indeed, in the eyes of many
Jewish people, the Holocaust was the culmination of centuries of Christian
persecution. But in the stories of the Wertheims and Jonathan Bernd, we do
not see an attraction to organized Christianity or a political system within
Christendom, but rather a compelling attraction to Jesus.

The Wertheim family tree goes back long before Nazi Germany, but that
is the setting where the story begins. Two families fleeing the ravages of
Hitler's horrors immigrated to New York. Their children, Laura Bing and
Fred Wertheim, met at their synagogue, a natural place for Jewish young
people to find eligible marriage partners in those days. Laura was still a
teenager when they married on October 22, 1949. By her account, she asked
him to marry her—though he had been pursuing her for years.

Fred was born in 1925, the son of a baker in a small German village.
With very few other Jewish families in the village at the time, Fred had no
Jewish playmates. As a little boy, he had non-Jewish friends. That changed
as the mindset of the German people became more and more anti-Semitic,
and Fred's one-time friends began shunning him. Initially, his parents
thought that Hitler's Aryan philosophy was a passing fad. Germany was their
home, and their bakery business was prospering. Like many Jewish people,
they held on to their hope that the climate of bigotry would change—but it

only got worse. By the time they realized how dangerous the situation was, their options were limited.

> Because of immigration quotas, they needed to apply to the Consulate for clearance. The family had no papers prepared by a United States citizen for them, and that made immigration difficult. They were given a number, a very high one—48,878, which represented the number of people allowed to come from Germany before them.[1]

Not long after Fred's bar mitzvah in 1938, the Nazis destroyed the synagogue where the ceremony had been held. Less than a week later, all Jewish children were expelled from school. Other boys Fred's age were being sent to labor camps, but due to his small size, he was thought to be younger and was overlooked. Whole families were being sent to death camps, and the Wertheims feared the worst. Then suddenly their immigration number came up. It was May 1941. They left Germany for America, thinking they had escaped Hitler's horrors.

Six-year-old Laura and her parents escaped and left everything behind, thankful that their lives had been spared. In 1936, they set sail on the *Manhattan,* which took them to safety in America. Her grandparents were not so fortunate; both were murdered for no other reason than the fact that they were Jews.

For Laura's parents, New York City was paradise—not because they had good jobs or luxuries to enjoy, but simply because they had escaped the constant fear of torture and death. Laura's mother worked in a leather factory, and her father spent his days cutting meat in a slaughterhouse. Yet for all the security they found in America, they were never free from anti-Semitism—a hatred that affected even the children. Unlike so many young girls who might have retreated into their own world of insecurity and fear, Laura stood her ground. "The children at school who made the mistake of calling me a 'dirty Jew,'" she recalls, "figured out in a hurry that I would rather use my fists than be bullied."[2]

## A STORY OF SURVIVAL

Fred was sixteen when he and his family arrived in America; two years later, he found himself back in Europe. Like other American eighteen-year-olds, he had been drafted into the army. After basic training, he was sent to England, where he was assigned to a frontline unit involved in removing land mines and building emergency bridges. In that capacity he took part in the D–day invasion of Europe. He fought his way through France, across the Rhine River, and back into his native Germany. There Fred's worst fears were realized when the Germans captured him, along with many others in his unit.

The first hours and days were sheer terror as the Nazis spoke freely in German of their intention to shoot the Americans. Fred, the only prisoner who understood German, was terrified. At the last moment, the plans inexplicably changed. Rather than shooting the men, their captors sent them all to Stalag 11B, a prisoner of war camp near Hanover. Though grateful to be alive, Fred wondered if he were merely facing a slower death by starvation. His one meal a day consisted of watery soup to which was added spoiled horsemeat and a few vegetables.

Back home, a woman dressed in black delivered the bleak news via telegram, informing the Wertheims that their son was missing in action. For months his family grieved, fearing their son was dead. But when the war ended, Fred was among those liberated by General Montgomery and his Ninth Division. His family received the news with indescribable joy; and when Fred returned to New York, there was a welcome home celebration at his synagogue.[3]

After their synagogue wedding in 1949, life was a struggle for Laura and Fred Wertheim. Fred was a partner in a delicatessen, a business that consumed all his waking hours from early morning until nearly midnight every day except the Sabbath. Yet in many ways life was good. They lived in a modest home in Washington Heights in upper Manhattan, where neighbors knew and looked out for one another. There was a sense of community as they shared the joys of bar mitzvahs and weddings and came together in times of sorrow and hardship.

## CONSIDERING THE MESSIAH

During the months and years following his return from war, Fred often thought about how God had saved his life. He believed in God and was convinced that he had spared him for a purpose. As he later reflected on his life, he saw the hand of God amid times of crisis:

> God has done so many good things for me. He brought my imme-
> diate family out of Germany. He kept me alive in a prisoner of war
> camp. And there was the time that I was in a German halftrack that
> turned over on top of me. Two Germans lay dead next to me. The
> halftrack was so heavy with equipment that I couldn't move. Then
> water started to come up as we were pressed down in the field. I
> thought my life was over. I said the *Sh'ma* and I spoke to God plead-
> ing for His help. At that moment, several of my German captors
> were able to lift the halftrack and slide me out from under it. I was
> safe once again.[4]

The births of Steve in 1951 and Rob a few years later brought great happiness to the Wertheim home. The boys grew up in what might be termed a stereotypical family of the 1950s—before the Vietnam era of rebellion and drugs. There was no reason for Laura to imagine that her boys would not grow up to marry nice Jewish girls and settle down in the middle-class lifestyle that was part of being a second generation European Jew.

But in 1974 that dream began to unravel when Steve decided to move to California. He was twenty-four years old and had been restless living in New York. Both Fred and Laura tried to discourage him from leaving, but they were convinced that he was levelheaded and would not pursue a California lifestyle that would bring disgrace to the family. It was simply not like him, they reasoned, to join a hippie commune or get involved with drugs or "loose" women. There was one kind of unacceptable behavior that they did not even contemplate—that he might get involved with Christians.

The Wertheims were not surprised to learn that soon after arriving in southern California, Steve found a good job in a bank and rented an apartment managed by a Jewish couple. As a good Jewish mother, Laura was subconsciously mapping out his life. This Jewish couple who had taken her son under their wings would introduce him to a nice Jewish young woman. They would marry, soon Laura would realize her dream of being a grandmother, and another generation would be added to their long family heritage.

But this Jewish couple was different—not like any of the Jews Steve had known while growing up in New York. They believed in Jesus as the Jewish Messiah. And instead of introducing Steve to a nice Jewish girl, they introduced him to Baruch Goldstein—a nice Jewish man who believed in Jesus. Steve's interest in these Jewish believers and their Jewish Messiah was tempered only by his strong loyalty to his family. He knew instinctively that a good Jew should not even consider the possibility that Jesus was the Messiah. But curiosity got the best of him, and he agreed to attend a Bible study that Baruch was leading. As Steve attended week after week, he realized that he was facing the decision of a lifetime. Either Jesus was the Messiah, or he was not. He could no longer ignore the issue. He could no longer go on living as if he had not read and studied Old Testament prophecies that he could see pointed to no one other than Jesus. Despite all the subconscious resistance he felt, Steve became convinced that Jesus truly was the one who could transform his life and bring him the peace and security he had never found in Judaism.[5]

## SOME SHOCKING NEWS

Both Laura and Fred were devastated by the news, and Laura's first instinct was to cut all ties with Steve. She would shun him. That reaction is not unusual among Jewish families whose children go to "the side of the enemy" in their religious faith. Indeed, Laura associated Christians with anti-Semitism and could not imagine how her son could renounce his Jewish heritage and become a Christian. She had never known a Jew who believed in Jesus, and she assumed, as most Jews do, that one cannot continue to be a Jew and believe that Jesus is Messiah.

Like Laura, Fred equated Christianity with everything anti-Jewish—particularly the Nazis. So when Steve sent word that Baruch would be in New York and wanted to visit with them, Fred agreed, though with a more-than-half-serious warning: "I want to meet the man who did this to you and throw him off our terrace." But Baruch and his wife Marcia were not surprised or offended by the resistance they encountered. It was a natural reaction of Jewish parents. The Wertheims asked questions, and the Goldsteins answered, emphasizing that following Jesus was a very Jewish thing to do and that the key to who Jesus was could be found in the Hebrew Bible.

"I was shocked at Freddy's response," Laura remembers. "He became so curious; it was like a light bulb was switched on from somewhere deep inside him. The Bible had never been very important to me, and it made me nervous to see my husband so interested."[6]

Indeed, so interested was Fred that he himself began going to a Jews for Jesus Bible study and studying the Bible on his own. In the fall of 1975 he professed his belief in Jesus as Messiah. It was only after Fred's profession that they learned that their younger son Rob had also come to faith in Jesus. He had kept silent, not wanting to disrupt the family further during such a difficult time.

## A FAMILY IN TURMOIL

Laura felt her life was caving in beneath her. Her once tranquil family was now in turmoil—at least from her perspective. Life had been so predictable. Now her future seemed so uncertain, as, for the first time in her marriage, she questioned her husband's love for her. "I resented the fact that my Freddy had made his relationship with God a priority," she recalls. "It's not that he was neglecting me; he was just as devoted a husband as ever. But...I began to suspect that Freddy loved God even more than he loved me."[7]

Laura attended Bible studies and church with Fred and Rob but vowed she would never join them in their commitment to Jesus. She reminded herself of the crimes committed against the Jewish people in Jesus' name, and vowed she would never betray her Jewish faith. But eventually she was challenged to reconsider her premise that believing in Jesus equaled betraying her own people:

> One night we went to see a film called *The Hiding Place*. It was based on a true story about a woman who risked her life many times to hide Jews from the Nazis during WWII. The woman, Corrie ten Boom, was a Christian. I cried throughout the entire film; I was so moved to see how Corrie put her love for our people into action. The film showed me the difference between following Jesus' teaching and

using his name as an excuse to hurt people. The barriers that kept me from accepting Jesus were starting to cave in.[8]

Soon after the film, Laura went to a Bible study. The lesson was on Isaiah 53. It was then that she fully realized how much God loved her and that the prophet had foretold the suffering of the Messiah. "That Tuesday night in December of 1975, I, Laura Wertheim, the 'last holdout' in our immediate family, accepted Jesus as my Messiah."[9]

Steve and Rob both married nice Jewish girls who also believed in Jesus. Both brothers joined the Jews for Jesus staff and continue to serve in key positions.

### ANOTHER LEGACY OF THE HOLOCAUST

The story of Jonathan Bernd's family depicts another household coming to faith in Jesus—though in a very different way than that of the Wertheims.

Jonathan's grandfather, Hugo Bernd, was the son of a wealthy businessman. Hugo became a doctor specializing in diseases of the ear, nose, and throat. Successful and affluent, the Bernds were contributing to German society, but like so many other Jewish families, their contributions were obliterated by the psychotic compulsion to "protect the purity" of the Aryan race. Hitler wanted them exterminated. Through the mercy of the Red Cross, Jonathan's father, Hans, at the age of ten was sent from Germany to England, along with his older sister and a cousin. There they found refuge with a foster family.

Back in Germany, the Bernds' livelihood and home had been confiscated. They were forced to live in the hallway of their own house before the Nazis sent them to jail for the "crime" of being Jewish. Finally, in 1943 Hugo and his wife, Senta, were deported to Auschwitz. Little is known of their last days, except that they were spent in that death camp.

Like many German Jews of the time, the Bernds had not been especially religious. And although Hans's foster family was Quaker, they did not emphasize religion much more than his parents had—except to send him to a summer camp sponsored by Scripture Union. There, in his late teens, he came to faith in Jesus. He later married a Christian woman, and they intended to raise their children as believers in Jesus.

However, Christianity held little appeal for his son Jonathan as he was growing up. Seeking his own way, he delved into Socialism and Communism and was satisfied—for a time. Eventually he concluded that the spiritual void in these philosophies rendered them powerless to address the deeper issues of life's meaning. Then there was always the question that haunted him. Was Jesus the Messiah, as his parents had taught him, or would he find his true spiritual roots in Judaism?

With his parents' blessing, Jonathan decided to spend a year in Israel. There he acquired a deep sense of his own Jewishness. Indeed, he began contemplating Orthodox Judaism, hoping to find therein the bedrock of his Jewish identity. Yet, all the while, the question of this Jewish man who lived two thousand years ago continued to torment him. When Jonathan questioned an Orthodox rabbi about Jesus, he was told that Jesus was an evil man, not a standard reply on the part of most rabbis. But that characterization did not satisfy Jonathan; if anything, it compelled him to look into the matter for himself.

He began reading the New Testament and, for the first time, realized that it was a Jewish volume and that Jesus and the apostles were really and truly Jewish. He was overwhelmed by the idea that belief in Jesus as Messiah was very Jewish. For the first time he understood that he could be Jewish and follow Jesus at the same time. But like so many Jews in this circumstance, he felt alone. The Jewishness of Jesus had not been part of his Christian upbringing. Further, Jonathan had developed his own Jewish identity apart from his father. He felt as though he must be the only Jew who had found Jesus as Messiah—until he met Richard Harvey.

## MOVING INTO MINISTRY

Richard, then the head of Jews for Jesus in London, introduced Jonathan to a large messianic Jewish family. After finishing his university education, Jonathan went to New York for training with Jews for Jesus and later toured with their evangelistic music team, The Liberated Wailing Wall. In that role, he met Cindy, a Jew for Jesus from Los Angeles. She would later become his wife.

Through his association with Jews for Jesus, Jonathan has encouraged his whole family to reclaim their Jewish roots. His father, who once downplayed his Jewish heritage, now speaks openly and proudly about being a Jewish follower of Jesus.

Yet, even as Jonathan has sought to reclaim his Jewish roots, he has found himself in a cultural "no man's land"—one that is shared by many Jews. Despite the loss of his grandparents at Auschwitz and the terrible stories of other relatives who survived, Orthodox Jews do not recognize Jonathan as a Jew because his mother is not Jewish. (In Bible times, Jewish lineage was determined according to the father.) To complicate his identity further, Jonathan is a Jew for Jesus—a far more serious issue for most Jews. This issue of identity has occasionally troubled Jonathan. It is uncomfortable knowing that people wishing to deny his Jewish identity have what they consider legitimate grounds to do so.

In recent years, however, Jonathan has come to see that what some might call a precarious Jewish identity has its advantages, at least from a spiritual perspective. Jonathan knows he is Jewish, whatever others may say. But most important, he knows the source of his deepest identity is, as Moishe would say, not his Jewishness, but his "Jesusness." Not that the two are mutually exclusive, but who Jonathan is will not make a difference in the long run; who Jesus is can change lives. Like the other Jews for Jesus, Jonathan chooses to make Christ's identity, rather than his own, the issue.

## ACCUSATIONS OF SPIRITUAL NAZISM

Identity under fire is part and parcel of Jews for Jesus, and whether staff members have one Jewish parent or two, they will not be exempt from that fire. The general attitude of Jonathan and company seems to be that "If we dwelled on what our opposition says about us, we would spend all our time licking our wounds rather than proclaiming the healing and forgiveness Jesus brings." Of all the accusations flung at Jews for Jesus, probably the most inflammatory is that they are "trying to finish the work that Hitler began." Some even say that Jews for Jesus are worse than Hitler because he murdered Jewish bodies while missionaries destroy Jewish souls.

Do not underestimate the pain and fear behind these accusations. While one might question whether or not their statements are hyperbolic, they truly see Jews for Jesus as a threat to Jewish survival. In a sense, it is a self-fulfilling prophecy because the consensus among the Jewish community is that you cannot be Jewish and believe in Jesus. Therefore, those who have a part in leading Jewish people to Jesus are seen as robbing them of their Jewishness.

Jews for Jesus recognizes that accusations of spiritual Nazism are used as an offensive defense. They say the issue of the Holocaust is so emotionally charged that the mention of it prevents many people from thinking critically about certain assumptions. "A Jewish person brings up the Holocaust, and of course he has the right to be angry," one staffer pointed out. "But the problem is, that anger is generalized. A person caught up in the emotion of remembering the Holocaust feels justified in linking Hitler and Jesus, because the Nazis said: 'You killed our Lord and so we are killing you.' It's not so easy to set aside that insidious lie and examine Jesus' true teachings, and the love that he showed to his own Jewish people."

For the Jews for Jesus, Hitler's most horrible legacy is this: From beyond the grave he has erected a hellish barrier between Jewish people and their own Messiah. But that barrier is not insurmountable, as evidenced by the stories of the Wertheims, the Bernds, and many, many others who not only survived the Holocaust but found eternal life and peace through Jesus.

When God is at work in a person's heart, he or she will search for the truth regardless of where it may lead. Even the specter of the Holocaust cannot frighten real seekers away from Jesus. And, Moishe points out, the obscene hatred Hitler unleashed, and the fact that so many willingly followed him, says something of the human condition and the need for redemption: "There is nothing as normal as hatred. The peace we have as Christians is planted in our hearts by the prince of peace.... You can't blame the teacher when the students don't learn the lessons."[10]

# CHAPTER EIGHT

# A MISSION
# WITH AN ATTITUDE

*Creatively Communicating the Gospel*

My initial reaction to writing the twenty-five year history of a mission organization was negative. I have read organizational histories and often find them boring. But when I began my preliminary research, it did not take long to realize that the history of Jews for Jesus was anything but boring. If this book is regarded as such, it is certainly not the fault of the organization. Most religious groups avoid controversy at all costs. The motto is, "Do nothing to shame Christ," which is appropriate. Perhaps what is not appropriate is the idea that anything deemed controversial is shameful. Jews for Jesus does not operate on that premise. The mission was born in controversy and has continued in that mode for the past quarter century.

How many ministries would put an ad in TV Guide spoofing a popular television sitcom just before its final episode? Or take a page out of radical antiwar literature for a training lecture? No other mission I know fosters such an "in-your-face" approach as Jews for Jesus. In a day and age when many tout friendship evangelism as the way to play the game, Jews for Jesus seems out of step. They do not try to placate those who have decided to view them as enemies; in fact, they use opposition whenever possible as a platform to proclaim the gospel. Their choice not to back down where free speech is concerned has resulted in numerous threats of lawsuits against them, something many ministries would do anything to avoid. The Jews for Jesus ministry is a mission with an attitude—and to me, that makes this organization truly fascinating.

*When I refer to the Jews for Jesus "attitude," I do not mean it in the negative sense this word often conveys. By attitude I mean the collective personality and mentality of this mission. The ministry has a very Jewish persona that exudes a forthright aggressiveness combined with humor.*

*This collective attitude is most evident in Jews for Jesus' style of communication: the Jewish flavor of their music, the humor that comes through in their dramas, and especially through their gospel literature called broadsides, which even their harshest antagonists concede are polished and clever and humorous. People who have no interest whatsoever in Jews for Jesus as a mission occasionally approach their missionaries on the street asking for a broadside with the explanation, "I collect these." I was fascinated to discover that some people regard the broadsides as collector's items, and that Moishe himself paid no less than $130 to buy back an original printed copy of his first broadside. It contained primitive artwork by today's standards, which made it all the more valuable. That tract, "A Message from Squares," was written in 1969, and it oozed attitude. It began, "Hey, you with the beard on your face! We think you are beautiful." That set the stage for a truly unique method of communicating the gospel.*

—ᗰᗯ—

Jews for Jesus has a single focus: proclaiming Jesus Christ as Messiah. They conduct their ministry in good Jewish fashion, using the Old Testament prophets as models. Like those prophets, their goal is not to win friends, but to declare a message—and their attitude and methods reflect that goal.

The prophets were often dramatic, their message delivered as more of a pageant than a pronouncement. God often commanded them to communicate in ways that exposed them to ridicule. Their messages were not generally preceded by a recitation of personal references or a resume of accomplishments to show why the Israelites should listen to what they had to say.

The Jews for Jesus attitude is not "How to Win Friends and Influence People." To the contrary, it is "If you really care about people, you want to win them to Jesus, not to yourself." That is the lesson Moishe Rosen has taught the staff over and over again.

Nevertheless, many people find the Jews for Jesus attitude somewhat winsome, probably in part because the staff has been taught not to take itself too seriously. This comes through in much of their public ministry and is an important part of their attitude. "You can't humiliate a humble person," Moishe is fond of saying. "A bit of self-deprecation has helped Jewish people survive persecution for centuries. It's part of our culture and it comes through in our sense of humor." It stands to reason that when people are looking to find fault with you, pride is a luxury you can ill afford. It also makes sense that Jewish culture and ways of relating do not disappear when a Jewish person accepts Jesus. So that humor, that *"haymishness"* (hominess, or family-style friendliness) comes through in much of what the Jews for Jesus say and do.

As far as what some call the in-your-face approach, if the idea of wearing brightly colored T-shirts to pass out gospel literature, or wearing clown outfits to do street drama strikes you as silly, you may be right. But these Jews for Jesus (most of whom, I am told are actually introverted and would prefer to be out of the limelight) do not mind being silly if it makes them approachable and gives people who want to know about Jesus the chance to ask them meaningful questions.

## PUSHING THE ENVELOPE WITH BROADSIDES

Jews for Jesus is known for its style of street evangelism, which uses humor as part of the drama to present the message of Jesus. For example:

> The collective sense of humor [of Jews for Jesus] is seen not only in the broadsides, but also in the street evangelism itself. During the 1994 New York campaign, while giving away free containers of "Juice From Jesus," from a sidewalk booth, pamphlets were also distributed, entitled "Beware of Religious Fanatics Handing Out Tracts."[1]

Broadsides are certainly not the only or even the best way to reach people for Jesus, but they are effective. They are gospel seeds, and the group expects that the majority of those they sow will not necessarily come to fruition. Nevertheless, when they sow five to eight million a year, they are bound to see fruit. And Jews for Jesus hear stories every year from Jews and Gentiles who received one of these tracts and kept it...only to reflect on it later as part of a process of coming to faith.

Some have suggested that the Jews for Jesus attitude or style is appropriate for the United States, but will not work in other countries. Richard Harvey, a former staff member from the United Kingdom, never thought that broadsiding would work there. He was forced, and gladly so, to change his mind when his brother received a broadside and found it useful in his journey to faith in Jesus. One of the most popular British broadsides was titled "Mad Human Disease," a takeoff on the "Mad Cow" controversy.

Moishe insists that Jewish people the world over have more in common than most people realize. Broadsiding is part of a straightforward but good-natured approach that Jews for Jesus have found effective for the past twenty-five years. It is certainly not their only approach, nor necessarily their favorite, but it has always been part of who they are.

A Moishe Rosen original style of communication, broadsides predate the founding of Jews for Jesus. Moishe began writing these tracts while he was still with the American Board of Missions to the Jews; in fact, they typify the type of communication that the parent organization felt was at odds with its image.

Other ministries have developed gospel literature, but probably few print and distribute the mass quantities that Jews for Jesus does. And none have pushed the envelope on humor and contemporary culture as have Jews for Jesus. Broadsides epitomize much of the Jews for Jesus attitude and outreach style.

William Willoughby, writing in the *Washington Times* in 1983, compared the traditional tract with those distributed by Jews for Jesus and called on other Christian organizations to learn a lesson:

> The independent missionary organization which Moishe founded in 1973 produces some of the cleverest gospel tracts I have ever seen—people not afraid to use humor to get the most serious religious point across. Some of these groups which think and act as if the whole lost world is on their shoulders could lighten the load

both literally and figuratively if they would take a cue from the Jews for Jesus. The point of the gospel tract, after all, is to have the recipient read it. The way so many of the conventional tracts are done, it's a wonder people receiving them aren't arrested for littering.[2]

The term broadside was first utilized by Moishe in order to differentiate his tracts from traditional tracts that are sold in Christian bookstores and stacked in racks in the foyers of many evangelical churches. He found the traditional tract inadequate for his purposes for several reasons:

- Most gospel literature was too wordy for a first contact. It tended to answer questions the average Jewish person on the street hadn't asked.
- Most tracts were not written in a contemporary style. Nor did they address themselves to contemporary life situations, problems, and concerns.
- Most had problems with the writing: poor transitions or no transitions. They rushed into the subject without bringing the reader along.
- They lacked creativity.
- They lacked a personal touch. A person who received a piece of literature would not feel the warmth of another human being behind the stilted language.
- Most tracts used Christian jargon and clichés that would alienate nonbelievers, particularly Jewish nonbelievers.

Missionaries describe broadsides as "invitations to interact with the gospel," and invitations ought to be engaging. That is part of what makes broadsides unique, according to the organization's training materials:

Broadsides are different from other Christian tracts, not only in format but in content. They are written for the purpose of provoking a response. They are written and drawn in such a way that they can be read completely in less than a minute. Serious truths are given in satire and in good-natured humor with contemporary illustrations.

The titles are designed as interest hooks; and the reader is moved along by whimsy to the consideration of the person of Christ.[3]

The instructions also include some hints for writing a good broadside:

- A broadside must make people smile first and consider Scriptural truth afterwards.
- A broadside wants to like people.
- A broadside would be embarrassed if someone said it was too preachy.
- A broadside is never arrogant or angry, but always accepting of where other people are at.[4]

One of the things that sets broadsides apart is their personal touch. They are not created by professional writers, but mainly by missionaries who distribute them themselves. Some are written by administrative staff and all pass through the ministry's own editors, only one of whom had any professional experience in writing before joining the staff. Broadsides are a very democratic form of empowerment. They give each staff member a potential voice and a platform in outreach ministry.

Some staff members even satirize themselves through broadsides. Avi Snyder wrote one titled "Man, These Guys Tick Me Off!" He begins with an infuriated cartoon figure saying, "You know who I'm talkin' about? Those Jews for Jesus, like the bullet-head who handed you that pamphlet you're reading." (The character is pointing his thumb at a balding caricature of Avi). The character continues:

> You know *what* ticks me off about those guys? I'll tell you.... First of all they're all over the place, like cockroaches.... Curse 'em out, and they say, "What if Jesus *is* the Messiah?"... Tear their *dumb pamphlets* up, and they say, "Why are you afraid to realize what we are saying? Tell 'em they oughtta be *ashamed* of themselves and they say, "Well, I'm ashamed of my sins but I'm glad *Y'shua*, the Jewish Messiah, forgave me.[5]

Again, the attitude: The message is serious, but not the messenger. That is why the street missionaries seem to care little about ridicule if they accomplish their task in urging people to think for themselves.

## THE DISTRIBUTION OF BROADSIDES

Writing broadsides is the first half of the equation; the second half is distribution. They are designed for mass distribution on a campus or a street corner, in a shopping crowd or a subway hole—anywhere there is a high amount of pedestrian traffic. Two people usually hand out between five hundred to a thousand broadsides within an hour—but you have to know how to do it.

Missionaries learn to hold the broadsides so that the person approaching can read the title or see a catchy illustration. They usually make eye contact before offering a person a tract. When one person rejects a broadside, the missionary does not continue holding it out in hopes that the next person will take it. He or she shuffles it back in the stack, having learned that people in crowds do not like to accept what someone else has rejected. Missionaries also learn to keep conversations brief and focused on Jesus. They hope people will stop and talk, but they have learned that most who are really interested will not stay to monopolize the missionary's time, although they will provide an address or phone number where they can be reached.

Broadsiding instructions caution the trainee to allow time for personal work, but not too much time. "One of the strategies of Satan is to get us involved in fruitless conversations for long periods of time so that we can neither distribute the literature nor be available for inquiries from another person."[6]

Other rules for distribution include reminders to pick up discarded tracts and dispose of them properly before leaving; to use only one title at a time so that each person receives the same broadside; and to have a person's name on the back so the individual receiving it can make a personal contact.

Perhaps the ultimate rule for distribution is just that—distribution. The broadside is of no value until someone receives it. Jews for Jesus encourages the widest distribution possible. "Any evangelical Christian group is granted, upon request, permission to reprint them...providing they give them away free and don't change copy or art without permission."[7]

Jews for Jesus has produced hundreds of different broadsides, and what is most impressive about them is the range of topics reflecting various points of interest including fads, sports, and even philosophies. From health foods to existentialism, from *Star Wars* to the Super Bowl, there seems to be a broadside for just about everything. Popular television series and movies also provided dozens of broadside topics. Several of these broadsides "struck a nerve" with some executives in the entertainment business. They often increased the effectiveness of the broadsides by having their legal department issue threats that caught the attention of the media.

Here are some examples.

### "MARY HARTMAN, MARY HARTMAN"

One example of Jews for Jesus' creativity, cleverness, and sense of humor is their lampooning of the "Mary Hartman, Mary Hartman" television show in the spring of 1976. The secular press was quick to jump on the story, as is evident by an article in the *Washington Post* by Marjorie Hyer, entitled "God and Mary Hartman." The opening paragraphs begin:

> A couple weeks ago a West Coast evangelistic outfit called Jews for Jesus put out a bright pink tract, spoofing the TV soap opera spoof, Mary Hartman, Mary Hartman.
>
> The cartoon style flyer had a light touch and—as evangelistic tracts go—was mildly amusing, keyed in the satirical tone of the latest Norman Lear success.
>
> "Mary Hartman, Mary Hartman, we've noticed how very exciting your life has been lately," it began. Then it recapped a typical week's woes of the show's heroine.
>
> "You certainly have problems and you think you'll never be happy; that you'll never fit in, and, you know, you're right, you're right," the flyer continued, warming up for the real pitch.
>
> "Mary Hartman, Mary Hartman, your REAL problem is sin, sin. God wants you to really repent, repent!… For more soap call or write Sue Perlman, Sue Perlman."[8]

The spoof made its way to the offices of Norman Lear, whose attorney wrote a letter to Susan Perlman demanding she "cease and desist" her publication of the tract. He threatened "legal remedies" if she did not comply within ten days. Moishe was not intimidated, insisting that he had no intention of ordering the tract discontinued "since we produce these for free distribution and they have no commercial value and since they amount to a review of public entertainment."[9]

Rosen summed up the whole tempest in the soap dish with the inevitable cliché: "They lampoon anything and everything; the most serious and solemn matters become the object of this spoof. However, they can dish it out, but they can't take it."[10]

## HOWARD HUGHES'S LAST WILL AND TESTAMENT

Another spoof that caught the eye of the secular media was a published "Last Will and Testament" of Howard Hughes. The dispute over his estate had made headlines, and Jews for Jesus sought to grab a little of the publicity. The will left seventy-five cents to each of Hughes's relatives and wives; $6 million to the National Heartbreak and Psoriasis Institute, $25 million to Jews for Jesus, and $2.6 billion to anyone who filled in his or her name on the phony will. It was, of course, signed by Howard Hughes.[11]

## PAC-MAN FEVER

The question in the editorial headline asked, "Will Pac-Man vs. Jews for Jesus be the legal battle of the century?" It was a tongue-in-cheek question, and the answer was no. But Pac-Man became one more episode in the Jews for Jesus' saga of pushing the envelope in a broadside spoof. The threat of a lawsuit by Bally Midway Manufacturing Company, the manufacturer of the video game, gave the organization free publicity. Indeed, Jews for Jesus made the matter public when they received a threatening letter from David Welsh, an attorney representing the company. The letter stated that the publication of "Pac-Man Fever" was not only unauthorized, but that it disparaged the Pac-Man and Ms. Pac-Man and characters.

How Pac-Man and company were disparaged was not disclosed, but the tract itself was relatively lackluster as broadsides go. It began "Jumping joysticks, everybody! It's Pac-Man, the A-Maze-ing video game—Yay!" and went downhill from there. But it brought threatened litigation, created interest, and as always, ended with a short gospel message.

Moishe responded to the threat of legal action with characteristic nonchalance: "We are not particularly worried.... Our pamphlet is a good-natured gospel tract which is handed out freely."[12]

### VANNA BANANA AND THE SPIEL OF FORTUNE

Moishe Rosen thinks Merv Griffin is a "sorehead"...although, "He always seemed like such a nice person on television."[13]

That was one more instance when Jews for Jesus captured the media attention with one of their broadsides. The pamphlet, about a puzzle called "Spiel of Fortune," satirizes materialistic values and—with the help of "Vanna Banana" and a couple of free vowels—provides the spiritual solution: J.E.S.U.S. T.H.E M.E.S.S.I.A.H. Attorney Antonia J. Robertson, who represented Merv Griffin Enterprises (MGE) and the television program "Wheel of Fortune" demanded that Jews for Jesus "cease and desist from using any form of advertisement or promotion which utilizes elements from Wheel of Fortune." The letter went on to say that MGE "views this as a very serious matter" and threatened to sue the ministry.[14] From the perspective of Jews for Jesus, this encounter with a high-profile Hollywood personality served as one more opportunity for publicity.

### BART SIMPSON

No cultural symbol is too sacred—or sacrilegious—and no Jew for Jesus is too young to spoof the giants of mass media. Thus nine-year-old broadside author Benjamin Wertheim received a letter in 1990 from a large California law firm representing Twentieth Century Fox. They were threatening to sue him for one hundred thousand dollars for copyright infringement. Bart Simpson, the obnoxious but popular TV cartoon character was the subject of dispute. A spiky-haired cartoon character wearing a "Bart for Jesus" T-shirt was pictured on a broadside, speaking in standard Bart lingo: "Don't have a cow, man, because we're telling you that Jesus is Messiah" and "Chill out! And ask God to show you if it's really true!" The pamphlet went on to explain that Jesus "is the *only* way to God.... After all, those cool dudes like Moses, Isaiah, Daniel, and David *told* us all about it.... Prophets are smarter than your mother, because *they're* always right."

As was true in previous threats, the incident drew the hoped-for press attention, and the official response was in keeping with the Jews for Jesus standard denial of copyright infringement—that such a message was "fair social commentary" and that Jews for Jesus has the same freedom-of-press rights as a newspaper because there is no solicitation of funds.

The response in the Jewish community was less than enthusiastic. One rabbi dismissed it as being "in poor taste" and went on to say: "As is the usual pattern for Jews for Jesus, it's trash."[15]

### "CHRISTMAS IS A JEWISH HOLIDAY"

Another broadside frequently mentioned in press reports was entitled, "Christmas Is a Jewish Holiday." It was brief, thought provoking, and humorous:

> Maybe Jews aren't able to celebrate because they see it is a Jesus holiday and they don't know that Jesus isn't prejudiced against them....
>
> Santa Claus is a capitalist agent who promotes the idea that happiness comes through THINGS.
>
> Santa Claus is a Communist agent. He dresses in red and only gives away things that are bought by other people.
>
> Santa is no friend of truth; you'll notice how he scrupulously avoids every mention of Jesus.
>
> Even if he has a beard, Santa is not Jewish, and such a no-good-nick should have no part in our Christmas as a Jewish holiday.
>
> All we need for Christmas or a celebration is Jesus.[16]

### THE X-FILES

Is Y'shua the Messiah? Truly a mystery to many—and one important enough for Scully and Mulder to investigate. In a broadside titled "The X-Files: Extra-Terrestrial Presence?" Mulder tells Scully that he has uncovered new evidence of extraterrestrials. She responds with her usual skepticism, but he has a document with the evidence: a translation of a Greek papyrus scroll that tells of astrologers following a celestial body that directed them to Bethlehem. Mulder goes on to read how an alien had come to earth—and that the alien was called Y'shua.

Scully is incredulous: "That's Hebrew for Jesus! Mulder, that's no alien you're talking about—it's Jesus the Jewish Messiah who came and died and rose again. And he's no hoax."

The broadside ends on the back panel with an offer: "Why not check out the Y-File on Him?" It is signed by Andrew Barron, a missionary, and gives the address, phone number, and e-mail of the Jews for Jesus headquarters in San Francisco.

## HOWARD STERN AND COMPANY

A broadside lampooning Howard Stern humorously made the case for the gospel, as did other broadsides including, "I'm So-So; You're So-So," (a spoof on the best-selling book, *I'm Okay; You're Okay*), "Forest Gump…You Do Have a Destiny," "Strange Facts about You, God, and Your Mother," "The Star Trek Fantasy," "Atheists: Some of Us Who Believe in God Appreciate You," and "A Message to Suits," which depicted early-morning pedestrians—men and women—all in suits, much like the broadsider would encounter at the subway station.

These and other Jews for Jesus' broadsides have made the group a target for threats of lawsuits. While Jews for Jesus does not produce its broadsides to incite legal action, the group has shown itself quite willing to go to court to defend its right to produce and distribute religious literature.

## FIRST AMENDMENT CONFLICTS

Next to the Bible, the Bill of Rights stands as a truly important document for Jews for Jesus. Those heading out into the streets and subways keep the "court order" with them at all times. It is stamped with a seal of the U.S. District Court, Southern District of New York, dated December 11, 1991. It lists Jews for Jesus, Inc., Mitch Glaser, and Efraim Goldstein as the plaintiffs; the New York City Transit Authority is the defendant. It is all they need to prove their constitutional right to "broadside" (hand out tracts) in the subway stations.

Many ministries seem determined to avoid litigation at all costs. Not Jews for Jesus. Those who oppose their ministry would curtail their outreach on the streets, in the media, and their use of cultural icons in their tracts if Jews for Jesus did not seek recourse through the court system. In many instances they appear to welcome court challenges. Though no one would admit that specific actions were taken to draw a litigious response, no doubt in some cases the ensuing free publicity was greeted with a certain amount of pleasure.

But neither is the organization frivolous in their court involvement. During a council meeting at the San Francisco headquarters in 1998, the discussion of a current lawsuit concerning the misappropriation of their web site by an antimissionary made it clear that the action had not been entered into lightly. Executive director David Brickner conceded that it was providing publicity for Jews for Jesus and free advertisement to the web site, which the group hoped would attract spiritual seekers. Nevertheless, the litigation was costing the organization a lot of money and consuming precious time that everyone would prefer to spend on a more direct proclamation of the gospel. The case has since been settled in favor of Jews for Jesus.

Jews for Jesus has been accused by some as being "too litigious," an accusation that conjures up mental pictures of frivolous suits filed by people looking for quick money. While Jews for Jesus probably is somewhat litigious in comparison with other Christian organizations, money is never their motivation. In reality, Jews for Jesus is more often than not the threatened party rather than the party threatening lawsuits—and they will do what they have to in order to protect their First Amendment rights of freedom of speech and expression. That includes protecting the right to produce *and* distribute the broadsides.

For example, in the late 1980s, an attorney representing MasterCard threatened legal action if Jews for Jesus did not immediately "cease violating Mastercard's trademark." Jay Alan Sekulow, who served as general counsel for Jews for Jesus, learned that the supposed violation was a broadside entitled "Shop Till You Drop," which included a likeness of a MasterCard logo.

Jay was convinced that MasterCard had no case at all. Still, when the credit card company's attorney threatened to get a restraining order, Jay recommended that Jews for Jesus discontinue distribution of the tract. After all, Moishe did not particularly like the tract, and why take any chances? But on principle, Moishe refused to back down. He felt it would set a precedent that could only lead to further compromise and infringement on the group's First Amendment rights. So the distribution continued—and the threatened litigation never materialized.

What did materialize was a "coincidence" that changed Jay's outlook for good. He was spending an evening with his Jewish (not-for-Jesus) parents in Los Angeles. His mother, an avid shopper, took Jay by surprise when she told him she had just received the tract in question—while shopping—from one of the Jews for Jesus. Mrs. Sekulow had found the tract amusing. "It was very well done, clever," she told her son. "It really explained what you believe and why." Jay later reflected:

> That incident reaffirmed something for me. While my mother did not immediately accept Y'shua into her life, it just goes to show that he really is the Master of our lives, and that we who believe in him must stick with our principles. If Moishe had followed my legal advice and had "run scared," my mother wouldn't have gotten the tract that is being sent out with this Newsletter, the tract that was just right for her.[17]

### A WILLINGNESS TO LITIGATE

Many Christians insist that the only biblical response to the kind of opposition Jews for Jesus encounters in court is to "turn the other cheek." They would apply that response literally, not pursuing legal action if someone strikes you physically; as well as figuratively, not striking back when others strike by ignoring or twisting the laws that give freedom to preach the gospel.

In response to such arguments, Moishe Rosen has often said, "It's right to turn your own cheek, but it is wrong to try to turn someone else's cheek. If someone physically assaults you while you are handing out tracts and he knows that no legal action will be taken against him, you've invited him to assault the next person he sees handing out gospel tracts." That is why Jews for Jesus missionaries involve the police when they are physically assaulted or threatened. They may or may not decide to press charges, but they send a clear signal that crimes will be reported to the authorities.

They take a similar view of protecting their First Amendment rights. Moishe has stated that the organization stands up not just for its own right to free speech, but for that of all Americans. "When it comes to preaching the gospel, if you don't stand up for your rights you will lose them," Moishe has stated unequivocally.[18]

If this point has been lost on some of the Christian community, it has not been lost on secular individuals and organizations that have shown themselves willing to defend Jews for Jesus. They recognize there is more than one organization's right to free speech at stake.

One example of this involved a legal organization that often is the object of scorn in some Christian circles: the American Civil Liberties Union, which has defended the First Amendment rights of Jews for Jesus on more than one occasion. One case involved Moishe's detention for passing out broadsides at the Portland (Oregon) International Airport. It was 1976 and Moishe, as was his habit, was handing out broadsides at the airport, having come to the city on ministry business. Officials immediately asked him for a permit, which he did not have. He was detained and ultimately went to court. The district court judge ruled against Moishe, but in 1981, the U.S. Circuit Court of Appeals ruled two to one that the Port of Portland has no right to require people to register before distributing pamphlets.

Another Jews for Jesus lawsuit involved an incident in an airport, this time in Los Angeles.

## BROADSIDING AT LAX

Avi Snyder was distributing broadsides near the main terminal at the Los Angeles International Airport on what should have been an uneventful day in 1984. For ten years, Jews for Jesus and other groups had distributed literature without harassment from airport security. But that day, an airport policeman stopped Avi and showed him a copy of a 1983 resolution banning such activity. He told Avi to leave or he would be subject to legal prosecution by the city attorney. Avi left, and soon afterwards Jews for Jesus sued in Los Angeles federal court and won. The airport commissioners appealed, claiming that their ruling of 1983 mandated that the terminal was not open for First Amendment activities.

Joel Covelman, representing Jews for Jesus, said: "They attempted to ban every kind of First Amendment conduct in the terminal—which includes having a conversation, reading a newspaper or wearing a button with a political slogan." In 1986, the three circuit court judges ruled unanimously in favor of Jews for Jesus.[19]

Jews for Jesus won in all the lower courts as airport officials continued to appeal the case. It went all the way to the United States Supreme Court, whose decision to hear the case seemed to be a knock. But once again, Moishe's saying, "every knock is a boost," proved true. Suddenly national news programs were interviewing Avi and others, giving Jews for Jesus a public platform they never could have afforded to purchase. One news commentator asked Avi why it was so important to hand out this literature. He answered that believing in Jesus is a "life-and-death issue." When asked what would happen if handing out literature became illegal, Avi responded that the day when handing out literature became illegal would be the day that Jews for Jesus would become outlaws.

The Supreme Court heard the case, then ruled nine to zero in favor of Jews for Jesus—on the basis that the ban was overly broad and vague. Basically, the Supreme Court overturned the statute without addressing the broader issue of whether an airport terminal is a public forum.

## BROADSIDING OUTSIDE THE OAKLAND COLISEUM

Another First Amendment case involved an incident outside the Oakland Coliseum. On July 9, 1987, two Jews for Jesus staff members were distributing broadsides when a security officer seized one of them by the arm and demanded that they both accompany him to the office where they were threatened with arrest if they ever repeated their activity. Five days later, Jews for Jesus returned to distribute tracts at the major league baseball all star game. Two members were arrested and five others were mistreated by security officers because they had not obtained the required permit, or submitted their leaflets for review, acquired an insurance policy, or paid the one hundred dollar cleaning fee the Coliseum demanded.

The U.S. District Judge ruled that such requirements were unconstitutional. The charges were dismissed, and the Coliseum eased its rules.

## PIERCE COLLEGE

Americans have constitutional rights, and Jews for Jesus has never hesitated to stand up for those rights, even when an arrest was inevitable. Such was the case in the fall of 1988 at Pierce College in California. Several staff members were arrested for distributing broadsides on the campus. Speaking for the group, Avi Snyder commented:

> The campus is a public forum. I have a constitutional right to be here and speak to students.... We don't need approval for something we have a constitutional right to do. We don't need permission to speak to students. Pierce students are intelligent enough to decide whether they'd like to speak with us or not.[20]

After their arrest, they pledged to sue the campus administration for infringement of their civil rights. Again, the greatest benefit that resulted from the arrests was the media coverage. From the Los Angeles Times: "A little hell is being raised by the Jews for Jesus." Reflecting on Moishe and his reaction to the school's requirement that he obtain a permit, the reporter wrote: "Rosen, who is not known for mealy-mouthing, said he already had a permit—the U. S. Constitution." The headline was: "A Campus Mix of Jews, Jesus and Cows" and the story read:

> Up until recently, the most serious problem confronting the student population at suburban Pierce College was the cow-tipping scandal of 1983. Tucked into a corner of the San Fernando Valley, Pierce is a community college with an agricultural tilt and is not known for the kind of uproars that traditionally shatter the serenity of most campuses.
>
> Students concern themselves with when to plant the corn and what to feed the cattle and how to get the most out of a chicken....

Only the cow-tipping incidents of '83 seemed to upset anyone. It involved, quite literally, the tipping over of cows. An ex-tipper told me that students taking night classes used to go out into the field after class, find a sleeping cow and shove it over....

Back to Jews for Jesus. I asked [Moishe] Rosen why they just didn't hand out their pamphlets from a booth the way Pierce wanted them to.

"It's the difference," he said, "between distributing 10 pamphlets in two hours or 750 pamphlets in two hours.... Jesus said go forth to all the world and proclaim the Gospel. He didn't say sit down in a booth and wait for people to come to you."

Someone at Pierce ought to stand up and admit that accepting or rejecting a pamphlet isn't going to make anyone late for anything they don't want to be late for.

Let the Jews for Jesus pamphleteer. Let anyone pamphleteer who wants to pamphleteer. That's the glory of freedom. Even if it's wrong, it's right.

But pray that cow-tipping never returns as a campus activity.[21]

Other cases involving Jews for Jesus and free speech include one filed against the Massachusetts Bay Transportation Authority and another against the Hillsborough County Aviation Authority at the Tampa International Airport. Without such lawsuits, the evangelistic outreach of Jews for Jesus would be severely curtailed. In fact, in at least one instance, a judge cited an earlier case involving Jews for Jesus when he ruled in its favor. When mission strategy calls for a forthright and public proclamation of the gospel, First Amendment rights of free speech are essential. And while Jews for Jesus protects its own freedom of speech, it also protects the rights of every other Christian to proclaim the gospel freely.

# CHAPTER NINE

# TRAINING AND DISCIPLINE BEHIND THE SCENES

## *"Think Tank" Evangelism*

I t's the economy, Stupid!" That was the catch phrase of the Clinton campaign in 1992, and it worked. "It's the strategy, Stupid!" might well be dubbed the catch phrase of Jews for Jesus—certainly more than any mission I have studied. Jews for Jesus is a simmering "think tank" that is ever processing new ideas and strategies.

Training, strategy, and principles—humanly speaking, these are the most significant aspects of Jews for Jesus. Moishe Rosen is quick to point that out, especially to anyone who would want to focus on people and personalities. It is this kind of information, he insists, that ought to be the focus of this book. It should be a book that could double as a training manual for missionaries, particularly those involved in Jewish evangelism.

My writing tends to be people oriented, but always with an emphasis on ideas, so in many ways, each chapter of this book rests on the philosophical underpinnings of the movement as it relates to the people who have made the greatest impact. Nevertheless, the focus on ideas and strategy deserves a separate section of its own

As a writer and professor in the field of missions, I would challenge missionaries and mission agencies to examine the strategy and methodology of Jews for Jesus, not with an uncritical eye, but as a case study. Investigate it on its own merits; compare and contrast it with other mission agencies, and above all, view it as a model for effective mission outreach.

—∿—

Talking about some of the strategies Jews for Jesus uses in its ministry, Moishe Rosen once said: "What's different about Jews for Jesus [is] we'll try anything as long as it's fun, good natured and makes people smile. In Miami, we had a plane fly a banner up and down the beach."[1]

Moishe has based his mission strategy on the firsthand experience of growing up Jewish and not knowing about Jesus. Of course he had *heard* about Christ. No one could live in Denver without being aware of Christianity and the gospel message—but he chose not to know. He contends that his choice was typical of his family and his community: "I had first heard the message in my teenage years, but it was my duty as a Jew to disregard it. It was a conscientious decision on my part not to deal with the issue. I feel that's where most Jews are today. That was the one thing I decided not to know."[2]

Moishe has always taken a very pragmatic approach to evangelism—especially Jewish evangelism: "Look, the fact that we say Jesus is the Messiah is not enough to make it so," he readily concedes. "And the fact that the bulk of the Jewish community says that He isn't is not enough to make it *not* so. Our job is to get out and let our people know that the issue is too important to be ignored."[3]

It is the philosophy of presenting the gospel in a way that cannot be ignored that drives Jews for Jesus to continually seek new ways to creatively communicate the gospel. And while making the gospel an unavoidable issue has put Jews for Jesus missionaries in contact with Jewish people who are receptive to their ministry, it has also attracted the attention of those who oppose them. Therefore, much of the training and philosophy have to do with handling opposition.

## UNDERSTANDING THE OPPOSITION

Saul Alinsky wrote a book titled *Rules for Radicals* in which he challenged protesters to seek to understand the mindset of their opponents. One of his "rules" was for protesters to formulate demands ahead of time and to attempt to anticipate any concessions they might make.

Moishe applied this rule in the early days of Jews for Jesus as his group carried out regular demonstrations outside topless bars in the North Beach section of San Francisco. Moishe never called these demonstrations protests because he wanted to emphasize the positive nature of the statement the group wanted to make. The group was not merely *against* smut, they were *for* Jesus. Therefore, their placards had slogans like "Love, not Lust."

Naturally, the bars' owners were concerned that these demonstrations would drive away potential customers. So, Moishe said, "With Alinsky's principle in mind, we decided that if they asked us what we wanted in return for staying away, we would request the right to preach the gospel inside the bars." Upset with the protest, the owner of the bar that Jews for Jesus most frequently picketed finally gave in to their demand:

> We filled up the place with a bunch of Jesus people and asked several Christian leaders to help us preach.… Needless to say, we were never invited back because we ran off most of the drinking customers. The bar owner apparently felt it was better to lose a little business from our demonstrations than to forfeit an entire evening's liquor by letting us preach.[4]

Opposition has always been a major factor in the ministry of Jews for Jesus. Some detractors would say they provoke it. But Moishe responds that anyone who is preaching publicly and forcefully will face opposition. What makes the people with Jews for Jesus unique is that they expect and prepare for opposition—and they take maximum advantage of it.

But in order to take advantage of it, they have to prepare.

## CAMPAIGN TRAINING

In the early days of the ministry, Jews for Jesus encountered the most opposition during what they called their Summer Witnessing Campaigns. The campaigns began in New York City, which is where Moishe expected revival to break out in the early days of Jews for Jesus.

Moishe always believed that his work in San Francisco was to train people who would one day reach New York.

The first campaign was conducted with the idea that if God poured out his Spirit, the band of Jews for Jesus would stay in New York and continue to minister in the revival. When the campaign ended with no visible sign of revival, one of the early Jews for Jesus told Moishe, "Well, we just need to have more campaigns."[5] And the summer outreaches became part of the group's regular strategy. So in 1974, almost the whole staff plus some volunteers left San Francisco and headed out to New York, driving across country caravan style.

The Jewish Defense League was especially active in those days and had not realized yet that Jews for Jesus would not respond in kind to violence. Therefore, Moishe wanted to make sure that the campaigners were prepared for the worst. Protective shoes were a must—no sandals. The street evangelists practiced blowing whistles and screaming at the top of their lungs in the case of attack. Everyone was trained to respond to his or her group leader quickly and without question. While questions were allowed—in fact encouraged—in many ministry situations, discipline was tight on the streets. The leaders had to respond quickly if a situation turned dangerous, and they could only do so if team members were ready to hear and respond to instructions quickly.

Campaigners were, and still are, also trained in how to deal with the rejection they encounter on the streets. Depersonalizing that rejection has been a key lesson from the start. "Always remember," Karol Joseph, who oversees the training program today, teaches the troops, "when people call you names or insult you, it's not you. They don't know you. It's the gospel they are reacting to. It's the gospel, not you, that they are rejecting."[6] This lesson is invaluable because it enables people to withstand a great deal of rejection. It also gives campaigners compassion for those who insult and spit at them (and they are insulted by Gentiles as well as Jews), because these people's response to the gospel shows that their eternal destiny is on the line. In addition, knowing that it is Christ who is being rejected gives campaigners the privilege of identifying with him, knowing that he understands what it is to be maligned and misunderstood. And finally, the realization that the rejection is not personal helps campaigners keep a cardinal rule of street witnessing: not to strike back, either verbally or physically, when attacked.

Yet when it came to physical attacks in those early days, Moishe did not want the campaigners to be "sitting ducks." While the campaigners were under strict orders not to fight back, they did learn how to fall, how best to protect themselves from a nonthreatening position, and most important, how to call for the police.

Jews for Jesus has always held the law in high regard. Moishe and now David are determined that all assaults be reported and prosecuted. The public knowledge that Jews for Jesus reports and prosecutes crime has served as a deterrent to many attacks. Nevertheless the campaigners need to be prepared physically and mentally for possible trouble.

The most controversial practice of campaign training that dealt with personally directed hostility during the twenty-five year history of Jews for Jesus was referred to as "pain training." It was instituted in response to threats of violence from the opposition. Most of the early campaigners would be kicked, punched, slapped, or otherwise assaulted at some point. Moishe was convinced that the campaigners needed to prepare for an attack—not only to steel themselves for the worst, but to have an idea of what to expect and thereby minimize the fear. Thus, pain training, a quick but painful exercise, was used to provide mental as well as physical preparation. How does one prepare to be physically assaulted? Lipson describes the training:

> At the final meeting before departure onto the streets, the members were asked to stand, whereupon Moishe struck [slapped with an open hand] each one across the face hard enough to knock him or her over. Almost no one flinched.... Observing this exercise disturbed me, but it attests to the strength of the members' commitment and their trust of their charismatic leader.[7]

The purpose of this exercise was to prepare the staff to endure physical attacks without flinching and without retaliation. Part of the training was to allow campaigners to separate the pain of a slap on the face from the emotional valence that could weaken an unprepared campaigner. Those who endured pain training knew there was no ill will behind the slap. They were instructed that should someone inflict pain on them in the street, they were not to allow that pain to provoke them to anger. Pain was a physical sensation that could be dealt with in a calm way. It was a harsh method of training, but, in Moishe's view, necessary in light of the circumstances.

Moishe's younger daughter, Ruth, recalling her first Summer Witnessing Campaign in 1975 describes the pain training:

> Tuvya Zaretsky was in charge of Campaign that year. I had just turned 19 and Tuvya was like a big brother to me. I remember when he got to me and our eyes locked for just a moment. I knew in that moment that this slap was going to be more of an ordeal for him than it was for me. Then it was over. The slap was hard enough to inflict a stinging sensation as well as a dull ache that lasted a few moments, but it wasn't that bad.
>
> I suppose the most remarkable thing to me about pain training was that it worked for me—in fact, I reaped the benefit from it the very first day of Campaign. We had been doing street drama in front of the 42nd Street library, and had broken up to hand out broadsides to the crowd that had gathered. Suddenly I felt a sharp pain in the back of my upper arm. It felt hot and cold at the same time, and there was a twisting sensation. I was amazed at how objectively I reacted. I wondered if someone had stabbed me with a knife. Touching my arm to feel for blood, I turned to face an elderly man who was holding a cigarette he had obviously just put out on the back of my arm. It took me a moment to put together what had happened. The man, with a look of utter contempt, said, "I'm sorry, you were in my way." He darted away before I could do much of anything.
>
> I kept remembering the slap from the day before. "It's only pain," I thought, "and it's over now." I felt sorry for the man who had burned me, and I prayed for him. Of course the burn blistered and turned ugly—popped in the subway about a week later when I was coming back from a sortie (tract passing expedition.) But I had endured the pain objectively and was grateful that I had been prepared.[8]

Jews for Jesus founder Moishe Rosen and his wife, Ceil.

Moishe Rosen in the early years
of Jews for Jesus at a rally.

Moishe Rosen and Baroch Goldstein
discuss strategy at a demonstration.

This man holds onto one broadside while reading another.

This homeless woman is intent on reading hers as well.

Avi Snyder (top) on 5th Avenue, and Jhan Moskowitz (below) near the New York Stock Exchange, preaching to the crowds that Messiah has come.

Early days of the Liberated Wailing Wall (1970s).

The team in London's Trafalgar Square (1980s).

The Liberated Wailing Wall (1990s).

Listening is an important part of evangelism.

Getting a contact in the '90s.

An animated discussion on a subway platform

and on the beach at Brighton.

Getting a contact in the former Soviet Union

and on the Champs Elysies in Paris.

A prophets procession was done with
solemnity one day

and with exuberance on another.

The Jews for Jesus council in the late 1970s.
Front: Kresha Warnock
2nd row: Baruch Goldstein, Mitch Glaser, Jahn Moskowitz, Susan Perlman
3rd row: Stuart Dauermann, Jeff Fritz, Moishe Rosen, Tarvya Zaretsky

Jews for Jesus get all kinds of reactions to
their gospel pamphlets.

A creative way of reading Scripture during a
New Age street fair

or of getting out the gospel and some cold
juice on a hot summer day.

Footwashing in Northern
Ireland during the "troubles"

and death threats in Los Angeles in the 1980s.

1970s demonstration outside a San
Francisco topless club

and gospel street drama.

David Brickner in his early ministry days

and years later selected to succeed Moishe Rosen as executive director as the rest of the senior staff pray over him.

The Jews for Jesus' board of directors discontinued pain training in the early 1980s. Without judging its merits, the board deemed it was potentially a hot issue that could easily be blown out of proportion.

Today, when challenged by a somewhat horrified interviewer, Moishe continues to explain the practice without being the least bit defensive. He says we are living in a different era now, when most Jews for Jesus staffers no longer face a daily threat of physical attacks. In the 1970s, however, preparation through pain training did not seem so shocking. Campus protests were the norm, and a countershow of force occasionally got out of hand. The campus radicals were prepared for attacks. Why not Jews for Jesus?

While pain training is no longer a part of campaign preparation, reactions to verbal and physical attacks still are. Though incidents are not as frequent as they once were, they still occur, and campaigners need to be mentally and spiritually prepared to take the knocks.

## BRAINSTORMING VERSUS LESSONS SET IN STONE

One unique aspect of Jews for Jesus is the balance they have tried to maintain between creativity and nonnegotiable principles.

From the very early days, brainstorming sessions were a must. Sometimes they would occur with everyone sitting on the floor of Moishe's office, and a tape recorder rolling. They would talk about strategies, dreams, and new ways of doing things. The only rule was not to shoot down someone else's ideas. "We can sift through the ideas later to see what's worth keeping or developing," Moishe would say. "Don't make sarcastic or cynical remarks about someone else's ideas. That stifles initiative and creativity."

The creative aspect of Jews for Jesus is one of the ministry's hallmarks, but so is their adherence to certain principles. Particularly among the older staff members, whenever a disagreement or argument about how to handle a situation arises, someone is likely to say, "Okay, what is the principle we are dealing with here?"

Some of the principles of operations are quite simple. Know what something costs before committing funds to purchase it. That principle plays out into a policy of getting three estimates anytime someone needs to make a major repair or hire an outside vendor to bid on a job. Another principle is not to make exceptions to a rule until the person wanting the exception has shown a pattern of upholding the rule.

Other principles have to do with ethics, accountability, and a Christlike response to opposition. These principles are part of the curriculum for new missionary trainees, but often their value is only learned through experience. Often the younger missionaries learn through informal times of fellowship and storytelling, when they have opportunities to hear veteran missionaries relaxing and recounting the "old war stories."

## "AVODAH"

By 1976 Jews for Jesus had become the second largest and fastest growing of any of the messianic Jewish ministries in the United States. There were branch offices in New York, Chicago, and Los Angeles, and a staff of sixty workers at the headquarters in San Francisco. It was no longer an organization made up of Moishe and a ragtag bunch of hippies. Professional education at a Bible college or seminary was encouraged, and the leadership team consisted of Moishe and a seven-member elected council. Much larger office space had been acquired with up-to-date equipment and all kinds of systems to keep the ministry wheels turning. The movement had gone from being a "family" to being a sophisticated organization—a sad state of affairs, according to some of the older members. Moishe lamented that much had been lost in the process: "As we develop the capabilities to do things ourselves, we rely less on prayer...."[9]

While Moishe often complains that he and the organization are not what they should be, he was always looking for ways to strive to be more. And so, in 1979, he brought the entire staff back together to do just that:

From San Francisco headquarters came the command: Pull back the troops, retrain, recharge, even cleanse the ranks when necessary, then go out fighting harder and more effectively.

With that, Jews for Jesus leader Moishe Rosen and his advisory board launched a militant new program, "Avodah" [Ah-voh-dah] (Hebrew, meaning "work and worship"), in which all the agency's methods and materials will be reexamined for greater effectiveness.[10]

Moishe's emphasis on training is evident in his 1979 proclamation of Avodah. It was a radical move. Volunteers continued in the cities where regional offices were located, and contact was maintained with supporters, but for all practical purposes the six-year-old mission was on training mode. Some sixty-five workers were uprooted and returned to headquarters. Jews for Jesus issued a news release:

> In order to grow, we have terminated the leases on our six branches and brought all our regular evangelistic staff, including our four Mobile Evangelistic Teams, back to San Francisco for nine months of retraining and intensive evangelism. We intend to double our activities in the next 18 months. However, rather than proceed piecemeal, we are doing what no mission has ever done before by making this move.
>
> Our new basis of ministry will involve intensive campaigns for extended periods of time. We need to be more thorough in our evangelism. We intend to discover what can be done right here in northern California in the next nine months before we redeploy the staff to branches.[11]

During that period, training took various forms, including formal teaching sessions conducted by well-known ministers and educators. The list included Dr. James Boice, pastor of the Tenth Presbyterian Church of Philadelphia; Dr. W. A. Criswell, pastor of the First Baptist Church of Dallas; Dr. Charles Ryrie, professor at Dallas Theological Seminary; and Rachmiel Fryland, a Jewish Christian scholar in rabbinics and apologetics.

Avodah was also a time of shaking up and sifting down as Moishe created a "level playing field" by putting a moratorium on the idea of group leaders. He wanted to give people an equal chance at leadership, and he wanted to see how the group would work together cooperatively without assigned leaders.

Older staff members still look back on Avodah and laugh at the term "duty light," which was applied to the nine-month experiment. There were regular exams to go with all the coursework; a certain amount of missionary work that was expected; and there was experimentation with different evangelism methods on nearby campuses. It was also a time for some of the young couples to begin their families and for some of the young people to begin courting one another. As a result, there were several marriages in the months that followed Avodah.

There was also an acceptance of ministry-wide standards and an understanding of ministry principles, policies, and procedures. The group learned from some of the best teachers, and they studied ideas as well as practical missionary techniques. The training covered a vast array of topics, from what character traits missionaries should possess to how far away from the door they should stand when doing door-to-door evangelism.

After 1979 the organization was too large to shut down for a period of nine months. However, on two occasions since Avodah, a special retraining week for the missionary staff has been held at a conference grounds in northern California. The organization plans a similar time of retraining, this time for two weeks at the close of the year 2000.

## DEPUTATION

Raising support is a necessary part of mission strategy. Since Jews for Jesus is an independent ministry with no formal denominational ties, they raise support through what is called deputation. Jews for Jesus defines deputation as "winning the hearts of God's people to our cause so that they will give, pray and witness to the end that Jewish people might be saved." Deputation includes communicating with churches and individuals and asking them to give needed funds. Moishe is convinced that deputation "is the scriptural method of raising support for ministries outside the scope of the ordinary parish." He and the others in Jews for Jesus have been well received in most churches. Yet, he has reservations and, in his typical style, he does not mince words:

> I have some problems with deputation. At the top of the list is [the fact that] doing deputation work makes me feel like a beggar. I have to write to the pastor and let him know that I would welcome the opportunity to speak to the church. Then I have to make arrange-

ments at the convenience of the church. In my presentation I'm supposed to maintain Christian dignity and decorum with such euphemisms as "prayer support," "personal involvement," "share in our ministry." Honesty and directness is crowded into a corner by "tact" for most mission speakers.[12]

Despite reservations, Moishe and his staff are among the most effective of independent missionaries in deputation outreach, and other ministries could learn from them. They present themselves well in churches—whether through a first-rate musical program, a well-rehearsed dramatic production, or a polished demonstration of the seder. These presentations stir people's hearts to give and pray in support of the organization.

While Moishe may not like having to ask for the support, the group has never taken the generosity of the organization's supporters for granted. Moishe speaks often of his gratitude for those who support the ministry, and this spirit of thankfulness has been passed on to the Jews for Jesus staff. Their gratitude is shown in tangible ways—most notably in the personal handwritten post cards they send to churches and individual supporters of the ministry. Moishe emphasizes that people should be given the opportunity to share in the ministry—but never be made to feel guilty if they do not. "The best way to interest people in the ministry," he counsels, "is to show them that your ministry is something you're excited about and believe."[13] He never liked the term *fund-raising*. He preferred a term used in a book title on the subject: *friend-raising*—which is essentially relationship building.

Jews for Jesus' deputation is designed to give something to the church as well as to ask something of it. Perhaps one of the most enduring gifts that Jews for Jesus has given to the church is the reenactment of the Passover seder as it relates to the Last Supper. But like virtually everything else in which the ministry has been involved, this Christ in the Passover presentation has not been without controversy. Jewish critics are incensed, charging that the seder is misinterpreted with Christian symbolism, and some would suggest that it goes so far as to make a mockery of Passover. David Brickner is quick to respond to such charges: "If we are guilty of misinterpreting the bread and the cup of the Passover, then I suppose Jesus could be accused of the same 'misinterpretation.'"[14] For Christians, however, there ought to be no contradiction or mockery of this Old Testament Jewish festival. It was a continuing celebration for Jesus and his disciples and has great significance for Christians today. Christians who see the presentation take away a deep awareness of the meaning and symbolism of Passover as it is translated into the Last Supper and communion.

Too often, when Christians think of the Last Supper, they envision Leonardo da Vinci's painting. Moishe recalls the first time he looked closely at that painting—or actually at a replica of the painting in sculptured wax. It was early in his ministry. He was speaking in San Francisco and staying with his family in a hotel near Fisherman's Wharf.

> Now I was sitting reviewing some notes when my two daughters came to me in a delegation and the older one spoke for both and said, "Dad, the Wax Museum is right close nearby and they have in life size, the Last Supper. Dad, could we go and see it?" And you know when you see such strong religious motivation on the part of your young ones, you just can't deny them, so I agreed and that night when we finished supper we went to the Wax Museum and as soon as I'd bought the ticket, the young one was pulling the older one around the corner yelling, "Where's Frankenstein?", and I was left to find the Last Supper alone…. I looked into the face of each of these disciples and…they all looked like Gentiles, Jesus looked like a Gentile…. Now there was one of the disciples that looked typically Jewish. You could spot him any place as being a Jew. Could you guess which one? Judas. And you know this is one of the problems that my people have. When they look at Jesus they see little that they can recognize as Israel's promised Messiah.[15]

Jews see only non-Jewish Christians in that last Passover, and that is what Christians see as well. The Christ in the Passover presentation helps Christians reevaluate their preconceived notions on this issue, but it is also a clearly evangelistic presentation to which they are encouraged to invite Jewish friends. Jews for Jesus missionaries have met many Jewish contacts at these presentations and have often had the joy of leading them to faith in Christ.

Critics of the Jews for Jesus' version of the Passover seder feel the presentation distorts and twists the meaning of Passover because the presentation shows how Jesus used this very Jewish celebration to point to himself as Israel's true redeemer. Among the harshest critics has been Jacqueline Swartz, a Jewish reporter. After attending one of these seders, she wrote: "This is a Passover from hell. A macabre parody, courtesy of Jews for Jesus."[16]

Despite such criticism, through these presentations communion becomes more meaningful for Christians. Equally important, they discover a deeper appreciation for the Jewish heritage and culture that permeates the New Testament.

In general, the mission strategy of Jews for Jesus is always in transition. A concept or program that works well one year may not work the next. Or one that works in one area of the country—or the world—may not work in another.

Jews for Jesus' key to success seems to be finding and implementing fresh ideas while at the same time retaining proven methods and strategies. One of their new programs is Christ in the Feast of Tabernacles. This involves setting up a full-sized booth in the host church, with traditional accouterments of the feast as celebrated in Bible times and Jewish homes today. The presentation is accompanied by Jesus' words, as recorded in the Gospel of John when he celebrated the Feast of Tabernacles (Sukkot).

The significance of this new Sukkot presentation for churches is that they will gain a wonderful insight into a holiday Jesus celebrated—a holiday that he used to make remarkable statements about himself. But it also has a tangential yet significant meaning for the Jews for Jesus' staff. All the staff are required to learn the new presentation—even the "old-timers" who have not, like the newer missionaries, had to memorize a script in order to do their Christ in the Passover presentations.

One thing that has been instilled in the staff is that it is crucial to keep on learning. Whether it is a new presentation, or taking summer courses for continuing education, or learning a new skill for a new phase of ministry; Jews for Jesus' staff are expected to continue to learn, to stretch, and to grow.

# CHAPTER TEN

# THE WISDOM OF
# A PATRIARCH

## Common Sense and Insight

## from Moishe Rosen

M oishe Rosen often dispenses wisdom as a father figure and friend, and in the course of researching this book I sometimes found myself at the receiving end of his advice. In one instance it related to money matters and income tax issues. He asked me pointed and personal questions and offered pointed and personal advice. I was appreciative—not offended—knowing he was concerned for my well-being.

Moishe's wisdom is forthright and personal. Those qualities also come through in his lectures. When I was in his home in San Francisco, he invited me to go through the file drawers in his basement office. Nothing was off limits or out of bounds. While perusing files, I realized that at least some of Moishe's common sense wisdom deserved a chapter of its own in this volume. I chose the folders and documents I wanted his assistant to copy. This wisdom is sprinkled throughout the book, but here I have consolidated excerpts from various lectures to show the force and range of issues with which he has dealt. Moishe's field of expertise is, of course, evangelism to Jews, but much of the wisdom he dispenses, particularly in training lectures, relates to ministry and community and behavior in general.

Jews for Jesus is a ministry with a collective mentality, and much of its strategy is based on the wisdom and street smarts of Moishe Rosen though Moishe is quick to admit that he has learned a great deal from the staff he trained. Colleagues who have stayed with him over the years have appreciated his style and gained much from his perspective on how to effectively reach Jewish people.

## ON LIVING IN COMMUNITY

Unlike Jesus People USA, Jews for Jesus' staff have never practiced communal living. Yet they do have a sense of family and community that I have not seen in most mission organizations. This is due in part to the fact that staff members have a common Jewish culture and in part because they have endured discrimination and misunderstanding from Jews and non-Jews alike. Perhaps most important, they need each other to accomplish a common task that is difficult and fraught with opposition. The bond that has emerged naturally from all these factors provides a foundation for community. Moishe, however, has not taken this sense of community for granted. He is committed to the concept and has made it a major part of his lectures to staff. What he means by community is not a new concept; it is based on what an apostolic church should be, as found in the second chapter of Acts.

Moishe's contemporary model for the ideal of community is not a commune, but a community of believers—frequently living separately—as in the case of the Navigators. They often share housing, which Moishe refers to as a "modified commune." He encourages staff families to purchase homes near one another and younger staff who are not married to share a house or apartment. He says that our principle is to live close to one another.

Moishe insists that even without the sense of a commune, as in the case of a socialistic commune, the commitment ought to be no less.

Moishe also talks about the importance of being vulnerable, insisting that a "can do" attitude is detrimental to the formation of the "I need you" sense of vulnerability. But next to vulnerability is accessibility and approachability, and here Moishe speaks of relationships beyond the community itself.

Community ties directly to ministry, and Moishe challenges the staff to seek out opportunities to minister: Do not invite someone to a meeting simply because there is a meeting and you want more people to attend. The only motivation should be because "We can bless people. We can lift people. We can help people. We can provide something in their lives. That's why we have meetings."

In seeking out people, Moishe insists, "Don't look for people you particularly like." Ministry, he says, is for the purpose of ministering. "You are there to be a mentor, a minister, not a friend." This becomes clear in Moishe's philosophy of whom the staff should seek out:

> In choosing people, look for people on the edge of the crowd. Our policy is the opposite from that of Campus Crusade for Christ. Campus Crusade goes for the leaders, for the campus presidents, for the "big men" on campus.[1]

## ON PANHANDLING

Frequently Moishe's teaching is common sense advice. He sometimes speaks in exaggerated terms with his own slant and bias—a bias that many of his own staff might challenge. Yet he speaks with such conviction and force that one cannot escape having to seriously consider his position. For example, in his lecture on "Jews for Jesus as Community" he deals with the issue of street beggars:

> I've told our staff in the home office never to give money to a panhandler. Never! People don't really meet their needs this way. Very often, panhandling is a form of dominance and aggression. Panhandlers set out saying, "I can get a quarter from that guy." Then they prove to themselves that they can prevail over you by giving you a good story, by an imposing presence, or just by your wanting to get rid of them. And they get that quarter....
>
> Go and seek out people who have needs. You meet their needs and be generous to them. But when people come to you...like I have just described, don't give.[2]

## ON CHURCH AND MINISTRY ETIQUETTE

Moishe insists that those who minister under the name of Jews for Jesus show proper respect when visiting churches. Street evangelism is entirely different. There the uniform is denims and T-shirts, and staffers' demeanor is often assertive with a strong dose of humor. But inside a church sanctuary, their dress and demeanor must be decorous at all times. There are rules to follow:

> One thing that I have constantly had to remind The Liberated Wailing Wall and other presentation groups is the necessity of respecting someone else's sanctuary.... The pulpit itself is a symbol, the place from which one hears God's truth.... When you take that pulpit and move it out of the way yet leave it in the sight of the people.... in effect you're telling them that what they're going to hear is not the Word of God. What troubles me more is the careless running of wires, tubes, and pipes. Some churches spend from $10,000 to $50,000 for a sound system. They're just waiting for a music group to come and use it so they can hear and see the full value of what they've purchased. To come in and set up all the tubes and wires and speakers in effect is to reject what they have prepared. It's like going to someone's home to eat a meal and bringing your own food.
>
> Likewise when you go to a church to worship, you should put on your best clothes. You're coming into the presence of the Almighty.... It's a matter of respect.... Before you come to church, if you're able, you might make yourself available to an adult Sunday school class. Show them that you're there as their servant not as a special guest. Contribute to the offering. Show that you support the local church.[3]

## ON RELATING TO OTHER MINISTRIES

One area that mission organizations often neglect is that of relating to other outreach ministries. Moishe has always counseled the Jews for Jesus' staff to form good relationships with other missions and not view them as competitors, as it is often so tempting to do. Nevertheless, he has little patience with

organizations he feels do not live up to their claims. In reference to one particular mission that he named, he bluntly stated:

> I don't think I have to tell anyone here that I have no use for
> [them].... I feel they're ersatz [artificial] missionaries, that most of
> their supporters think they are doing missionary work but they're
> duds.... So, what would happen if we met someone who was from
> [this group]? We don't need to level an accusation at them, but we
> may need to explain that we are not the same kind of people doing
> the same kind of thing at all.
>
> Generally speaking it's known throughout Jews for Jesus whom
> we regard as co-laborers.... Always give a person the benefit of the
> doubt. When a new worker starts up a work in the city, it's up to
> that person, even as part of his planning to know what other Jewish
> ministries there are.... [When you move to a new city] Pay a call on
> each of them. During the call extend courtesy, ask for their counsel
> and ask for their prayers. Tell them where you can be found. Ask if
> there's anything you can do to help them.
>
> Say that a person belongs to a separatist fundamental group but
> they do witness to the Jews. They still deserve our respect. They are
> not going to give us any of their referrals. They are not going to give
> us any support and they're not going to attend any of our meetings.
> We should still support them as best we can because they're out
> there witnessing to Jews, they're fulfilling our purpose. They're co-
> workers.[4]

Moishe has an easy way with people, and he suggests many ways to deal
properly with others on a one-to-one basis. For the missionary visiting someone at home, Moishe has all kinds of hints on how to relate. For example, if
the missionary is visiting a Jewish family and they do not offer any refresh-
ments—even a cold drink—"it means they don't want you to stay." That
does not mean the missionary ought to leave immediately, he says, but
"you've got just a few minutes either to make them want you to stay, or to
leave."

What if the television is blaring so loudly that the missionary cannot carry on a useful conversation?

> You don't have the right to get up and turn it down, nor should you tell someone else to turn it down. Instead, just start talking softer and softer. [If they want to hear you] they'll either get a chair and get closer to you or they'll turn down the television set. In other words, you always let each person control their own situation.

Moishe includes the topic of physical contact in his lectures on etiquette. Some of his advice seems almost simplistic to adults who move freely in social and professional circles. For young people barely out of college who might feel somewhat unsure, the suggestions can be very beneficial. For example: "In greeting someone, is it appropriate to hug or kiss?" he asks. His answer is:

> I think you have to know if that kind of attention is welcome. There are certain signals that it is welcome. You'll know the purity of your own heart if you're willing to hug and kiss the men as well as the women if you're a man. In general, women should not be physical with men. Men might misunderstand it and consider it an invitation.

For women and men his counsel is simple: "A ready smile helps." Having said that, he pointedly criticizes some of his own staff:

> If I would fault certain people in this group, it would be [because] they go for laughs, not smiles. Laughter can sometimes be a distraction and can sometimes say we're not serious. I notice that those who go for laughter mostly want personal attention and personal admiration rather than to use their humor as the oil to lubricate relationships. The smile will do.[5]

## ON ORGANIZATIONAL ENCOURAGEMENT AND LOYALTY

Moishe emphasizes the staff's need to encourage one another in order to build team spirit. "We should be encouragers. We should be a force for good." He also insists on loyalty; that the staff members should be loyal to one another, especially when dealing with other ministries or outsiders in general. It is all too tempting to agree with an outsider's criticism of fellow members when you know the criticism to be true; but if you care about your colleagues, you will confront them about their weaknesses rather than discussing those weaknesses with others. "You don't have to uphold that colleague," he counsels, "but you can bring a stop to an unwelcome conversation by saying, 'I'll have to talk it over with him.' In other words, you show that your colleague is part of you."

Moishe went on to place himself (then executive director) at the center of this unwanted criticism, and he did so with typical brash and self-deprecating humor:

> Those who dislike Jews for Jesus are going to personalize an attack. They're going to say Moishe Rosen is this or Moishe Rosen is that. I expect you to behave properly. At one time I would say, don't defend me, I'll defend myself. But the organization has become too large and the criticisms are too many.... You have to demonstrate loyalty. Even if they say something that is true, like "Moishe Rosen is a fat slob," you would be obligated to say, "Yes, but he's a competent leader." If something is questioned that you are not sure about, just say, "I'll ask Moishe Rosen about that."[6]

## ON LIFESTYLE ISSUES

Jews for Jesus staff members are well paid in comparison to many others who serve with independent missions. They are professionals, and Moishe always believed that they should be compensated as such. But he had warnings regarding their lifestyle:

> Live in modest good taste. It depends a lot on the individual. Frankly, I don't think anybody should own a yacht on our staff. I don't see how they'd have time to use it. But what about summer homes? I don't know about summer homes. You know, everybody's got choices, but I'll tell you one thing that burdens me about the

staff and standards. Luxury and convenience becomes a standard very quickly. After certain staff families began to have a second car, it became the culture and it was expected.[7]

## ON RULES FOR EVERYDAY LIVING

Some critics might argue that the Jews for Jesus' staff has too many rules governing their personal lives, but in many cases these rules are common sense. As such, they are very beneficial to those they are meant to help. For example:

A supervisor must be careful not to be rude.... I have to ask anyone who does my typing to take the hard edge off some of my memos.

Jews for Jesus has a rule where we don't loan one another [a substantial amount of] money. We do have a staff benefit fund where if there is a small emergency we'll meet that. It's just a rule that we don't loan one another money.

Don't make excuses. Even if the dog ate your school paper, you still don't have it. Even if the fire truck was in your way...you're late. Telling a person the reason why only exacerbates the problem because in effect you are saying they must accept what you've done.... [Simply say "I'm sorry."] "I'm sorry" means "I did wrong" or "I was inadequate." If you started out ten minutes earlier, maybe the fire truck being in your way wouldn't really matter. If you'd fed the dog, maybe he wouldn't have eaten your paper.[8]

I believe that you can do the job that I've assigned you or I wouldn't have assigned you. I'll always assign the kind of work that you have to expand yourself to do. You must keep growing in your ability to function in order to keep up with the rest of Jews for Jesus.

Don't tell me that I don't understand something when you don't get your way. Make me understand. You can count on me to try.

It's not wrong to hurt people if you're trying to help them, but if they can't benefit from the hurt you cause, then it is wrong.[9]

Moishe has much to say, but he also listens. He is in his element among thinkers who confront issues and ideas and debate his perspectives. His words of wisdom and advice gain substance through interaction. Those who know him best have found that questioning his words often stimulates even deeper thought and yields a more valuable insight than the original.

# CHAPTER ELEVEN

# EXPANSION AT HOME AND ABROAD

## Taking the Message Worldwide

F rom the early 1970s, Moishe was convinced that the ministry would not be confined to San Francisco. In fact he often said, "I had to come to San Francisco to reach New York." He fully expected to build a work in New York, which he saw as the hub of worldwide communication. As such, a strong work in New York City would have effects around the world. From New York it was inevitable that the ministry would expand beyond the borders of the United States though Moishe never planned that Jews for Jesus would be a worldwide ministry.

My interest in missions is due in part to a movement that played a key role in my own spiritual pilgrimage. In the 1890s A. B. Simpson founded the Christian and Missionary Alliance. A tiny part of that movement's legacy reached into a 1930s farming community in northern Wisconsin through two home missionaries ("lady preachers" as they were called). The work they started became the Green Grove Alliance Church, where I came to faith in the 1950s. My "call" to missions came some years later at an Alliance Bible camp, through the moving challenge of an Alliance missionary. I began my college education at St. Paul Bible College (now Crown College), an Alliance institution. Although I did not become a career missionary, much of my writing and teaching has been about missions.

As I focus on missions in this volume, I find it most interesting that Jews for Jesus has been influenced by the legacy of that same man—A. B. Simpson. In the early years of Jews for Jesus, Moishe strongly urged the Jewish hippies who had *gathered around him to pursue formal Bible training. He recommended Simpson College, an Alliance school then located in San Francisco, and it became the college of choice for many of the early Jews for Jesus.*

*Such is the history of missions. It takes only one person with a vision—an A. B. Simpson or a Moishe Rosen—and the legacy goes on. The ripple effects are felt around the country and around the world by the generations that follow.*

—⟊—

Jews for Jesus expanded worldwide as needs arose and opportunities developed. Branch locations depend largely on the Jewish population in a given area. The decision to expand abroad came well after the home base of operations in North America was firmly established. And, unlike many faith mission organizations, Jews for Jesus sends missionaries abroad with the intent that they work their way out of a job as locals come to faith and take over the responsibility of further evangelism.

But before they expanded abroad, they had some growing pains at home.

### OPERATION BIRTHDAY CAKE

Bigger is not always better, and that is a lesson Jews for Jesus learned during their third annual Summer Witnessing Campaign. In the summer of 1976, Jews for Jesus launched "Operation Birthday Cake" (OBC) to commemorate the nation's bicentennial. The campaigns in 1974 and 1975 were known as New York City Witnessing Campaigns, but the 1976 event involved additional "satellite campaigns" in Chicago, Philadelphia, New York, Washington, D.C., and Boston. The combined Jewish populations in these urban centers represented two-thirds of the U.S. Jewish population. Most of the campaigners departed from San Francisco and crossed the county on interstate highways in a caravan of eleven vans emblazoned with 'Jews for Jesus' in fourteen-inch-high letters. They aroused much curiosity—and sometimes hostility—even while they traveled. Their first stop was Trinity Evangelical Divinity School, north of Chicago. There they spent one week in intensive training, for which they received seminary course credit.

The outreach in the various cities was in typical style: The Jews for Jesus stood on busy corners, passing out broadsides and talking with anyone who would talk back. They did street drama, music, parades. As usual, there were some violent reactions, but Moishe's response was typical: "The thing we fear most on the streets is not violence but rather indifference.... Some of our tactics may seem brazen, yet we don't want to make it easy for people to ignore us."[1]

Naturally, Jews for Jesus encountered opposition in this campaign.

The plans for Operation Birthday Cake were "top-secret," according to Hesh Morgan of the *Jewish Press,* who claimed that a newly organized Jewish group calling itself the Anti-Missionary Institute had uncovered the plans. "The operation is a secret," Hesh revealed. "Only the elite leadership knew." Such counterintelligence, he went on to say, arose out of a long tradition:

> Ever since the days of Joshua, the Jewish people have had the most effective intelligence gathering units of any people.... The tradition of knowing of the plans of the opposition has been perpetuated in the Anti-Missionary Institute (AMI). This secret division of AMI is responsible for the ingathering of material concerning missionary movements and activities.[2]

The name "Operation Birthday Cake" was far more mysterious than the campaign itself, and in fact was typical of Jews for Jesus' tongue-in-cheek humor. Nevertheless, certain details were kept under wraps to prevent the opposition from preparing a counteroffensive, which is exactly what the Anti-Missionary Institute was planning to do, according to Hesh:

> Sam Nadler and his wife Miriam will be leading in the New York campaign; the question is whether they will lead effectively after AMI publishes listings of their daily activities. If the Jewish community is made aware of the fact that during the campaign, a team of missionaries will make the New York Public Library on 23rd Street a focal point, the element of surprise will be withdrawn. Rabbis can be present to contradict the barrage of missionary propaganda before the ideas sink in.[3]

Apparently there was a mole in the New York office of Jews for Jesus, if Hesh and AMI are to be believed:

The secret intelligence section of AMI would like to publicly thank the leading New York "Jews for Jesus" representative and his wife (who will remain nameless) for providing us with a copy of the confidential letter [from Moishe to his top staff] as well as other secret material.[4]

The staff enjoyed Hesh Morgan's series of articles, knowing that the confidential and top secret documents he referred to were nonexistent (although the leadership was not above classifying some of their documents as confidential for the fun of seeing the opposition crow over routine information).

Although there were some physical attacks made on members of Jews for Jesus during "Operation Birthday Cake," the worst opposition could probably best be termed bureaucratic harassment.

Officials at the airport in Chicago told the group they needed a permit, which could be obtained only between 9:00 to 9:30 A.M. Moishe arrived at the permit office at 9:00 A.M. and was told that the person handling such permits was in the washroom, and would not be available until after 9:30—past the daily deadline for the permit. Before the effort was over, seventeen members of the group had been arrested and jailed. They were charged with "resisting an officer" and "failure to obey the police"—even though their literature distribution itself was not illegal.[5]

Similar harassment occurred in New York. The hotel where they had a reservation suddenly refused to honor the agreement, and the group ended up having to stay at a motel on Forty-second Street, near the docks. To make matters worse, five thousand dollars worth of sound equipment was stolen, several vans were involved in accidents, and sanitation inspectors (with police power) "started issuing summonses right and left. The charges were for 'littering' and distributing circulars.'"[6]

In the final analysis, Operation Birthday Cake was not one of Jews for Jesus' finest moments. Indeed, after looking back, with more than twenty years of experience and hindsight, some would list it as one of the organization's least successful ventures. It failed to accomplish the purpose it set out to achieve—that of making a profound difference in the American Jewish community through the proclamation of Jesus as Messiah.

## EXPANDING THE MESSAGE THROUGH SECULAR MEDIA

Moishe learned some lessons about the secular media from his time with the ABMJ.

In the spring of 1971 the American Board of Missions to the Jews bought television air time on WOR-TV in New York City. They were going to present a dramatization of the Passover seder from a messianic Jewish perspective. In response to Jewish protests, the station cancelled the program three days before it was scheduled to air. This same scenario was played out at ten of twelve television stations in cities around the country, and suddenly the messianic Jewish movement was in the headlines—of the *New York Times,* no less.[7]

When the television programs were banned, the ABMJ decided to focus on the print media, specifically on full-page newspaper ads with the title message "So Many Jews Are Wearing 'That Smile' Nowadays!" The ads featured a group of smiling Jewish people and included a free offer for a compilation of their testimonies. The first of these advertisements ran in the *New York Times* in December 1971 and drew some four thousand replies the first week.

With that response, the ABMJ placed the newspaper ad in cities all over the country that had a Jewish population of at least one hundred thousand. More than fifteen thousand people responded, requesting literature. Jewish leaders responded as well. Rabbi Marc Tanenbaum of the American Jewish Committee accused the American Board of "trying to sell Christianity the way you sell toothpaste."[8] In comparison to previous evangelistic efforts, which resulted in few more than a dozen baptisms a year, the endeavor was viewed a success.[9]

Many Jewish leaders reacted in ways similar to Rabbi Tanenbaum, but their outcry only brought more attention to the messianic movement in general and the ad in particular. The National Conference of Synagogue Youth placed an ad of its own: "Yes Many Jews Are Wearing 'That Smile' Nowadays!" and went on to warn Jews not to "stray in distant waters, in far off places in search of your treasure." One rabbi, without organizational money, published his own ad entitled, "Wipe That Smile off..."[10]

The ABMJ did not continue the strategy in the following years, and the fledgling Jews for Jesus could not afford to place ads in secular newspapers. But Moishe had been impressed by the success of the ABMJ's ad and recognized the value of secular media for evangelism. Jews for Jesus was three years old before they began placing a full-page gospel statement in secular print media. On June 1976 they put their first ad in the *New York Times,* and for many years they seemed to be the only Jewish mission interested in this form of outreach.

In 1982 they went beyond placing a gospel ad in one or two papers; they carried out a full-fledged media blitz called the Y'shua Campaign:

> As part of its aggressive mission strategy, in December of 1982 Jews for Jesus launched an unprecedented nation-wide newspaper ad campaign. Costing an estimated quarter of a million dollars, the full-page advertisements ran in seventy major papers, with the announcement: "The Messiah has come and his name is Y'shua (the Jewish word for 'Jesus')."[11]

In 1983 the media advertising blitz known as the "Y'shua" campaign was even larger. In addition to appearing in about one hundred newspapers in major cities across the country, the ads ran in major news magazines. More than twelve thousand people, almost half of them Jewish, responded, and all received a copy of Moishe's book of messianic prophecies, *Y'shua.*[12]

The 1984 ad campaign included full-page ads in four December issues of *Time* magazine. The first of these featured the attention grabbing headline, "Sure I'm Jewish. And I celebrate Christmas." The text went on to present the Jewishness of Jesus:

> Have you ever noticed that Y'shua (that's the Jewish way to say Jesus) was born of a Jewish mother, spent all of His life in Israel, said that He was the Jewish Messiah and backed it up with evidence from the Jewish Scriptures?

That ad alone garnered more than six thousand responses; the four-part series elicited fifteen thousand. Were they worth the expense at more than thirty thousand dollars each? Yes, according to Susan Perlman, who spoke for the organization. The cost was approximately what it would require to fund a full-time missionary for a year, and the ads brought in many more contacts than a missionary could. Not all magazines were willing to accept the controversial ads. The *New Yorker* refused, as *U.S. News and World Report* had done the previous year.[13]

Jews for Jesus media campaigns have become a regular part of their outreach, and more importantly, have become part of the testimony of many Jewish people who have come to Christ after seeing them.

The ministry's outreach continued through the eighties, and near the end of the decade, its influence expanded overseas.

## SOUTH AFRICA OUTREACH

Jews for Jesus' first overseas branch was launched in South Africa in 1989 when Andrew and Laura Barron arrived in Johannesburg. Yet the groundwork for that outreach had been laid nearly a decade earlier when The Liberated Wailing Wall music team visited South Africa on its first world tour.

As with most of Jews for Jesus' outreach efforts, this one was met with some resistance.

"Leaders Slam 'Jews for Jesus.'" This was the headline of an article in the Johannesburg *Times*, September 16, 1984. Pictured were team members David and Patti Brickner distributing broadsides. Many people defended the organization's religious freedom, but Jewish leaders were outraged, calling the evangelistic efforts "blasphemous" and a "slur" against Judaism.

One newspaper reported that the group faced severe opposition:

> Three of their scheduled meetings in the Johannesburg area had to be called off or reconvened and the group was barred from performing on university and college campuses for fear of provoking the wrath of their Jewish students.
>
> Police were called in to remove over 100 Jewish protesters from disrupting a meeting in Pretoria on Tuesday.[14]

Protesters interrupted a concert by The Liberated Wailing Wall in Pretoria as well. *The Citizen* reported that the concert resumed after the protesters "were shepherded away" by the Pretoria Flying Squad. "If we went to a synagogue and did the same thing, there would be cries of anti-Semitism," drama team member Lee Fraum told a reporter. "It's a disgrace that Jews are persecuting us for our beliefs when they have been persecuted for over 4,000 years for their own."[15]

Indeed, so strong was the opposition in Johannesburg that The Liberated Wailing Wall and its dramatic counterpart, the New Jerusalem Players, had to cancel two appearances. Yet, the press reports were favorable. One reporter wrote that the music was "very Hebraic in content…a Christian version of 'Fiddler on the Roof.'" His evaluation of the New Jerusalem Players was even more positive: "The drama group presents much humour with their message, such as the bringing up to date of the "Book of Acts," which is done in the form of an American TV news service. Precise, funny and to the point."[16]

In summing up the South African leg of their world tour, David Brickner confessed to a reporter that the group had not expected the angry outbursts. Yet, as always, they refused to be intimidated: "I am amazed at the rioting and harassment we encountered in South Africa—Jewish people are usually fairly open-minded. But we are not going to allow this to stop us from spreading the word of our Messiah."[17]

Following the 1984 music tour in South Africa, a mission society called Hope of Israel, already based in that country, requested assistance from Jews for Jesus. This was the beginning of a partnership between the two organizations. In 1986, David Brickner began a series of visits to South Africa for the purpose of training and encouraging the Hope of Israel staff. The following year, at the request of Hope of Israel, negotiations for a merger began, and in 1989 the two organizations became one, using the name "Jews for Jesus, South Africa."

Andrew and Laura Barron led the team of workers. When the Barrons arrived in Johannesburg on November 10, 1989, they came with a five-year mandate. Their job was to work with South Africans to put the ministry on a solid footing and then turn the work over to them. Two months later the

Barrons were joined by Lawrence and Louise Hirsch, South Africans who had participated in the 1988 New York Campaign. The Barrons continued their partnership ministry in South Africa for the next several years until the work became indigenous and self-sufficient.

## ENGLAND AND THE LIBERATED WAILING WALL

In almost every instance where Jews for Jesus has opened new areas of ministry, The Liberated Wailing Wall has been actively involved. The somewhat aggressive and forthright style of distributing broadsides is balanced by the softer approach of this musical team's presentations. But The Liberated Wailing Wall pulls no punches, and their outreach ministry has resulted in some of their most interesting encounters. On one occasion the group was giving a concert at a large retirement home for Orthodox Jewish people in London. As was typical, the traditional Jewish music was well received by the residents, and they even politely listened to the music that focused on Jesus. Then it was time for Joel Kleinbaum's testimony:

> There were about eighty people in front of me, all Jewish except for a few staff members. Most of the old men wore *yarmulkes,* Orthodox prayer caps.... I fearfully envisioned about thirty of those nice elderly people suffering simultaneous cardiac arrests when I told them that I believed in You-Know-Who!...
>
> I began with my childhood memories from the synagogue and my early attempts to know God. I mentioned Hebrew school, singing in the synagogue choir, keeping kosher along with the rest of my family, and wanting to be even more Orthodox and observant than they were. I explained how all that changed when I became an atheist in college. As I talked about atheism, I saw them beginning to murmur and whisper to one another, *"What's he trying to tell us?"* Then, *"Shhh...let him finish!"*
>
> I was fast approaching the "punch line" as I began to tell them about my college roommate, how his life seemed different to me, how I saw that he had a personal relationship with God. Suddenly my audience became very, very quiet as I told about this friend

showing me certain Messianic prophecies from the Jewish Bible that seemed to describe Jesus."[18]

Joel went on to tell them how he began reading the Bible to check out these biblical prophecies and how he himself then acknowledged Jesus as Messiah. This was his pilgrimage of faith, and there was no other way to tell the story. "When I finished," he recalls, "they actually applauded. Nearly eighty Orthodox Jewish people were applauding my testimony about receiving Jesus!"[19]

Through this and other encounters, the group helped to lay groundwork for future Jews for Jesus in the United Kingdom.

### GREAT BRITAIN OUTREACHES

The news announcing the opening of a London office of Jews for Jesus in 1991 was met with negative publicity. An editorial in the *Times of London* by Bernard Levin, entitled "Clodhoppers on Crusade," characterized Jews for Jesus' promotional endeavors as "oafish vulgarity" and "revolting hype." Levin was primarily reflecting on "a large advertisement" with the heading, "You don't have to be Jewish to celebrate Christmas, but it helps." That ad introduced Richard Harvey, the new London director of Jews for Jesus. It said:

> Richard Harvey was born Jewish, brought up Jewish and even looks…Jewish…. He loves Borscht, gefilte fish and…chicken soup, and will admit—privately at least—that his mother's the best in the world….
>
> With such a pedigree it might surprise you to discover that Richard is also a follower of Y'shua (the Jewish way to say Jesus). Not that it should be a surprise. After all, Y'shua was Jewish. He was born 2,000 years ago of a Jewish mother in the Jewish town of Bethlehem.[20]

In the years since the London office opened, the opposition has continued. Vandals have sprayed graffiti on the windows and walls of the building and have defaced and torn down posters. But the ministry, one of several messianic Jewish organizations in Britain, continues its evangelistic outreach to an estimated 285,000 Jews living in the United Kingdom. As elsewhere around the world, the message of Jews for Jesus proclaims Jesus as Messiah, challenging British Jews to think for themselves and to consider biblical claims.

## NORTHERN IRELAND

That Jews for Jesus would go to Northern Ireland in an effort to bring peace might appear curious to some people, but much of what the organization does could fit into the category of the unusual. In 1976 Bill Dooner, an Irish American, contacted the organization almost on a whim. In a conversation regarding the plight of Northern Ireland, someone had told him that "peace will come to Northern Ireland the day Jews come preaching the gospel." It was said almost in the same vein that someone might say, "the day hell freezes over." But Dooner took the comment to heart and called headquarters in San Francisco, inviting them to preach the gospel in the strife-ridden little country.

Dooner's invitation sparked a chain of events that became public when billboards appeared in Belfast with the message: "I Love You, Is That OK?" signed Jesus with the byline, "Sponsored by Jews for Jesus." When confused residents inquired, "Why Jews for Jesus?" Sam Nadler explained:

> We in Jews for Jesus believe that the solution to the fighting has to begin with a change of heart on the part of the individual. The only way we can truly love one another and be at peace with ourselves and our brothers is through Jesus Christ. No doubt we will be criticized for being outsiders with no real understanding of the problems, and to this charge we plead guilty. All that we do wish to convey is that Jesus Christ, the Prince of Peace, can bring peace to Catholics and Protestants in Northern Ireland on an individual basis.[21]

## OUTREACH IN FRANCE

France is a very difficult field for any evangelical ministry, but even more so for one like Jews for Jesus whose strategy involves a very public proclamation of the gospel. Distributing tracts on the Champs-Elysées, for example, is prohibited, but Stephen Pacht and his staff and volunteers in Paris did not let that stop them.

It was Bastille Day, 1997, and police would be out in full force. There was no way to avoid them. So one of the campaigners decided simply to ask for permission to broadside. After all, the broadside was entitled, "Liberty, Equality and Fraternity." After the campaigner "explained that the tract told how the ideals of the French State are only possible in Christ," the police-man "not only gave permission to distribute the tracts but told her to come to them should she encounter any problems." The team continued its cam-paign in the days that followed with few problems with authorities. And there were positive results: "We met Jews from all over the world there, par-ticularly Israelis. One Canadian Jew, Adam, found his Messiah as we sortied at Champs-Elysées."[22]

## MISSIONS TO ISRAEL

Because of the sensitive nature of missionary activity in Israel, Jews for Jesus prefer not to publish all the details regarding their work in Israel at this time, though they will admit that they have half a dozen missionaries and are growing. The organization's first venture into Israel was in 1975 and was known as the "Jews for Who?" campaign. Sporting T-shirts with that slogan printed in Hebrew, nine team members went out into the streets as shops were reopening following the close of Shabbat at sundown. When passersby inquired about the identity of "Who," (Many asking, "So—who's the who?") the Jews for Jesus did not answer directly at first. In some cases they would say, "It's a secret, but if you guess correctly, I'll tell you." Or, "I'll give you a hint; he walked on water." To that hint, one person responded, "George Washington," apparently remembering the coin toss over the Potomac.

The purpose of the T-shirt brigade was to stir up interest on the streets of Jerusalem, and it accomplished that end. But there were also opportuni-ties for more in-depth interactions with Israelis, one of which involved the music ministry of The Liberated Wailing Wall at Kfar Blum, a kibbutz in the Huelah Valley. The chairman of cultural activities at the kibbutz had accepted the team's offer of a free concert, knowing that they presented Christian music. However, it seemed the residents themselves were unprepared for what was coming. They clapped and sang along with the traditional Jewish folk songs, but "as the music progressed their conversations grew more amazed." Were these young musicians really Jews? They looked like Jews, and their music sounded Jewish, but they were singing about Jesus. For many people at this kibbutz, it was the first time they truly understood that some Jews who are proud of their Jewish identity are also unashamed believers in Jesus.

Following the concert, Slava, a woman who lived in the kibbutz, invited the team to her home for an evening get-together with a group of her neighbors. They shared stories and found common ground in their struggles. There were no spectacular decisions made, but the conversation continued on into the evening, and there were promises to keep in touch. The seed had been planted on that once malaria-infested marshland west of the Golan Heights.[23]

Israeli believers are quick to remind people that messianic Judaism began in the land of Israel almost two thousand years ago, and that it flourished up until the seventh century, when believing Jews assimilated into the Catholic church. Some two hundred years ago there was a new emphasis on messianic Judaism in Europe and North America, and a small number of messianic Jews immigrated to the Holy Land and became a part of Christ Church, "an Anglican institution established in 1833 with the express purpose of introducing Jews to Jesus." The modern messianic movement saw a resurgence after the Six Day War in 1967, in part as a result of what some Christians believed to be prophetic fulfillment pointing to the end times.[24]

"Private to the point of paranoia just a few years ago," writes Michele Chabin, "many of the 30 to 40 messianic Jewish congregations operating in churches, meeting halls and private homes throughout the country have come out of the closet in recent years." She goes on to say that "messianic Jews have lived quietly in the Holy Land since the early 1800s. Only in the past decade, however, have they become a force to be reckoned with." But few Israelis are even aware of the messianic movement, except for "two well-publicized court cases involving messianic Jews wishing to immigrate under the Law of Return."[25]

There is far more recognition today as a result of an antimissionary bill introduced in the Knesset in the late 1990s. Though unsuccessful, it sparked much publicity in Israel and abroad, and in recent years more and more missionaries have entered Israel. Many of them would say that they have not come primarily for evangelistic purposes, but rather to settle and build their homes in Israel. Much of the missionary work done in Israel is carried out by non-Jewish evangelicals. However, many observers concede that Israel's several thousand messianic Jews also conduct evangelistic outreach and that there is a growing desire to train Israeli believers for ministry in the land. There is an antimissionary law on the books, but the problem, according to Shmuel Golding, director of an "anti-cult" organization, is that the law "isn't worth the paper it's written on." The law forbids anyone from offering anything of value in an effort to convert someone, and Shmuel said no one has ever been arrested, much less convicted, on the grounds that they were breaking that law. It does not prohibit lecturing or handing out pamphlets. Golding cites the tourist revenues brought in by missionaries and Western Christians, insisting "the government doesn't see anything wrong here—as long as [messianic and Christian missionaries] put money into the economy. Who cares about a few Jews here and there?" Golding and his associates admittedly "harass" missionaries, but his efforts are small compared to that of the missionaries. A colleague who also does "anti-cult" work laments:

> We don't have the financial resources of the missionaries here. If we did, we could put advertisements in the Israeli press and rebut messianic quotes. It's impossible to fight enormous Christian organizations all over the world. Our work is one on one." He concedes that he has little effect.[26]

## CONTINUED GROWTH THROUGH THE 1990S

In 1993, Jews for Jesus, according to Moishe Rosen, "logged exactly 1,000 recorded Jewish decisions.... The year before, there were exactly 841 Jewish decisions and about 5,000 to 5,400 Gentile decisions." He explained his terminology: "The reason that I say 'about' and 'exactly' is because we follow up on all Jewish decisions ourselves, whereas the churches follow up on those who are not Jewish."[27]

By 1996, Jews for Jesus had a thirteen million dollar annual budget, and David Brickner was reporting nearly one thousand converts for the previous year. Statistics in the New York office for the first quarter showed that "Missionaries distributed 64,921 leaflets and obtained addresses and telephone numbers of 257 potential converts. Of the 45 Jews who converted, 28 were Russian Jews."[28]

A 1997 report from Philadelphia in the *Post & Opinion* quoted Mark Powers, head of Jews for Judaism, who declared that "Jews for Jesus has the budget and manpower to do a great deal of damage to our people," claiming the organization was operating with a budget of $14 million and had a staff of 150 full-time workers. His organization, devoted to combating evangelism to Jews, had a budget of only $300,000 and a staff of four. "How many people have joined Jews for Jesus and other like-minded Christian groups?" the article asks. Powers "estimates the number at a quarter of a million."[29] Jews for Jesus have never estimated such a high number and do not present themselves as being as successful as their opposition does.

Nevertheless, by 1998 there were nearly one hundred and fifty full-time staff members working at sixteen separate offices across the United States, Canada, and overseas. Overseas offices include London, Paris, Tel Aviv, Sydney, Johannesburg, Buenos Aires, Odessa, and Moscow. How does an independent mission fund such an enterprise? Jews for Jesus is very effective in appealing for funds in ways that do not sound like appeals at all. The secret is simple. The organization conducts an effective ministry and effectively publicizes its success to churches and individuals. A promotional pamphlet offers the following challenge to Christians in words they easily understand:

> We trust God for the financing and funding of Jews for Jesus and He has provided through caring Christians. Jews for Jesus is not a church, nor do we take the place of the church. Therefore, we ask that our Christian friends support their local churches first.... Then we ask people to prayerfully consider giving to our ministry as well.... We deplore "crisis appeals" and manipulative devices to raise needed funds. God has shown us that all we need to do is

present the opportunity for involvement, and He will move the hearts of those who are obedient to Him.[30]

# CHAPTER TWELVE

# OUTREACH TO RUSSIAN JEWS

### *Following a Vision*

s I write my introductory thoughts on this chapter, I am on board Lufthansa flight 3213, returning from Moscow to my home in Grand Rapids, Michigan. My host on this journey has been Avi Snyder, whom I came to know through reading his story and some of his writings. He has a quick sense of humor and a strong sense of security—both of which come through in broadsides he has written. One, for example, opens with the disarming "confession":

> "Okay, okay, so if I had half a brain, I'd get a real job instead of passing out these cockamamie little pamphlets.
>
> Okay, okay, so I ought to be ashamed of myself...so I'm a disgrace...so I'm an insult to your intelligence."

If Avi is anything, he is an enthusiast, and he always maintains a very positive demeanor. For this book, I insisted we talk about some of his disappointments and failures. Nevertheless, Avi is most comfortable with his optimistic side, which serves him well for the ministry he has chosen. To him, almost everything is a "real blessing," and God always seems to answer prayer in the right way. He told me how his fourteen-year-old-son had asked him what he was going to do when he retired. Avi had replied, "How can you retire when you don't have a job?" That quip represents more than Avi's casual humor; it represents his philosophy of life. "Jews *for Jesus is not a job; it's a life," he told me. Then without missing a beat, he added, "I love my life. I can be who I am and be as creative as I want to be, and there are no restrictions."*

*I saw Avi's philosophy demonstrated less than an hour later during an evening service at a conference near Stuttgart. "Those are my children, not that I'm boasting," Avi insisted, with all the pride of a father. The children to whom he was referring were members of Messiah's Shofar, the music team from Odessa. He had trained them, and now they were ministering at a messianic Jewish conference in Germany. Avi had good reason to be proud of their performance. It was an upbeat, well-rehearsed professional sound that typifies the music of Jews for Jesus.*

*Yet another side of Avi surfaced when I pressed him. There were the disappointments, the failures, and the tough family times—including his misgivings about not being more attentive to his wife, Ruth. Indeed, the story of the Russian ministry of Jews for Jesus cannot be summed up as a glowing account of total success. It is a mixed bag of trials and errors—and blessings as Avi would be quick to remind me. It is a story of Avi's enthusiasm, of disciple making, and of millions of broadsides distributed. Yet it is also a story of Ruth's loneliness, Sergei's denial of the faith, and many "decisions" that bore no lasting results.*

—m—

The ministry to Jews in the former Soviet Union is a fascinating case study of mission outreach in the latter part of the twentieth century. It corresponds with the most significant event of that era—the breakup of the Soviet Union.

The idea of a Jews for Jesus branch in the Commonwealth of Independent States (CIS) was born not out of a committee agenda in search for another project, but out of spontaneous concern for a people who seemed to be on the losing end in every turn of events—a people then known as "Soviet Jewry."

The main character in this unfolding drama has been Avi Snyder.

## A MAN WITH A VISION

Raised in a conservative Jewish home in New York, Avi Snyder first encountered Jews for Jesus when he was given a tract on a sidewalk in New York

City during the 1975 campaign. "I thought it was trash," he later recalled. But, oddly enough, he kept it. He had grown up with "a proper reverence and respect for the Scriptures," but the focus was on tradition. His own questions, however, went beyond ritual and tradition.

Reflecting back, he remembers: "I was always looking for the Messiah." In fact, at his own bar mitzvah, he asked the rabbi, "How will I know the Messiah?" That question faded as Avi drifted into existentialism in his early twenties. To him, life was meaningless. "Whatever I accomplished essentially was pointless," he later said, reflecting on that time in his life. Finally one day, amid anger and confusion, he came to a turning point in his life: "I cried out to God, 'How dare you make a pointless universe?' Then I thought to myself, 'Wait a minute—if you don't believe in God, who are you talking to?'"[1]

In the days that followed, Avi began reading the Old Testament—including prophecies that were cited in the tract he had regarded as trash. This interest in fulfilled prophecy combined with his introduction to Ruth, the young woman who would later become his wife, turned his life around. He remembers: "Here was a nice gentile girl, who claimed to have a relationship with the God of my fathers, the God of Abraham, Isaac, and Jacob, through the Jewish Messiah." Avi was convinced. He found the God of his fathers by trusting in Jesus as Messiah. Soon after that he once again encountered Jews for Jesus, who were handing out literature on a street corner in Los Angeles.[2]

Fifteen years after he received that tract on the streets of New York, Avi was heading the Jews for Jesus staff in Los Angeles. He had previously traveled with the New Jerusalem Players (coworkers say he wrote and directed dramas that brought the team to a new level of expertise), and he served as a missionary in Chicago. His unflagging love for the work was obvious; when others would grow weary of street ministry, Avi's enthusiasm never appeared to wane. His personalized broadsides managed to be humorously self-deprecating, while lifting the name of Jesus. The *Jewish Advocate* summed up one of his pamphlets as follows:

> "Okay, okay, so I'm ugly and my mother dresses me funny," says this man, who is called "Avi (ugly person not to mention sloppy dresser) Snyder."

Throughout the pamphlet he calls himself "a disgrace…an insult to your intelligence…a *nasty, terrible* no-goodnick…*too* stupid to be easily offended."

He is shown being ridiculed for his belief that Jesus in the Messiah, and ends by saying, "What you think about me really doesn't matter. What you think about Y'shua does," because "he happens to be the only one who can pardon us for all the ugly, shameful, disgraceful, and insulting things we've done before God."[3]

In Los Angeles, Avi found himself stretched not only administratively, but creatively. He wrote and performed a one-man show, *Watchman for the Morning,* based on the life of the apostle Paul. These opportunities made good use of his background as a Broadway and off-Broadway actor and as a writer and director in Los Angeles.[4]

Avi's choice to portray Paul was intentional. He is quick to point out the apostle was one of his predecessors—one of the first Jews for Jesus. Many Jewish people assert that Paul corrupted Jesus' teaching and that Christianity is a Pauline invention. Not so, insists Avi:

> There is a school of thought that says, "Jesus we can accept. He never intended to start a new religion. His message was Jewish. But Paul took the Jewish message and allowed all kinds of pagan influence. It lost touch with its Jewish roots.…" They paint a picture of him turning his back on his people. But he never ceased to identify himself as a Jew. He said, "I was born a Jew and I'll die a Jew." He never lost his burning desire to see his own people turn to Jesus."[5]

While he was heading the branch office in Los Angeles, Avi caught a vision for reaching Russian Jews. The idea began to percolate in 1989, as the Communist grip started to loosen. The media made much of the fact that some East Germans were taking holidays in Hungary, where restrictions were not so tight and people could slip through to freedom. In the Soviet Union, Gorbachev was demonstrating a groundbreaking openness to outsiders. Avi pondered these things along with one of his colleagues, Elizabeth

Terini. A Jewish believer born in Uzbekistan, she had left the Soviet Union in the 1970s and had found faith in Jesus some years later. Avi recalls:

> One morning at staff meeting, I started to play with a thought that simply seemed like a good, strategic idea. I turned to Elizabeth and said, "You know, we ought to try to get a team into the Soviet Union." I expected a look of sour bewilderment.... I knew she had no lost love for the life that she had worked so hard to escape. But instead of registering bewilderment, her face brightened, and she nodded "Yes."[6]

Avi presented the idea to Moishe, who said it was unrealistic. Jews for Jesus is not a jump-on-the-bandwagon type of ministry, and Moishe was generally not impressed with ideas until they had been seriously thought through. The ministry's outward flair for the outrageous disguises a nuts and bolts practicality. Avi's hopes—passing out broadsides in Red Square, encouraging new Jewish believers in the faith, bringing these Jewish believers out of the Soviet Union to train them, and sending them back to the Soviet Union to evangelize—struck Moishe as little more than a pipe dream.

> "Snyder," Moishe said in a droll voice, 'IF you could get into the Soviet Union, and IF you could hand out broadsides in Red Square—and live to tell about it—and IF you could find any Jewish believers and encourage them, and IF you could bring anyone out and train them...they'd never go back."[7]

Avi assumed that Moishe had ruled out his impetuous idea, but Moishe was merely forcing Avi to face reality. To his question, "Should I forget about it?" Moishe responded: "No, I'm just telling you why it's impossible. Go ahead and do it anyway."[8]

When his challenges did not dampen Avi's enthusiasm, Moishe had to consider that this "dream" might be from the Lord—and he had to consider it very prayerfully.

So in 1990 Avi, Ruth, and Elizabeth embarked on a three-week visit to the Soviet Union. They encountered an unexpected freedom and openness as they boldly distributed their broadsides to the crowds lined up to visit Lenin's tomb in Moscow. Police stopped the team—not to arrest them, as they had expected—but to move them away from the tomb to the exits and entrances to Red Square. Three weeks of evangelism sealed the vision for the Snyders and Elizabeth. While Ruth did not share Avi's passion for ministry in the Soviet Union, as a strong Christian she knew that the best place to be was in God's will, and she was convinced that he was orchestrating Avi's yearning to go. The opportunities for ministry in the Soviet Union were too great to ignore:

> We made two remarkable discoveries: Yes, we could be as bold in our outreach over there as we were in the States (we passed out broadsides and preached in the open): and even more exciting to us—we discovered that our Jewish people were eager to hear about the Lord. Once they understood that we were Jews, they gathered to us and plied us with questions about Y'shua.[9]

But Moishe was not yet convinced. Avi was conducting a very effective ministry in Los Angeles, and a transfer to the Soviet Union could not be made lightly. "Avi had hoped to return six weeks later for the Lausanne Committee on World Evangelization meetings, which were being held in Moscow that year, but instead Moishe sent Elizabeth Terini and Tuvya Zaretsky, admonishing Avi to keep his eyes on Los Angeles so that work did not suffer and die."[10]

Avi accepted the decision, but kept the vision of Russian Jews close to his heart. Avi and Ruth knew that he had a special calling, and their goal was to return to the Soviet Union, leaving behind their California lifestyle. Avi recalls how the future suddenly snapped into focus when they returned from that first trip:

> I remember the night that my wife and I reentered our home in the San Fernando Valley. We stood on the porch and looked at each other. Ruth said, "We have a nice home." It was not just an acknowl-

edgment of how graciously the Lord had allowed us to live in comparison to the lack that characterized the homes of our Soviet counterparts. Her comment was the first admission between us of what we would be giving up.[10]

Later, Avi would realize that the dream of reaching out to Russia had been born long before his conversations with Elizabeth and Moishe. A couple of years after the big move, he was able to articulate that realization to a group of Russian Jewish believers in Jesus:

"When I was a boy in America, every year at Pesach we talked about the Jewish people who were still imprisoned in the Soviet Union. And every year at the seder, we recited special prayers for the liberation of all people who were still enslaved, especially for our people behind the iron curtain. Now we're here together." I stopped for a moment. Then I added, "You're an answer to my prayer.

"When I was a boy, I had no idea of the freedom I would one day find...or that I would travel thousands of miles and learn a new language to help bring it to my Russian brothers and sisters.

"Real freedom is not found in a place. It's found in a Person. Real freedom is not a license to pursue our personal goals. It's a responsibility to perform the will of the One who purchased us. Real freedom is not liberation FROM service. Rather, it is being set free IN ORDER to serve."[11]

In 1991 Moishe brought up the issue of Russia again. He was convinced that the time for Russia was right, and the Snyders began preparations to move. Elizabeth Terini was eager to accompany them, but Moishe was concerned; she was older than the others and the difficult lifestyle could take its toll on her health. He was also concerned that as a former Soviet citizen, once there Elizabeth might never be allowed to leave. So he decided to bring the matter before the Jews for Jesus council. Elizabeth gave an impassioned speech that stirred the hearts of everyone present. To hear a woman who had fled the harsh life in the Soviet Union, who had become a United States citizen and made a life for herself in the West—to hear such a woman pleading to return to the Soviet Union to bring the gospel to her people was remarkable. The entire group sensed God at work and unanimously endorsed Elizabeth's request.

The commissioning of the Snyders and Elizabeth Terini was scheduled for August to coincide with a staff retreat. But the very week of the commissioning, David Brickner entered the lounge where Avi and others were "schmoozing" with startling news: "There's been a coup in the Soviet Union." The reports that followed were bleak. The State Department issued travel advisories, and it seemed like the worst possible time to make the move. Yet the Snyders and Elizabeth were determined to proceed, and Moishe and his advisors agreed that it was no time to pull back. The team arrived in the Ukraine on September 25, 1991.

## A Surprising Openness

Their arrival coincided with the fiftieth anniversary of Babi Yar—a horrifying World War II atrocity in which the Nazis slaughtered one hundred thousand Jewish people in a wooded area outside Kiev. Elizabeth had heard stories of this massacre as a child. She wanted to attend the fifty-year memorial observances, and the Snyders joined her. Avi later wrote about the visit:

> Upon arriving in the Ukraine we made our way immediately to Babi Yar.... Elizabeth and I quickly stationed ourselves at two sites near the entrance to the grounds and began to offer literature to those who passed by. Our clothing, with *Jews for Jesus* written on the front and back in Russian, Hebrew, and English, made our identity clear before anyone began to read what they received from us.
>
> In America, some might have seen our presence as an insensitive, opportunistic intrusion. Certainly that was not our intention, and most of those who noticed us did not seem to regard us as insensitive or offensive. Rather they were inquisitive, and instead of avoidance we encountered eagerness for our message.
>
> What could account for such openness?... Perhaps hearts that have withstood tragic ordeals know that it is not enough to look

back. One must look forward in order to live. One must believe that there is a purpose in both the present and the future to validate the experience of the past.[12]

They had no idea that within three months the Soviet Union would collapse, opening up remarkable new opportunities for evangelism. In fact, Avi was amazed by the openness of Russian Jews, most of whom had never heard that Jewish people are not supposed to believe in Jesus. Their enemy was not the Christian church, but Communism. As one man explained, "All our lives we have been told, 'Don't read, don't take.' Today we are free. We want to know the truth. We want to read and decide for ourselves." That is all Avi and Elizabeth were asking them to do.[13]

From the earliest days of the ministry, Avi encountered a greater spiritual hunger than he had ever seen in the West: "In Odessa alone we are seeing people make decisions for Christ virtually every week. Jewish receptivity to the gospel is probably greater in the CIS than it is anywhere else." This is a remarkable turn of events, especially considering the history of Jews in the former Soviet Union. An article by Gary Clayton pointed out:

So much has been done to the Jewish people by the Cossacks, the Tsars and even the church that, humanly speaking, there is no reason for them to be so open to the gospel. But God, in his grace, is doing a sovereign work among post Soviet Jewry.[14]

According to Avi, one of the reasons that Russia is an open field for Jewish evangelism is because the people have not been told that being Jewish and believing in Jesus are mutually exclusive. "People here are less likely [than in the West] to be afraid to look at the issue. They're not afraid to find out who Yeshua [Jesus] is. They don't believe that looking at the question with an open mind is equivalent of treason."[15]

Jews for Jesus' greatest successes in the former Soviet Union have not been in Moscow, but Odessa. Avi purposely chose Odessa over Moscow as a starting place, despite Moishe's initial reluctance. Odessa is Galilee, says Avi, not Jerusalem. It is an outpost—virgin territory for the gospel. Indeed, Jews for Jesus was the first Western ministry to take up residence in Odessa in modern times. Avi had visited and built ties with Central Baptist Church and the Odessa Theological Seminary during the 1990 trip and continued building those relationships when he moved there.

The Odessa work most closely mirrors Moishe's early ministry in San Francisco. Like Moishe, Avi needed a place to experiment, and Moscow was not that place. He had been successful in missionary outreach in the States, but bringing Jews for Jesus to the former Soviet Union was an entirely new venture. Avi was a rookie, as he readily admits, and he was not prepared to deal with criticism from other more established missions in Moscow.

## THE TRAILBLAZERS WHO WENT BEFORE

Avi was not the first "Jew for Jesus" in Odessa; other messianic Jewish believers had gone before him. Avi unexpectedly learned more about one such believer from a woman whose family he had touched. It was 1994, and Avi was handing out tracts near the train station when an elderly Jewish woman came to him with a worn and yellowed booklet titled, *Can a Jew Believe in Jesus as the Messiah?* The author was Leon Rosenberg, a Russian Jew who had raised up a thriving Jewish ministry in Odessa early in the twentieth century. Avi had heard of Rosenberg's ministry and was deeply moved as he held the evidence of that ministry in his hands. The booklet, which had been in the woman's family for three generations, confirmed what Avi already knew— that he was standing on the shoulders of a giant.

On the surface it looked as though Leon Rosenberg's work had died, and perhaps it had for all practical purposes. But the booklet confirmed to Avi that he was not alone in this work; it also affirmed the power of literature. Some might have been discouraged to think that for all Rosenberg's efforts, all that seemed to remain was a worn-out booklet. But Avi, who tends to look at things from a positive angle, saw in that booklet a powerful symbol— a confirmation that the literature his team was distributing would remain long after Jews for Jesus departed.

The story of Rosenberg's ministry is fascinating. Like Avi, this man faced opposition on both political and religious fronts. Not only Jewish people, but professing Christians of Rosenberg's day insisted that "a Jew can never be

a Christian and a Christian can never be a Jew." The Orthodox church leaders were particularly upset about Rosenberg's evangelical fervor. He
responded to the opposition by issuing a public statement:

> It was based entirely on Scripture and made clear the fact that the
> great Apostle Paul himself, after his conversion from Judaism, called
> himself a Jew.... Becoming a Christian, he gave up Judaism, accept-
> ing the teaching of Christ, according to the Gospel, but he never
> ceased to be a son of his nation and remained a Jew."[16]

Almost immediately there were divisions among the Jewish believers;
some "wanted to remain in the synagogue, to live and act as Jews.... Others
sought a middle ground, and a third group, the Hebrew-Christian church
that Rosenberg led, aligned itself with the Christian church. His church was
culturally very Jewish, but "they made no distinction in the realm of spiritual fellowship between themselves and Christians of other nationalities." By
1914, when the church celebrated its tenth anniversary, it had grown considerably in size and outreach. But storm clouds loomed on the horizon.[17]

With the outbreak of World War I, the church was used for a Red Cross
center. Rosenberg was exiled to Siberia, but through government connections he was able to return to Odessa, where he continued a house church
ministry. But that ministry came to an end with the Communist Revolution
of 1917. Rosenberg was expelled from his homeland, and he was forced to
leave behind the remnants of his congregation in Odessa. The believers in
Odessa held together as best they could, but by the 1930s all churches had
been closed by the Communists.[18]

When Avi arrived in Odessa, there was no evidence of this once-vibrant
congregation of Jewish believers. Nothing remained—except that worn and
faded booklet by Leon Rosenberg.

### BEGINNING WITH BROADSIDES

The work of Jews for Jesus in Odessa began with broadsides. Avi had fifty
thousand tracts printed in Kiev. Every day he went out to distribute tracts. He
carried with him a little index card explaining that he did not speak Russian,

but that those who were interested could give him their address, and someone would contact them. Every time he went out, crowds would form around him, and he would get eight or ten contacts. Then Elizabeth Terini would follow up. Less than a month into the work, they scheduled their first public meeting. Seven people came. Avi preached through a translator, and all seven raised their hands at the invitation and then prayed with Avi. One of these went on in the faith and relocated to Israel. The others continued to come to meetings but later lost interest. There were disappointments from the very beginning, but the broadsiding, visits with contacts, and the public meetings continued.

The meetings quickly grew in size because, as Avi put it, "We were the new game in town and the only game in town."[19] At one point in those early months, more than one hundred were attending, but the average ranged between eighty and ninety. Later, two of the most faithful attendees formed a discipleship group. That group grew and eventually became the training school for the budding staff of Jews for Jesus. It marked the difference between "decisions" and disciples. When invited to receive Christ, many were willing to raise their hands; fewer were willing to learn what it means to follow Jesus. But slowly, handfuls of people were showing evidence of changed lives.

Jews for Jesus held its first messianic Passover seder six months after its arrival in Odessa. This celebration was very possibly the first public seder since the implementation of Soviet repression. Some two hundred and fifty people attended—the vast majority of whom were Jewish and not yet for Jesus.

In the first year, dozens of people made professions of faith and went on to join with a congregation of believers. In September 1992, the School of the Messengers was inaugurated. This three-week training program resulted in four trainees joining the Jews for Jesus staff.

## THE OPPOSITION

There was little opposition in the first eighteen months of ministry. The first real opposition arose when Hasidic Jews from Brooklyn came to do their own missionary work in Odessa. Although they had not come for the purpose of opposing Jews for Jesus, they quickly developed that focus and began printing tracts against the organization.

That opposition continued for some time and culminated in "the Felix Melstein incident." The incident involved a Purim celebration. Jews for Jesus had been distributing their literature outside the festivities, which were cut short by a bomb scare. Melstein, a leader of the Jewish community in Odessa, accused Jews for Jesus of making the bogus bomb threat. Instead of defending their innocence, Jews for Jesus launched a campaign with the slogan "Jesus Loves Felix Melstein." Many in the Jewish community were amazed at this reaction to such a serious accusation. As Ukrainian officials investigated Jews for Jesus in months ahead, the Odessa team "redoubled their efforts to preach the gospel," Avi wrote. "If the officials were going to shut us down as a consequence of something we didn't do, then at least we would be 'guilty' of telling as many people as we could about Jesus."[20]

Five months later, Felix Melstein's name was once again in the newspaper; this time, on the other end of an accusation. It seems Felix had been apprehended in Odessa and his wife taken into custody in Israel. They had allegedly defrauded Jewish people in Odessa of thousands of dollars that they had promised to take to Israel for safekeeping. Following this news, the opposition to Jews for Jesus in Odessa declined.

## MOVING ON TO MOSCOW

The Jews for Jesus' work in Moscow began in early 1993. That same year, Avi launched the first Moscow campaign. Following the campaign, four volunteers joined the staff, and in January 1994, Avi and his family relocated to Moscow, leaving Elizabeth Terini in charge of the Odessa work. The advantage of being in Moscow was that it raised the visibility of Jews for Jesus. Yet that work did not flourish as was hoped. In terms of discipleship and recruitment, there were disappointments and setbacks.

The most heartrending of these setbacks regards the young man Avi had chosen for the Moscow work. Sergei had publicly confessed faith in Jesus at a John Guest evangelistic campaign in 1990 and was doing translation work for various organizations when Avi met him in Kiev. In 1991 Avi was searching for a worker who would ultimately serve as a missionary. According to Avi, Sergei was the best. He was efficient and effective, and as the first indigenous staff member in Odessa, he worked very closely with Avi. Indeed, he became like a member of the Snyder family, living in their home and taking part in family activities.

In 1993 Avi sent Sergei to open the Moscow work. As Avi reflects on that decision, he now sees it as a mistake. Perhaps he was pushing Sergei into leadership too quickly. Within a matter of months, Sergei announced that he could no longer do the work and that he wanted to resign. It was not that he had other ministry or job offers—as talented as he was. The suddenness of his decision baffled Avi, and Sergei gave him no valid reason for his hasty departure. It seemed as though he were running away from something. And he was. It was a crisis of faith. Months later, Sergei confessed to Avi that he simply did not believe in Jesus anymore.

Despite Sergei's departure, the work in Moscow has continued to grow. In many respects, it is the hub of the Russian work with its efficient office staff and its well-publicized campaigns. Yet it has not reproduced itself as has the work in Odessa. None of the "decisions" made in Moscow have resulted in recruits for the organization. The entire outreach staff has come either from outside Jews for Jesus or outside Moscow. Indeed, this has been per-haps the biggest disappointment for Avi. But he reflects on this and other disappointments philosophically:

> I used to live in fear of failure. But I now have a healthier concept of what constitutes failure and what constitutes success. No one can ever take away from me what I believe has been built here—for what I know we did. If it all died tomorrow, no one could ever take away the fact that these people have handed out over twenty mil-lion pieces of literature and conducted over seventeen thousand one-on-one visits. This is genuine ministry, and no one can take it away from me. God will do with it what he wants to. I was faithful, and that constitutes success. Some of the most significant things I've done, I may not even know about.[21]

From the day he arrived on his first visit in 1990, Avi was in his element amid the teeming throngs of people whose language he did not understand. They were his people, and he had the privilege of sharing the Good News with them during that historic time. As he learned the language and built friendships, his enthusiasm only increased. The opportunities in the former Soviet Union were limitless, and he was the captain of the ship, so to speak. But his enthusiasm for this Russian ministry had not consumed his family to the extent it had consumed him. Ruth was a realist who brought balance to Avi when his idealism and optimism turned to anxiety and pessimism. Although she was constantly occupied— with the children's schooling, teaching at a Christian academy, and serving in the ministry—she often felt lonely and isolated. The work in the former Soviet Union involved sacrifice as well as a great opportunity for service.

For Avi Snyder and his family, the work in the Ukrainian port of Odessa and the work in Moscow has come to an end. He and his family returned to America in 1998. Avi continues to supervise the Russian work of Jews for Jesus from the New York office. His work in Russia, for all practical purposes, is done except for periodic visits. His Russian coworkers have taken over the leadership, as he originally planned. "It is a special blessing to me," he writes, "when I remember that so many of our colleagues [from Odessa] are actually the fruit of the evangelistic work. They heard the Gospel through Jews for Jesus, they came to faith, and now, many are serving in full-time ministry themselves."[22]

Since the first visit to Russia in 1990, the work has grown significantly and has main offices in both Moscow and Odessa. From its inauspicious beginning with five missionaries passing out literature in Moscow's Red Square, the organization now has an indigenous staff of thirty workers stationed in Odessa, Moscow, Kiev, Kharkov, and Dnepropetrovsk.

These Russian colleagues are not merely keeping the work going, they are expanding it in ways that are suited to the Russian and Ukrainian people. In both Moscow and Odessa, the ministry publishes two quarterly journals that deal with issues of particular interest to Soviet Jews and non-Jews alike. Music teams tour from city to city, presenting the gospel not in a North American package, but in a way that says first and foremost, *We're home-grown*. The staff conducts mini-campaigns to reach out beyond the major cities, and some of these campaigns have been the most effective to date.

Avi purposely left before the 1998 campaign got underway so that those he had trained would not look to his leadership. When he returned to Russia and the Ukraine for two weeks in September—amidst newspaper stories of the country's financial collapse—he found that his Russian coworkers were doing very well without him. Indeed, the night before his arrival in Moscow he received a fax from the Odessa office giving the results of nine days of campaigning in Lvov, a city of one million people in western Ukraine. In those nine days, the team of eleven campaigners had distributed more than a quarter million broadsides and received more than two thousand contacts (people willing to give their name and address), nearly one quarter of whom were Jewish. Nearly one hundred people had indicated that they wanted to repent and receive everlasting life in Jesus. This was the work of a second generation of Jews for Jesus in the former Soviet Union.

# CHAPTER THIRTEEN

# NEW YORK CITY

## *Where the Action Is*

Sunday is a day off for the New York campaigners, and it was for me as well. Having flown into LaGuardia late Saturday night, I slept until after 9:00. By 10:00, I was out on the streets with millions of other New Yorkers, enjoying the beautiful day. My wanderings took me to the Flower and Garden Show at Rockefeller Center, kitty-corner to St. Patrick's Cathedral. The noon hour service at St. Patricks's drew me in and set the stage for the next few days of my observation and ministry with Jews for Jesus. The words of the opening hymn said it all: "Lift high the cross, the love of Christ proclaim, till all the world adore his sacred name."

The Old Testament reading was Genesis 18:20–32, which narrates Abraham pleading with God to spare Sodom. In the passage, Abraham asks God if he would spare the city for the sake of fifty righteous people; then he asks if God would still spare them if only forty-five are found; and so on, down to ten. God responds, "For the sake of those ten, I will not destroy it." Father Thomas Nielson's homily reflected on a Jewish legend—that in every generation ten righteous people would rise up so that God would not destroy humanity because of sin. A nice legend, but not for us, he emphasized. We have a solitary man—Jesus—who has risen up and paid for the sins of all generations. What a powerful truth. That homily further prepared me for my time on the streets with Jews for Jesus. This was why I was in New York: to better understand Jewish people who had risked so much in committing their lives to Jesus and to see them tell of the one who paid for the sins of all generations.

Monday morning I was up at 5:30 to shower, dress, and walk the six blocks to *the branch office for the team leaders' meeting at 6:20. "This must be a cult," I grumbled, as I crawled out of bed. "Who else would call a meeting this early in order to have us out on the streets by 7:00 A.M?" But if there is anything I have learned about Jews for Jesus, it is that they demand a high level of commitment regarding ministry.*

*I spent the next three days in subway stations and on street corners observing and handing out broadsides. It is hard work. It is not easy to smile and be enthusiastic at 7:00 in the morning in a sweltering underground that has never cooled off from the previous day. But you make the best of it. And it helps if someone with the same mission, the same T-shirt, and the same stack of broadsides is standing nearby with a quick wit and a playful spirit. In fact, it can be downright fun.*

—m—

New York, in many ways, is where the action is—ground zero for Jews for Jesus. They encounter intense opposition in New York, but it is an exciting place to minister. The New York assignment requires courage and just plain *chutzpah*, as well as a good sense of humor. The Jews for Jesus Newsletter underscored the need for humor in a short piece titled "How to Witness on the Streets of New York City." The tongue-in-cheek article contained some half-zany, half-practical tips. For example:

> Smile a lot. That always makes everyone in New York wonder what you're up to and will confuse potential adversaries.
>
> If someone yells, "Whaddya crazy?" he doesn't want a notarized certificate about the state of your mental health. It's merely a non-committal way of saying, "May I have one of those pamphlets?"
>
> The weeping and gnashing of teeth you may hear in the subway does not indicate that the world has come to an end. It's the sound of commuters reading the *Wall Street Journal* on their way to the Financial District.
>
> You will need to learn to interpret some of the New York dialect:
>
> Donder is not one of Santa's reindeer. It's a direction as in, "I already got one of those pamphlets don-der on 32nd Street."

Canchasea is not a swimming beach near Brooklyn. It's an admonition like, "Canchasea my hands are full of packages and I can't take a pamphlet?"[1]

## A RETURN TO THE CITY

In 1974 Moishe took Jews for Jesus back to New York City, his old stomping ground, right under the nose of his parent organization, the American Board of Missions to the Jews. He was not abandoning San Francisco. In a real sense, the Bay Area had been a laboratory to try out methods and materials for New Yorkers. Moishe always had a sense of anticipation about reaching New York City with a Jewish population second only to that of Israel itself. A team of thirty Jews for Jesus prepared for a summer campaign to capture the attention of the city. Armed with posters, broadsides, arguments, and answers, they fanned out in all directions, working fourteen-hour days. Through street preaching, drama, and music, New Yorkers learned about Jews for Jesus and their message. The opposition was harsh and vocal, yet, as hoped, many people were willing to stop and talk to these outspoken Jewish believers who were fearlessly declaring that their Messiah had come.

As the campaign drew to a close, Moishe was somewhat disappointed that there had not been the outpouring of God's Spirit he had longed to see. Nevertheless, he returned the following year, and the year after that; and the organization has conducted witnessing campaigns in New York City ever since (except in 1979). In 1975, Jews for Jesus opened up a branch in Manhattan, and the focus on New York has continued to the present. New York City is marked by "saturation" ministry, especially in the summer.

With a Jewish population of nearly two million, the city is home to the largest urban Jewish population in history. For that reason, the New York branch office is the training center for all missionary recruits. In fact, to be accepted as a missionary with Jews for Jesus, a candidate is expected to complete a successful witnessing campaign in New York, and he or she can be assured of being assigned to at least two more New York campaigns as a new missionary. Many of the veteran Jews for Jesus enjoy a change of pace during the summer and circulate in and out of the New York campaign in two-week shifts. They normally do not lead teams, but encourage and support the

younger leaders and volunteers. Those who have been around since the seventies have the option of going on three "sorties" (tract-passing expeditions)
a day rather than four.

In the two decades since the first summer campaign, Jews for Jesus have
handed out more than thirty million tracts, resulting in some seventy thousand contacts. The staff uses every parade and street fair as an opportunity
to proclaim the message. But distributing tracts is only a fraction of the year-
round ministry conducted in a Jews for Jesus branch. There are daily phone
calls to make, appointments to set up with contacts, Bible studies to prepare,
and one-to-one follow-up visits to be made with those contacts. The 1995
Jews for Jesus Journal describes that kind of workday evangelism:

> Annette Sofaer does missionary work throughout the New York
> metro area. In typical Jews for Jesus fashion, she uses the subway
> system for double duty: handing out tracts as well as getting to her
> daily appointments. She says, "Every morning, I tune my radio to
> the 'strap hangers' report, which warns of any problems with a par-
> ticular subway line. Millions of New Yorkers travel the subway each
> day, and I can distribute up to 1,400 tracts in two hours' time."[2]

## A NOON HOUR ON THE STREETS OF NEW YORK

Street evangelism seems as natural and normal as breathing to the Jews for
Jesus staff and volunteers. Many if not most would admit that they still get
butterflies in their stomachs before going out to distribute tracts. It is not that
they are braver than anyone else; it is just that for them, it is all in a day's
work. For the outsider, the endeavor often seems bizarre. Yet outsiders'
descriptions—even those with a strongly negative slant—sometimes offer
the truest picture of the group's effectiveness. In a 1986 article in *New York*,
Jan Hoffman described a typical noon hour for staff members assigned to the
New York office:

> Noon, 42nd and Fifth: It's one of those brilliantly sunny spring days,
> and like everybody else with an urgent message, five Jews for Jesus
> are handing out leaflets. They wear T-shirts, they're young, and

they're friendly. A few spoil-sports make faces at the proselytizers, rip up their pamphlets, or even spit. A few others, the curious and the spiritually confused, will stop and inquire. But most New Yorkers, on a tight lunch-hour schedule, give them a polite, empty smile, accept a pamphlet, and keep moving.

After about an hour, the Jews for Jesus return to their base; a seven-story brownstone at 109 East 31st Street (off Park Avenue), for which the national organization paid $1.6 million in cash in 1984. "It's too small for us," complains [Baruch] Goldstein. They gather in the first-floor conference room for their regular debriefing session. "Okay, how many did you give out?" asks Goldstein, adding that he "did 450." The others have distributed only 400 each: 2050 leaflets, an embarrassingly slow day. "Any good contacts, names and addresses?" he asks.

"One GB [Gentile Believer]!"

"One UG [Unsaved Gentile]!"

"One JB [Jewish Believer]!"

"One UJ [Unsaved Jew]!"....

The members of Jews for Jesus are the most skillful and aggressive proselytizers in the Hebrew Christian movement.... In 1986, the organization's traveling missionaries will give nearly 3,000 fund-raising presentations and sermons in American churches and fellowships.

Last year, they handed out 5.5 million pamphlets, 2 million in New York City alone.[3]

## 1998 SUMMER CAMPAIGN

The New York summer campaign of 1998 clearly demonstrated that after twenty-five years, the ministry of Jews for Jesus has continued to move forward. In many ways, things looked the same as in previous years. Teams of broadsiders were in place and ready to greet the morning commuters by 7:00 A.M. Jeans, T-shirts, and sneakers were standard uniform. As in past years, the broadsides offered contemporary humor and a pithy gospel message. And there was good fun in lighthearted comments to early morning commuters suggesting that they use the tracts as fans (in the stifling air of the under-ground); asking if they wanted some religious propaganda; singing a silly ditty while passing them out; or passing them out "acrobatically"—under the leg, over the shoulder, behind the back (while spinning around). There was opposition, but for the most part, not nearly as mean spirited as in years past. And as always, team leaders turned in reports of the numbers of broad-sides distributed and contacts made. The campaign was a success, and in some respects it was also a turning point that set the stage for the twenty-first century.

## A MEASURE OF SUCCESS

The success of the campaign was calculated not only in numbers of tracts, contacts, and people who prayed to receive God's salvation through Jesus, but also by the number of volunteers who decided to continue with Jews for Jesus and by the profile of those volunteers. They were young, and they had a vision for the future. They were not the cause-oriented hippies of the previous generation, nor could they be described as cynical and self-absorbed members of Generation X. No, these were the millennium generation—fun and free spirited and optimistic about tomorrow, not thinking too much about the future beyond that. They volunteered for the campaign, and many went on to join the ministry.

Such has not always been the case. After working fourteen-hour days, many of the early volunteers chafed under the rigorous schedule and found the prospect of full-time ministry for Jews for Jesus unappealing. But the summer campaigns of recent years have had a different flavor, and a different tone. Practically speaking, the tiring work of packing tract bags and taking care of details such as laundry, cooking, and cleaning have been handled by stewards since the mid-eighties. These stewards often greet campaigners returning from sorties with bottles of water, smiles, and assurances that they have been praying for the sorties. The food—always abundant—is prepared by a skilled chef, often a professional. In addition to the meals, fresh fruit, dried fruit and nut mix, a variety of juices, and soft drinks are always on hand, along with ice cream bars and other frozen treats to cool off the troops. The campaigners feel cared for.

There is also a growing emphasis on doing things to draw on the strengths of young volunteers, such as sidewalk art during a noon hour at a corner of Central Park. This year there were still four sorties each day, but the eighth sortie was a sabbatical—personal time.

In addition to the campaigners, in the past couple of years there has been another group involved in the summer outreach. A program called Halutzim involves high school youth who come to New York not only to help with the campaign, but also to learn about their Jewish heritage and have fun. Most are second generation Jewish believers in Jesus; many are children of staff or former staff members. The program offers them an opportunity to have a part in the ministry. It is a training ground for future campaigners and missionaries as well as a time to form or strengthen relationships with other young people who understand the challenges of being Jewish and believing in Jesus. There is hacky-sack in the park, pizza parties, and late night talks. Watching these young people gives a taste of what the future of Jews for Jesus might be.

## THE MINISTRY TO NEW YORK'S RUSSIAN POPULATION

Reaching Russian Jews, particularly in Brooklyn and Queens, is also part of the focus of Jews for Jesus' New York branch. The time is particularly opportune for this ministry because many thousands of Jews have been immigrating to New York since the early 1990s. These people have a new sense of religious freedom and are wary of any system that tells them what they can and cannot believe. They do not automatically buy into the dogma that Jewish people cannot believe in Jesus, and they are often more open about spiritual matters than their American counterparts.

Since the summer of 1998, New York has become the headquarters for the ministry to Russian Jews. Headed by Avi Snyder, it is a ministry that reaches far beyond New York City to Germany, Russia, the Ukraine, and other places.

## THE TEAM AT THE TOP

Avi Snyder is not only in charge of Jews for Jesus ministry to Russian Jews, he is the senior leader in the New York branch. Working alongside him,

Karol Joseph is in charge of the training program, and Mitch Forman over-sees the regular Jews for Jesus staff and day-to-day branch operations. This three-part leadership team is new to Jews for Jesus, and it shows, among other things, the importance of the New York branch to this ministry. New York has not been an easy place to minister, and it has been especially diffi-cult on many of the leaders who have served there. Jews for Jesus staffers have come to see that where opportunities for evangelism are greatest, oppo-sition also tends to be greatest. There are some who would contend that opposition is not only from the Jewish community, but that there are also spiritual forces working against them.

The leadership "team at the top" is not only for a division of labor in this flagship branch; it is for the sake of mutual support and community build-ing. To that end, the ministry has purchased two buildings so staff and trainees can have affordable housing and a sense of community with one another.

Moishe got his training in New York, and Jews for Jesus staff have fol-lowed in that tradition. It is an exciting city, the setting for many Jews for Jesus family stories of trial as well as triumph.

# CHAPTER FOURTEEN

# THE MISSION FAMILY

*Behind the Office Facade*

W ho are Jews for Jesus? Not the organizational entity, but the people
who, individually and collectively, make up the mission family?
The opposition literature often claims they are misfits, mentally
unstable young adults from dysfunctional families. In actuality they appear to be
anything but that, though many of them joke about being misfits. In some respects
it could be argued that Jews for Jesus demonstrates the survival of the fittest when
it comes to their staff, though it could also be argued that some of the fittest have
gone on to head up other ministries or have taken secular positions. Moishe always
considered Jews for Jesus a leadership cadre, but not everyone is born to be a leader.
The organization has room for some members to continue on a nonleadership
track. On the other hand, some did not "survive" to serve in leadership positions
because they either were not able or willing to endure the rigors that Jews for Jesus
expects of its full-time staff members.

In some ways, Jews for Jesus is typical of a countercultural, youth-oriented
mission family growing out of the "Jesus-freak" generation. Like Jesus People USA,
it is more of a "family" than traditional mission agencies are. It demands a high
level of commitment and expects a high level of loyalty. And while some people
have left the ministry on good terms, others have left with hard feelings. Sometimes
individual members have been hurt—badly by some accounts. In some cases, fractured relationships have yet to heal.

This has also been the situation with Jesus People USA. Sociologist Ron Enroth
took that organization to task in one of his books. After interviewing members who

*had left the movement, I challenged Enroth in print, pointing out that his research was faulty. He had focused his attention on disgruntled members only, and he had failed to understand the dynamics of a mission that is truly a "family."*

*Some would characterize Jews for Jesus as a great big dysfunctional Jewish family. But what is a dysfunctional family—if the term has meaning at all? What seems dysfunctional to one may seem perfectly, or at least acceptably, normal to another. It is all subjective.*

*The stronger the family ties, the more pain there is in separation. What is the solution? To place less emphasis on camaraderie and togetherness? The answer for Jews for Jesus is no. That answer means the struggles and hurts and tears will continue to be woven together with the sense of security and fun and oneness that only a family can offer.*

—m—

Sue Perlman once said, "Jews for Jesus is an all-encompassing lifestyle. Although we have friends and associations outside the ministry, we tend to prefer one another's company."[1] The Jews for Jesus family orientation arises from a number of factors, but three of these stand out above the others.

The first factor is that the organization is largely Jewish in personnel and in character. That alone gives it a sense of togetherness unique among missions. Staff members come from similar backgrounds and experiences. In many ways, they stand apart because their beliefs differ from those of most Jews, and their culture differs from that of most Christians. They share stories of their upbringing before coming to Christ, and they share stories of their experiences in Jews for Jesus. They laugh and cry over the same things in their shared culture.

A second factor that contributes to the sense of family togetherness relates to opposition. Because of their up-front—some call it aggressive— evangelistic style, Jews for Jesus faces more opposition than many other ministries. Opposition commonly works to unite the opposed. Some people would say that the Jewish community has held together not only *despite* persecution, but to some degree *because* of it. Many have observed the same phenomenon with Christians who struggle with persecution, particularly in totalitarian states. Likewise, Jews for Jesus pulls close together in the face of opposition.

A third, and very significant factor, has been Moishe's past leadership.

## LOYALTY AND LEADERSHIP

Moishe's strong leadership and the staff's loyalty to him, especially in the early years, contributed greatly to the family mentality of Jews for Jesus. For many years, Moishe was the father figure of the family. (He has now taken on a more "grandfatherly" role.) As with his own family, he was a loving father, but that love included a stern side. He often used the term "discipline," and he often treated his young adult staff and volunteers as much like his children as his employees. That was part of the organization's family mentality, and Moishe's fatherly role came naturally because in many ways he felt responsible for their well-being—especially in the face of fierce opposition. He demanded compliance to rules, whether they related to punctuality or wearing an identifying blue denim jacket, the proper "uniform" for street ministry. "This is like an army," he exhorted in a group meeting; "you'll be fined in New York if you are late or improperly dressed. We're on wartime footing."[2]

Moishe pointed out prior to the first New York campaign that some of the group were getting lax with the rules and with their responsiveness to his leadership. He warned that they were going into a difficult and potentially dangerous situation in which the group's safety could depend on orderliness and quick response to authority. The members then drafted a statement entitled "resolution of recommitment" and submitted it to him. It was a document written in a very specific context, yet many critics claimed that it gave credence to their charges of cultic practices:

> We have prayed individually and together concerning this recommitment and agree that full submission to the leadership of Moishe Rosen is the will of God. We agree to accept his judgments, directives, and decisions, upholding him at all times. We agree to accept and obey all orders concerning both professional and personal matters for the benefit of the effectiveness of the entire group in the furtherance of the Gospel of the Lord Jesus Christ.[3]

It is difficult to imagine today's Jews for Jesus staff writing such a document, especially for anyone who has observed the lively interchange and
democratic debates during Jews for Jesus council meetings and in less formal
settings. Yet it is not surprising that this type of commitment would have
been made in the earlier years. Sociologists confirm that in the early stages
of all new religious movements there is a pattern of holding a high standard
of commitment and work ethic. Most such movements would not last
beyond a decade without strong leadership at the top.

## GROOMING NEW LEADERSHIP

As strong as Moishe's leadership was in those early years, what stands out in
Jews for Jesus' history is the fact that he groomed all the members of his
youthful ministry team for leadership. He invested in, rather than stifled,
their strengths. That investment has served the movement well, developing
rough—and in some cases, unfocused and undisciplined—followers into
confident, capable, and independent leaders. At the same time, some of
those strong-willed leaders eventually challenged what they perceived to be
Moishe's authoritarian leadership, and in some cases, turned against him,
leaving the ministry on rather unhappy terms. Most went on to other ministries. A few who left the accountability of the Jews for Jesus family/ministry
did not make themselves accountable to any other Christian community and
eventually abandoned their faith. Whatever their reaction, all of their lives
were irrevocably changed by the father and the family of Jews for Jesus.

Some names that once filled the stories in newspaper articles and organizational literature are no longer featured in the headlines. The names are
by no means forgotten. The family photo album still has all the old snap-
shots, but many of the smiling faces that were so prominent in days gone by
have moved on: Baruch Goldstein, Sam Nadler, Amy Rabinowitz, Mitch
Glaser, Barry and Steffi (nee Geiser) Rubin, Stuart Dauermann—all gone, but
never forgotten.

Many of the "old-timers," those old hippies, are still part of the Jews for
Jesus staff. Today, however, they are anything but the stereotypical old hippies with long, stringy hair, tie-dyed T-shirt, and worn-out blue jeans. Those
old hippies and flower children of the counterculture have matured and

found their places individually and collectively in Jews for Jesus. A profile of a few of the early Jews for Jesus traces changes as well as consistencies over the years.

## Susan Perlman

One who has endured the rigors of Jews for Jesus' ministry from the early days is Susan Perlman, who was born into a traditional Jewish family in Brooklyn. After college, Susan worked in New York, and life was good. Unlike many young people who joined the movement in the early years, she was not doing drugs and was not part of the hippie counterculture. Nor was she going through bad times that might have made her vulnerable to the deceptive tactics of a cult. She simply did not have the stereotypical profile of a joiner of Jews for Jesus. Nevertheless, she was an activist with high ideals. And she was not finding fulfillment. "My life fell far short of what I thought it should be," she recalls. "I recognized my need for God and prayed very simply—God I need you in my life. If you're real and not just thin air, somehow let me know."[4]

God revealed himself to Susan, but not at all as she might have expected or hoped: "My life was inundated with Christians and signs of Jesus, which wasn't the answer I was looking for. I was terrified. It was not the conventional thing for me to believe." During that time in 1971, a folksinger Larry Norman introduced her to the Jesus Movement. It appealed to her "anti-establishment sentiments," and she never looked back.[5]

The road to Jesus was not an easy one for Susan. Her family and friends rejected her new beliefs out of hand. They had no desire to discuss the issues much less debate them seriously. "My family considered me a traitor," she recalls. "They were ashamed; they were angry. They wanted me to keep it a secret. My roommates thought I went off the deep end."[6]

Susan moved to California in the early 1970s to become a volunteer with Jews for Jesus. She, like most of the group, was in her twenties. Moishe likes to tell the story. Friends in New York had encouraged Susan to contact Moishe. She sent him a letter that he never received. When they finally hooked up in a phone conversation, the only paid position Moishe could offer Susan was that of a secretary, which she declined. She wanted to write, to do drama, to be an evangelist. So Moishe invited her to come to San Francisco and begin as a volunteer. His offer was simple and straightforward: "I can promise you that if I have food on my table, you will also." How could she refuse? "When can you come?" was his response to her silence. She told him she would have to give her supervisor two weeks' notice. "I'll see you in two weeks, then." That was the end of the brief phone conversation.

Moishe was out of town when Susan was due to arrive, but he returned to find that no one had heard from her. He was concerned, particularly when he learned that she had indeed boarded a flight from New York to San Francisco a few weeks earlier. Through further investigation, he tracked her down. She was staying at the home of her boyfriend's parents—Chinese immigrants who spoke no English. She had been hiding out there for two or three weeks. When asked how old she was at that time, Moishe responded lightheartedly, "As I remember she was twenty-one—going on fifteen."[7]

Susan worked as a waitress to make a living but still had plenty of energy for the ministry. She found her volunteer niche, a self-created position heading up publicity and media relations. She quickly made a place for herself in the cramped headquarters office space in Corte Madera. She spotted a long, narrow storage closet, and after shifting some boxes and books, she had her own "office." Unfortunately, there was only one phone—with a hold button—in the office. ("We didn't need another phone," says Moishe.) Susan persuaded Amy Rabinowitz, the office manager, to allocate funds for a long phone cord. Moishe left town again, and this time returned to find Susan in her own "office," taking press calls for "Miss Perlman." Amy would answer the phone, put the caller on hold, and carry the phone into Susan's closet.[8]

From that inauspicious beginning, with no real background in public relations, Susan very quickly moved Jews for Jesus into the limelight.

The fact that Susan had accepted Jesus as Messiah did not make her any less Jewish, so it seemed natural to her to become part of a local Jewish congregation. She chose a conservative synagogue in Marin County. "I enjoyed the worship there," she recalls, "but [then] my picture came out in the local paper as a volunteer for Jews for Jesus. When I came into the temple one Shabbat morning, the president of the congregation and the cantor were yelling out 'traitor' and 'we don't want you here, we don't want you as part of our congregation.' I was so upset that I just left." The rabbi, however, was less drastic in his response and eager to make a compromise with Susan.

> The rabbi was very troubled because he knew that I had been a loyal member of the congregation. That night he called me and told me that they were very upset that I was doing missionary work, but that he would stand and support me in front of the congregation if I would extend my promise not to evangelize anywhere in the county in which we lived. He knew I wasn't evangelizing to the members of the synagogue, but once he asked me that, of course I said "You know you're asking something of me that I can't do. You're asking me not to come back again." The cantor had given him an ultimatum and he had been willing to support me, if I would have made this promise. It really hurt me, because I didn't expect it. We have never left the Jewish community. We've been tossed out, rejected, abandoned."[9]

In Jews for Jesus, Susan quickly found her place in a ministry that rewarded talent. She moved up through the ranks, specializing in the area of publicity and public relations, with the title of first assistant to the director.[10] She also found her place in the broader evangelical world. Leighton Ford, World Chairman of the Lausanne Committee and longtime associate and brother-in-law of Billy Graham, listed Susan ten years ago as one of the promising newcomers in evangelicalism. This recognition came not only because of her high profile at Jews for Jesus, but also because of her involvement in activities and on boards outside the organization.[11]

Susan's achievements have not come without a willingness to make sacrifices in other areas of her life. She has chosen to forgo marriage and children, though she concedes, "Marriage is a very Jewish thing." And she is well aware that her "singleness hasn't always been understood." Yet, she can confidently say, "I feel quite complete," and she encourages other women to consider their options:

> It is important that Christian women realize they have a choice. To me, being married would mean being less of what I can be for God.

I hope that won't be misinterpreted. But being single, I am also more
available. I can pick up and go when needed. I usually keep a suit-
case packed.[12]

Unlike many independent mission organizations, Jews for Jesus provides a very positive working environment for single women. According to
Susan, "Men who come into our ministry realize that they will advance on
the basis of merit, and not because they are male." Most evangelical mission
agencies pay salaries according to family needs. Not so with Jews for Jesus.
The pay scale is based on merit.[13]

Like all members of Jews for Jesus, Susan is caught between two
worlds—the world of her Jewish heritage and the world of modern American evangelicalism. Susan blends those two worlds in her own unique way.
She is Jewish in her personal mannerisms, outlook, lifestyle, and tastes. Her
home, in Moishe's description, is in many ways a very Jewish home with a
very cultural slant. Her walls have become almost a museum for the works
of the Jewish artist Marc Chagall, as well as several Israeli artists. For all that,
she moves very comfortably in the evangelical world as was demonstrated
by her election to the office of president of the Interdenominational Foreign
Missions Association (IFMA).

## Jhan Moskowitz

Jhan Moskowitz, who currently heads the Chicago branch of Jews for Jesus, was
one of the "originals." He was the last of a pot-smoking threesome to turn his life
around, and he is the only one remaining in the organization. Baruch Goldstein
has gone on to other things, and Mitch Glaser now heads another Jewish mission.

Jhan, like so many other youths of the 1960s counterculture, was cause
oriented. His cause was Zionism, and he went to Israel hoping to defend her
in the 1967 war with Egypt:

I decided I'd rather die in Israel than in Vietnam, but I never was
officially admitted into a combat unit. I stayed in the reserves and
lived on a kibbutz, but then I began to realize that war wasn't where
it was at for me. Although I still supported Israel, I saw a subtle

racism over there. The Arab refugees were treated pretty poorly, and I didn't like that. So, disillusioned, I started looking for personal truth in the youth subculture.[14]

Jhan's first contact with Jews for Jesus came in 1971 when Mitch Glaser invited him to a Bible study Moishe was teaching. Jhan's decision to follow Jesus, however, was not clinched through biblical arguments, but rather through a coincidence. He had a strange dream of a woman seducing him, and there was something of a supernatural or spiritual overtone in the dream. When he awoke, he later recalled, "At first I thought God had seduced me." Later, he returned home to his commune, where a party was in progress. When a young woman came up behind him and put her arms around him in a seductive manner, he had an eerie sense that the dream was coming true. Just then, a sign of the cross appeared on the frosty window that looked out on the sidewalk leading up to the door. A supernatural mystical experience? Not really, as Jhan later explained: "Baruch and Mitch had been walking outside just at that moment. Mitch, as was his custom, drew that cross on the window, but neither of them could see me through the glass. Coincidences were one thing, but this was too much."[15]

Walking outside to a nearby park, Jhan was still dazed when he talked to his two buddies. "Hey, man, the dream really came true. What should I do?" Baruch had a ready answer.

When they reached the park, Jhan got down on his knees, and Baruch and Mitch laid their hands on his head. Jhan prayed. "Father, forgive me for pretending I knew You, for being the imperfect person I am. Come into my life, take it over, I'm Yours."[16]

"People say I'm a Christian. Absolutely, I am!" insists Jhan. "But that doesn't mean I'm a Gentile. I'm a Christian, but I'm also a Jew.... My wife Melissa is Jewish as well, and both our daughters have had messianic bat mitzvahs." In response to Rabbi Mordecai Simon, who claims he cannot be both, Jhan argues: "It's not his prerogative to take it away from me. Belief in Jesus doesn't make a person stop acting like a Jew, or thinking of Jewish causes." Ask Jhan why some people would accuse him of misrepresentation when he claims to be Jewish, and he would respond:

They assassinate the messenger so they don't have to deal with the message. And that message is whether you are Jewish or Gentile, God loves you and sent his messenger Jesus, to be your sin bearer. And if you really believe, you can have a forever relationship with him.[17]

Jhan has come a long way from his early hippie days. He is one of the ministry's most dynamic speakers and receives invitations to address various groups such as the Promise Keepers.

## Tuvya Zaretsky

His Hebrew name, given on the day of his circumcision, was Meyer Leib Tuvya ben Avraham, but he grew up as Lloyd Carsen. Like many immigrants in the early years of the twentieth century, his grandparents, Alex and Bessie Zaretsky, changed their name so they would fit more easily into their new environment. Zaretsky became Zarsky, which eventually was changed to Carson. When he became an adult and found Jesus as Messiah, Lloyd Carson reclaimed his Jewish roots, and with his roots, his Hebrew and family name, Tuvya Zaretsky.

Alex and Bessie Zaretsky emigrated from their home in Belarus and Poland in 1910 for the "promised land" of America. They settled in Toronto, Canada, where they lived most of their lives. Their son Abraham (Tuvya's father) grew up as Al Carsen. Al studied medicine, served in World War II, and returned home to marry his sweetheart, Vicky. Al and Vicky were an all-American couple who also held tightly to their Jewish heritage and identity.

Tuvya remembers his bar mitzvah at age thirteen as the first time he truly sought God. He slipped away from the family reception afterwards and went back into the sanctuary to "talk to God quietly and personally." The lights were out, and the room was dark. "I believed that His presence was there and powerful in the darkness," recalls Tuvya. "I've said 'hineni,' here am I, but where are you?" he asked God. It was this experience that signaled the beginning of his search for God.[18]

Tuvya grew up believing in the God of Israel, yet he did not know God in a personal sense. During his college years at the University of Redlands in Southern California, Tuvya joined the antiwar protest and the hippie counterculture, with little focus on the things of God. But following his graduation, he encountered a number of Christians who influenced his spiritual journey. One of them sent him a copy of Hal Lindsey's popular book, *The Late Great Planet Earth.* Tuvya later said:

> It presented some startling new facts to me. I had never heard Jesus cited as the focus of Old Testament prophecy or called the Messiah of the Jews. I never understood the nature of sin until it was described, particularly through the words of Jesus in that book. I heard for the first time that Jesus Christ is God's answer to sin, and the provider of a new life.[19]

Incredibly, no sooner had Tuvya finished the book than he noticed a poster announcing that Hal Lindsey would be speaking in the area. Tuvya attended the meeting and talked to Lindsey briefly afterwards.

Soon after, Tuvya attended a Festival of Lights pageant. His initial reaction to the pageant was negative: "I had been angry because I knew the Festival of Lights as Hanukkah, a Jewish festival. These Christians had it all wrong! But I went that night and heard a message...." The message was from John's Gospel, focusing on Jesus as the light of the world. From Tuvya's perspective, that message had been coming to him from a number of sources, all of which were convincing, but there were still obstacles. One was the issue of professing Christians Tuvya saw as hypocrites because their lives "had never been a testimony of love or grace." Speaking half out loud, Tuvya reasoned, "If these people are the product of this message, why should I ever want to be a Christian!?" The person sitting next to him spontaneously replied, "The relationship that you have with God will be your own. It will not necessarily be like that of anyone else. It is just between you and Him."[20]

For Tuvya, that was the answer he needed, and "the last barrier fell." His journey was not over; it had just begun. "I could no longer say, 'It's not for me, I'm Jewish.' I saw that it was a personal relationship that was available to anyone, including me."[20]

Tuvya went off to Israel, where a Christian couple took him in and helped him grow in his new faith. Like many other Jews who have recognized Jesus as Messiah, Tuvya initially felt alone, and he prayed to God for direction. Then he heard about Jews for Jesus. "People were coming together," he remembered. "The excitement was our discovery that other Jews believed in Jesus, too, and that we were going to continue being Jews together."[21]

Like all of those involved in Jews for Jesus street ministry, Tuvya has encountered thousands of people each week, rarely knowing whether a tract or a brief conversation might be a catalyst to change their lives. However, in one memorable instance, he learned the results of a brief encounter—sixteen years later. Tuvya describes these encounters as "Divinely appointed moments when the Lord is quietly and effectively touching someone, often when we are least aware of it."[22]

The first encounter had occurred in the very early days of Jews for Jesus and was a less-than-pleasant experience. It was during a public protest to draw attention to the gospel. The setting was "The Garden of Eden," a bar in the North Beach area of San Francisco that featured topless dancing and sex shows—one featuring "Adam and Eve." Tuvya later recalled:

> In those days, all of us were volunteers who would go down to North Beach in a car caravan after work. We used to gather outside the Garden of Eden, and carrying placards with messages like "Love, Not Lust," "Real Love in Jesus" and "Jesus is Lord," we would begin a demonstration march in front of the place. We were a small, ragtag group back then, and most of us were out on the streets publicly proclaiming our faith for the very first time.[23]

Moishe preferred to call these attest demonstrations because the point was not so much to protest as it was to make positive statements about the gospel. He chose the Garden of Eden because he wanted to counter their perverted reference to Scripture.

Demonstrations became a regular activity for Jews for Jesus and friends. One night the frustrated club owner decided to try to cut a deal. He agreed to allow the demonstrators a chance to preach for ten minutes in the bar—

if they would leave as soon as the preaching was over. Not surprisingly, the small crowd was less than receptive to the message. But what was happening outside the bar turned out to be more significant. Billy, a young man who played the part of Adam in the sex show, was irritated by the turn of events. He had walked out to the parking lot to harass the young women who were attesting. There he was, dressed only in a loin cloth, sparring with Jews for Jesus, and hearing, perhaps for the first time, that he would have to face the eternal consequence of his sinful activity.

Sixteen years later, Billy approached Tuvya while he was distributing broadsides on the Santa Monica Pier. He reminded Tuvya of that night and told him how the message he heard later changed his life. When his wife's life was in the balance due to a drug overdose, he promised God he would turn away from his life of sin. "She lived and Billy never forgot his promise. In the months that followed, Billy and his wife both became followers of Jesus Christ." That was the good news that he gave to Tuvya—a "divinely appointed moment" that Tuvya didn't know about until sixteen years later.[24]

Among his many gifts, Tuvya brings a strong sense of organization to the ministry, a quality that has earned him respect and recognition beyond Jews for Jesus. He was recently elected president of the Lausanne Consultation on Jewish Evangelism, a networking organization comprised of various mission societies and congregations from all over the world.

## Bob Mendelsohn

Bob Mendelsohn joined the staff of Jews for Jesus in 1979, eight years after he became a follower of Jesus. He had already served as senior pastor of a Christian congregation in Kansas, an unlikely job for one who grew up in an Orthodox Jewish home. But as the title of an article about him suggests, Bob has "A Foot in Two Faiths."

> In many ways, Mendelsohn fits the description of a good Jew. He was raised to read the Torah, keep kosher, and keep holy the Sabbath. But in one important respect he is different from his parents: Mendelsohn accepts Jesus Christ as the divine Son of God. For his

involvement in Jews for Jesus, Mendelsohn's family, which forbade reading the New Testament, disowned him. Friends, too, no longer speak to him.[25]

When Bob was serving as the director of Jews for Jesus in Washington, D.C., his pastor, the Reverend Bob Creamer, responded to critics who insisted Bob and his family should not mix two separate faiths:

> Because they choose to celebrate the Jewish holidays doesn't make them less a Christian.... I think one can be French and Christian, you can be Japanese Christians. Culture has religious roots. What is happening in our culture is people are saying that Jews as a culture are unique, they shouldn't talk about religious matters outside of Judaism and I think that's bunk.[26]

Bob is a creative self-starter, and is known within the ministry for his pioneer spirit. In the fall of 1998, he and his family relocated to Sydney, Australia, where Bob directs the ministry. Almost immediately, a flurry of news stories appeared expressing the fears of local Jewish leaders. Bob evoked quite a response as he distributed a broadside declaring that "Jesus is what makes some of us want to be more Jewish." Condemning the evangelistic endeavors as "harassment," Peter Wertheim, president of the Jewish Board of Deputies, asked the Archbishop Harry Goodhew to intervene. Others were more reserved in their assessment. Professor Richard Kohn of Sydney University, a self-proclaimed expert on messianic Judaism, refuted one of the more volatile accusations regarding Jews for Jesus activities. According to Professor Kohn, "to say it is a form of spiritual genocide is too strong; it is an inevitable outgrowth of the many scholarly developments of the 60s."[27]

The controversy raised the image of Jews for Jesus in Australia, and Bob was quick to answer charges that he was concealing his Christian faith: "I don't deny that I'm Christian. For most, being Christian is being a Gentile, and I'm Jewish."[28]

## BOUND BY THE FAITH

It is the kind of Jewish-Christian faith seen in these Jews for Jesus that makes the ministry unique. The Jews for Jesus family is diverse. It is not a church, and staff members attend various local congregations—some Lutheran, some Baptist, some Messianic, to name but a few. Their upbringings also vary with regard to the way their parents observed Jewish customs. Their personalities differ one from the next; their gifts and abilities represent a wide spectrum. Their disagreements with one another can be loud and long, and most of them would admit to being stubborn.

Yet the Jews for Jesus family is also a picture of unity and oneness. They love to sit together and recount old stories, not only of victory and triumph, but of embarrassing moments, funny moments, and situations that taught them life lessons. They reflect on hardships and blessings together. They share prayer requests and remind one another of spiritual priorities. They rejoice over the births of one another's children, and they mourn one another's losses.

As with any family, there is sadness over those who have broken the ties that bind, particularly when long-term staff members have left angry. Those breaks are quite painful, and continued relationships are awkward at best. On the brighter side, many former staffers remain on good terms with Jews for Jesus, continuing to enjoy friendships and cooperative ministry opportunities.

As new staff members join the family, they enjoy hearing the old stories. But what the old-timers enjoy as much as telling their own stories is hearing the newer ones begin to tell stories of their own.

# CHAPTER FIFTEEN

# PERSPECTIVES ON LIFE

## *Political, Social, and Spiritual*

One of the most refreshing aspects of Jews for Jesus is its open-ended stance on issues of the day—whether theological, social, or political. I found a wide range of views as I talked with the old-timers as well as with some who have joined the organization more recently. I heard strong and diverse opinions on matters like party politics, health care, and the women's movement, but there is no ministry policy, written or unwritten, on these issues. In many Christian organizations I have known there is at minimum an unwritten expectation that all those in good standing would, for example, support conserva-tive Republican Party candidates. Indeed, some years ago at a seminary faculty retreat, I heard a long-term insider state publicly that he did not believe a person could be a Christian and vote for the Democratic ticket. His statement went unchallenged, even by me, because I was too intimidated to do so. Something like that would not occur in Jews for Jesus. Moishe has strong political views, as does Susan Perlman. That they are at almost opposite ends of the spectrum is nobody's concern.

*Jews for Jesus' lifestyle and practices (so long as they do not violate biblical principles) are much more free and easy than in most evangelical mission organi-zations. There is also a very broad range of stances on theological and ecclesiasti-cal issues, as I have come to discover in discussions with various people on staff. Persuasions range from free-spirited charismatic to liturgical Episcopalian. There is no presumed right way to go as long as one agrees with a basic statement of faith that covers those things Jews for Jesus consider essential. One rule that is made quite clear is that staff are not to force their opinion regarding nonessentials on other staff.*

*The same latitude is afforded those who would incorporate Jewish religious rituals into their worship and those who would not. How people express their Jewishness is up to them. Just as in the general Jewish population, there are some in Jews for Jesus, like Susan Perlman, who are very much in tune with a normative Jewish culture and heritage; there are also others, like Joshua Sofaer, who grew up with a totally different experience.*

*Some think of themselves as messianic Jews, others as Jewish Christians. Quite a few really do not care about labels at all, so long as it is clear that they are Jews who are for Jesus.*

—ɷ—

Having grown out of the Jesus Movement and the Faith Mission Movement, and as a member of the Interdenominational Foreign Missions Association (IFMA), Jews for Jesus is planted firmly in conservative evangelical soil. Yet in many ways, the organization does not follow the scripted line to which many faith mission organizations conform. Jews for Jesus enjoys a freedom of thought and practice that is uncommon in evangelical circles. This may be due in part to an often-repeated theme in the organization's evangelistic outreach: "Think for yourself." Many Jewish people have simply refused even to consider Jesus as Messiah because such a consideration is taboo. Freedom of thought is an essential ingredient in the process of recognizing Jesus as Messiah, and that freedom is not left behind as an individual matures in faith. It is only natural, then, that an organization like Jews for Jesus would be composed of free-thinking Jewish believers.

The best sources for the wide-ranging perspectives represented in the organization are, of course, the staff members themselves. Another valuable source is the four-color, eight-page mailing entitled *ISSUES*. It is a quality piece of literature, edited by Susan Perlman, that deals with topics ranging from "Jesus in Jewish Art" to angels and the women's issue. An evangelistic periodical—though not conspicuously so—*ISSUES* is designed for Jewish seekers, and its title reflects its content.

## JEWISHNESS AND JUDAISM

On issues relating to Jewishness, Jewish heritage and customs, Jews for Jesus represents a wide span of lifestyle and loyalty. Most of the old-timers would place more emphasis on their Jewishness than the younger generation does, and this tends to reflect the current position of the Jewish community at large.

It was very important for the first generation of Jews for Jesus to demonstrate that they were not in any sense renouncing their Jewish heritage. They frequently chose to use the Jewish names given them at their circumcisions or naming ceremonies: Moishe rather than Martin, for example, or Avi rather than Alan. Younger staffers, in many cases, have been raised in mainstream American society, often with less emphasis on a Jewish identity. In some cases, joining Jews for Jesus gives them an opportunity to explore the heritage they missed, and many are eager to learn more about their Jewishness. Others are very matter of fact about their Jewish identity and do not feel the need to take it beyond what their parents gave them.

How Jewish a lifestyle a staff member wants is left entirely to the individual. For most, there is a mix of what is Jewish and non-Jewish—whether in celebrating holidays or in food tastes. There is no pretense of purity of tradition. Tradition is tradition—no more. There is nothing sacred about tradition.

Regarding Judaism, which some would term the actual belief system of Jewish people, there is not so much latitude. Moishe has made it clear through the years that Jews for Jesus does not speak for or represent Judaism, nor, he believes, do messianic Jews in general. They are not a fourth branch of Judaism. Judaism as a religion insists that Jesus is not the Messiah. Therefore, as far as Jews for Jesus are concerned, religious ties are with Christianity. There are many beautiful traditions and truths within Judaism, but Jews for Jesus regard the basic religion as a human construct that has largely departed from its biblical base. This is a somewhat controversial issue in the broader messianic movement, but it is not an openly controversial issue within the Jews for Jesus organization.

New executive director David Brickner takes essentially the same position. His ties are very close to evangelical churches. "I do not oppose messianic congregations," he writes. "I am a member of a messianic congregation myself. However, I believe it is healthy for many Jewish believers to be members of evangelical churches as well. I base my view on the doctrine of the Universal Body, which we find throughout the New Covenant." David goes on to challenge strongly the concept of a dual church—one of Jews and another of Gentiles:

> We recognize differences between ourselves and others, but those differences do not give us the right to create divisions. For example, I keep hearing a misnomer that causes me to cringe. It's the phrase, "Gentile church." For many that is nothing more than an observation that the majority of people who claim to be Christians are not Jews. But I really think we have to stop using that term because it is just plain unbiblical. Regardless of the intent, the term allows creeping prejudices—and makes it difficult for many Jewish believers to be at home in the church of their choice. I don't think it is intended to be rude; nevertheless it's a divisive term.
>
> Y'shua established one church.... The Church is a new organism that is neither Jewish nor Gentile, though it is made up of both....
>
> Just imagine if Gentiles started referring to the "Gentile church." Picture them naming congregations "First Gentile Presbyterian Church," "St John's Gentile Lutheran Church" or "Grace Gentile Baptist Church." We would be livid if they implied that Jews ought to be excluded! Yet, if we use the phrase "Gentile church," are we not implying that Jews don't belong? We can be thankful to God that the Church is not like that. Let's be careful not to foster the kind of separatist thinking that we would find hurtful if it were directed at us from others.[1]

## AN HONEST APPROACH

Although critics of Jews for Jesus insist the organization uses deceptive tactics and language, downplays its Christian identity, and pretends to adhere to Judaism—such is not the case. It is very clear in the literature that they see a distinction between Jewishness and Judaism and that Jews for Jesus is a Jewish Christian organization. They are fully aware of the radical nature of Jesus' teachings—that he not only fulfilled the law, but he transformed it.

One helpful source relating to this issue is a book by Rabbi Jacob Neusner, *A Rabbi Talks with Jesus*. It focuses on Jesus' teachings from the Gospel of Matthew. Neusner argues very convincingly that what Jesus taught his disciples and the crowds was a significant departure from the teachings of Judaism, in other words what the rabbis of the day were teaching. He wrote the book "because he believes Christians and Jews rarely argue openly about the substantive issues dividing them—especially about Jesus. Interfaith dialogues are, for him, largely dishonest exercises in which both parties pretend to take the other side seriously but do not."[2]

Rabbi Neusner's evaluation of Christianity and Judaism would correspond in many respects with Jews for Jesus' perspective. Christianity and Judaism are two very distinct religions. Both sides would agree that Jesus, among other things, made a "radical claim to divine authority," that his message was not directed exclusively to the Jewish people, and that he opposed the rituals and rites that got in the way of "interior moral righteousness."[3]

## JEWS FOR JESUS AND FUNDAMENTALISM

In the early years of Jews for Jesus, Moishe defined his organization as "evangelical fundamentalist," and he sought to gain the friendship and support of fundamentalist churches and individuals. He quickly discovered that it was impossible to gain strict fundamentalist support while developing relationships in the broader Christian community. In 1976 Lyle Murphy, at the request of Moishe, came on board with Jews for Jesus for the express purpose of reaching out to the fundamentalist community. But Murphy resigned his position after little more than a year. He summed up his reasons in an interview featured in a magazine published by the Independent Fundamentalist Churches of America (IFCA):

> Compromise means something different to Rosen than it does to IFCA men. In Rosen's mind, there is no compromise if he is free to believe as he will and to teach his ministry to the Jews unhindered.

This means to him that he is free to speak tonight in a liberal denomination, tomorrow night in a Bible Church, the next night in a Pentecostal camp meeting and the night after in the liturgical robes of a creedal church. I've told him again and again that fundamentalists insist that you walk in their camp or in the ecumenical, charismatic, liberal or compromising camp but that you can't expect fundamentalists to tolerate an admixture of these.[4]

Murphy's disaffection with Jews for Jesus was strictly an issue of separation—nothing else, as his answers clearly indicate. In response to the question, "What do you see as the future of Jews for Jesus?" he offered a straightforward answer:

The young people are creative and highly entertaining. Many churches will be open to their ministry. Rosen is a good pulpit speaker and presents his ministry in a very lucid, interesting way. He, too, will have pulpits open to him throughout the country. I believe, however, that he has openly hazarded the prayer and support of fundamentalists who have given liberally to sustain the Jews for Jesus ministry.[5]

Murphy's references to liberal churches are probably not relevant since Jews for Jesus have never expected or sought support of churches that take a low view of the Bible or do not believe that Jesus is the only way of salvation. Nevertheless, the charismatic and noncharismatic debate is one that the staff refuses to be pulled into. Jews for Jesus will regretfully forgo a relationship with any church that requires them to avoid Bible-believing Christians in other churches.

## ORDINATION WITHIN JEWS FOR JESUS

Moishe is ordained as a Baptist minister. Throughout his years as director of Jews for Jesus, he has strongly encouraged male leaders to be ordained. All missionary staff are commissioned as church workers. This apparent discrimination between men and women has related more to the practices of churches with which staff members have identified than with any position of Jews for Jesus. The organization itself has no official statement or position on women's ordination. The reason for the ordination and commissioning was "partly to avoid being called an offbeat cult by critics."[6]

Rarely are ordained staff members identified as such by the use of "Reverend" before their names, and none would identify himself in that way. Moishe himself has set the standard on this issue, and others have followed.

## THE WOMEN'S ISSUE

As with most controversial issues, there is no consensus on issues relating to women's equality. Jews for Jesus does not confirm ordination on anyone, so the issue of women's ordination is not one upon which the organization has needed to take a position. However, in one edition of *ISSUES,* a lead article entitled "A Woman's Place," by Elisabeth Hill affirms an egalitarian position in the church.

She points out that "Throughout the Bible, women are joint participators and heirs of the promise along with men" and that "God's promises culminated in the very special person of the Messiah." It is the Messiah— Y'shua—whom Hill identifies as the "liberator" of women. She reminds her readers that "His first recorded utterances concerning his messiahship were delivered to a Samaritan woman," and he went on in his ministry to include women among his close circle of disciples.[7]

Moishe was always very supportive of women in ministry, as is seen by his own appointment of women to important roles in the organization. His position is also evident in his writing. In a recent article on the history of Jewish missions, he wrote about women and the important roles they played, especially in previous generations. He also points out that they were not always given the respect due them.

At any given time, there were probably more single women missionaries in Jewish Evangelism than there were men. Female missionaries of the past did not fit the stereotypical caricature of stern prudishness. They generally wore nice clothes and their hairdos were not especially severe.

Nevertheless, if women were partners in mission, they were treated like junior partners. For example, Hilda Koser built a work in Coney Island that had two hundred people, almost all Jewish, worshiping with her on Sunday mornings. Yet that body couldn't be called a congregation or its worship a church service. Instead, it was called Sunday school. And though Miss Koser was quite a capable teacher and rousing preacher, she was not the principal teacher at the Sunday service she had built. The service featured Dr. Henry Heydt, a Gentile scholar and the former president of Lancaster School of the Bible.

The attitude of the mission leaders of that day seemed to be, "Women can do work of which they're capable in mission, as long as they know their place."

Moishe and David have been careful to communicate a different message. David says, "I am committed to developing our young men and women in their gifts. The laborers are few and we cannot afford to devalue a significant segment of our missionary force because of gender or age. I believe that women are treated as equal partners with men in this ministry and I am proud of that."[8]

## Spiritual Warfare, Signs, Wonders, and the Charismatic Movement

The current debate over spiritual warfare and signs and wonders has not had a significant impact on Jews for Jesus. They focus on tangible plans of action: street evangelism, music, drama, print media. They do not deny powers of darkness in the unseen spirit world, and they certainly emphasize that individual staff members should follow biblical principles to avoid becoming spiritual casualties. Nevertheless, they are not interested in drawing more attention to the devil than they do to the gospel.

One chapter in Moishe's book, *Jews for Jesus*, is entitled "Prayer Power and Holy Ghost Stories." Here he relates some answers to prayer and one very powerful dream that paralleled a criminal attack that was occurring at the very same time. But perhaps the most significant aspect of this chapter is its lack of emphasis on the supernatural—especially when "spiritual warfare" was a hot topic. On this issue, as with many others, Moishe was not inclined to be faddish, and he warned the reader of subjectivity and dishonesty in this area:

> Some believers tend to see supernatural interventions when they're not really there, or to embellish or exaggerate actual encounters with the supernatural. They fool themselves into thinking they have seen or heard or experienced something that never occurred. A person who is good at telling these "Holy Ghost stories" may find that he has a power over others, especially those who are younger and less experienced. Also, although we have experienced a great deal of startling supernatural interventions, I am reluctant to emphasize these incidents, because I don't want to lead others to rely on miracles instead of making an effort to trust God and then work hard to solve their problems.[9]

Moishe has high regard for the Jewish mission outreach of the neo-Pentecostal and Charismatic movements. Of their work, he states: "More than half of the Jews coming to Christ do so through the charismatic movement. Three-quarters of the messianic Jews identify themselves as charismatic. This, in one way, validates the charismatic movement.[10]

### POLITICS OF THE RIGHT

Rosen declined to discuss political subjects such as school prayer and abortion and said Jews for Jesus stays clear of politics. "I will say that if such a thing should happen that the government became 'Christian' and legislation was passed that all residents must worship Christ, we would be in the forefront of the dissenters. Christianity is a matter of conscience. People under compulsion don't really believe."[11]

As in the case of women's issues, political views vary greatly. One cannot say, however, that political views span the spectrum since staff members are not pro-choice when it comes to abortion. But you will find a variety of opinions on various other political issues, and this in itself makes Jews for Jesus peculiar among conservative faith missions. In the title of an *ISSUES* article, Alan M. Shore asks the question, "Is the Religious Right Good or Bad for the Jews?" While the title question does not refer merely to Jews for Jesus, but to Jewish people in general, Jews for Jesus have roots in the Jewish community and identify in many respects with Jewish ideals.

Shore begins with the fear that many Jewish people have regarding conservative Christian political activism. In other articles, the organization points out that this fear is ungrounded and that conservatives are often at the forefront of support for Israel and take moral positions in line with what Jews for Jesus understands to be biblical perspectives. Of course, there is an "ancient, well-grounded fear that a reunion of Christian doctrine and political power spells hardship for Jews." In the past, Jewish people have been persecuted when the church and state have been closely allied. He also points out the long history of liberal political activism in the Jewish community. "If you were poor, downtrodden and a minority [as Jews often were in generations past], your home was in the Democratic Party, the party of the masses, or some party or movement further to the left."[12]

In the last paragraph, Shore asks "Where do Jewish believers in Jesus fall on the political spectrum?"

Most are caught between two poles, each of which exerts a powerful pull. Most resonate with Jewish activism in the righteous social causes of our day and want to be "on the side" of those championing the poor, the powerless, and the disenfranchised. The pull transcends party affiliation as a motivator.... Their question goes beyond "Is this good or bad for the Jews?" They must also ask, "How does this person or position line up with the biblical values I hold?"

For this same edition of *ISSUES,* Susan Perlman wrote an editorial subtitled, "confessions of a politically liberal, theologically conservative Jew for Jesus." Although she makes very few "confessions" in this brief piece, she does reflect back on her civil rights activism and her antiwar stance with a good conscience. And the subtitle itself is provocative—especially in evangelical circles.[13]

Regardless of a variety of strong opinions among the staff, Jews for Jesus has refused to take official opinions on any number of concerns. Why? "We are a one-issue organization," staff members firmly assert. The organization's first core value is: "We commit to direct Jewish evangelism as our priority." Fleshing out this value in their February 1999 newsletter, David Brickner wrote, "Direct evangelism occurs when there is a clear presentation of the facts of the gospel to the unsaved and an appeal to receive salvation through faith in Christ. This is the best and only hope for my Jewish people, indeed for all people everywhere."[14] This does not mean that other issues are unimportant, and it does not mean that individuals on staff cannot support other organizations that champion certain causes or viewpoints. But as far as Jews for Jesus is concerned, there are too many "good causes" that can distract them from their primary cause—and that is telling the gospel to Jews and Gentiles.

# CHAPTER SIXTEEN

# THE CHANGING OF THE GUARD

## Moishe Steps Aside, David Steps Up

How does the founder and director of a large organization step aside with dignity? Moishe Rosen did. His early retirement from the directorship of Jews for Jesus is one of the most remarkable aspects of this man and this ministry—and it was early. Moishe was not even sixty-five when he stepped down. He easily could have stayed on until age seventy or beyond. Many executives do—sometimes to the detriment of their organization.

When is the time right? For Moishe, it was when he felt God was directing him to step down. Not that he did not have his own thoughts on the matter; he felt he had done what he could do as the executive director and had brought the ministry about as far as he was able. He had trained others for leadership and felt one of them would be able to take the ministry farther. The bottom line is that Moishe had the confidence to step down because he believed it was God's timing for him to do so. And he gave fair warning. He did not wait until there was a crisis and leave the organization in turmoil.

David Brickner was the council's choice as successor—and more importantly "God's choice," as Moishe and others I have talked with are quick to emphasize. I have no doubt of that. Though at first I thought David rather young to fill those size sixteen shoes, I soon observed the force of his personality and his maturity in dealing with difficult issues. I have seen him relaxed in his home with his wife, Patti, and the kids—a devoted husband and father. I have noticed the camaraderie he has with his extended Jews for Jesus family, the easy manner and quick wit. I see *in him not only a leader of a Jewish mission organization, but also a leader in the broader Christian world as we move into the twenty-first century.*

*The Lord said in Zechariah 12:10: "I will pour out a spirit of compassion and supplication on the house of David." David surely would not want Jews for Jesus to be referred to as "the house of David Brickner." Yet in a real sense, this organization is the house of Messiah, David's Greater Son. As such, it has received God's blessings—past, present, and hopefully future.*

*The passage in Zechariah foretells a time when the Jewish people, "the inhabitants of Jerusalem," will "look on the one whom they have pierced" and "mourn for him, as one mourns for an only child.... On that day a fountain shall be opened for the house of David and the inhabitants of Jerusalem, to cleanse them from sin and iniquity." In reflecting on this passage, David Brickner writes: "That is our destiny. That is where Jews for Jesus is headed. We don't know all the steps between the here and now and the future God promised. We have a sense that God is using us to pave at least part of the way for the great events to come."[1]*

—Ⓜ—

In 1996, at age sixty-four, Moishe Rosen stepped aside as executive director of Jews for Jesus. He had announced his plan to the senior staff some four years earlier, but to those outside the ministry it came as quite a surprise. In fact, the event was seen by some observers as extraordinary. Marcia Ford of *Charisma* magazine wrote, "In a move virtually unheard of in ministry circles, Jews for Jesus founder Moishe Rosen stepped aside as executive director in May and gave the ministry's nine-member advisory council control over who his successor would be..." Moishe later said:

Our people have been trained to discern God's leading.

They didn't need me to tell them who God wanted in this position. I expressed no preference....

I realized that our organization needed a younger, more dynamic leader. When you're the founder, your own shortcomings become incorporated into the organization. I had taken Jews for Jesus as far as I could.

It was time for a change—though I'm still probably the most radical person on the staff.[2]

Moishe insists that he has not retired; he has merely relinquished his position of executive director. Since stepping down, his life has not been filled with golfing, fishing, or lolling on the beach. He never learned to golf; too much sun makes him physically ill; and he hates sand between his toes. While he enjoys the idea of fishing, he has not had much time for that. He continues to serve on the board of directors, writes and speaks for the organization, and spends quite a bit of time witnessing to people on-line.

## AN ASCENSION TO LEADERSHIP

The leadership [of Jews for Jesus] has been transferred to David Brickner, one of the young people Moishe trained. Moishe did not make the decision. There were a number of leaders who were qualified to assume the directorship, and their names were nominated for the position. Of the seven final candidates, David was the youngest. It was not until the fifth ballot, however, that David received the most votes. It was a matter of voting once, voting twice, and again, and again, and again until the process ended in a unanimous decision. But it was far more than a political process. The election had been preceded by a full day of fasting and prayer.[3]

From the testimony of a local pastor who observed the proceedings that night, but who did not vote, it was a deeply spiritual experience. When the vote was decided on the fifth ballot, "It just seemed as though the Holy Ghost fell," he recalls. With the unanimous vote the weeping began, and they all gathered around David to lay hands on him and commission him for the work. Susan Perlman, one of the seven candidates, later reflected on the process: "It was beautiful to see brothers and sisters not jockeying for position but looking to see what God wanted to do."[4]

Citing Romans 11:5, where Paul speaks of the Jews as "a remnant according to the election of grace," David, a fifth-generation believer in Jesus as Messiah, testifies of the deep roots of his Jewish heritage:

I am a modern-day echo of Paul's ancient refrain. My great, great, grandfather Rabbi Levi Yitzhak Glaser (on my mother's side) was a chief rabbi in Zhitomir, Ukraine in the 1800s. First his daughter, and then his wife became believers in Jesus. My great grandmother Esther and her husband Julius Finestone (also a "Jew for Jesus") had a fruitful ministry among the Jewish people in Odessa. After Julius passed away Esther married Wolf Kendal—another Jewish believer. They ministered to the Jews in Odessa, London and eventually Toronto, Canada.

My grandfather, Fred Kendal, grew up in Toronto, attended Moody Bible Institute and was married in Toronto. After my mother was born, he moved to Detroit where he started a ministry called "Israel's Remnant." People used to come into the store looking for pieces of carpet from the Holy Land! Yet God used my grandfather Fred's ministry to bring my father and his entire family to faith in the Messiah. My heritage is indeed beautiful to me as I stand on the shoulders of giants of the faith, those who have gone before us and have served so faithfully.[5]

## A JEWISH-CHRISTIAN HERITAGE

This brief reflection on David's family background gives only the outline of a remarkable story. The drama began in the nineteenth century in the Jewish quarter of Zhitomir. The lead character was Esther, one of three surviving children of parents who saw six of their little ones die. Esther's father was a rabbi and a distinguished leader of the Chassidim, a very devout Jewish sect. Disappointed that his son was not devoted to the faith, he took great pleasure in little Esther's depth of spiritual discernment. She, in turn, revered her father as one who could do no wrong. Esther's happy childhood ended at fifteen when her beloved father died after a brief illness. On the tenth day after his death, as was the custom, she went with her mother to her father's grave.

As she stood there, she felt as if her heart would break. Then tender memories came to comfort her. As she thought of her father, she could almost feel again his hands laid on her head in blessing and hear him say,

"May God bless you my child and make you as Sarah, Rebekah, Rachel, and Leah." She pictured him as he had looked on seder night, robed in white, seated on a throne of cushions teaching the beautiful Passover service from the yellowed pages of the *Haggada*. What a good man he had always been.[6]

Soon after her father's death, Esther learned that her beloved second cousin, Julius Finestone, had become a Christian. She had always looked up to him, and the two had been very close. The news of his seeming defection devastated her. "One shocking fact stood out for her. Her idol had fallen. Julius had forsaken the Faith of his Fathers and was now *posch Israel* (apostate)!"

When Julius left the village, Esther was glad he was gone and that he had taken his new Messiah with him—out of her life forever she assumed. But two years later, she received an unexpected letter from Constantinople. Julius was lonely for home—and for Esther. He enclosed a photo of himself, and she responded with a photo of herself. His next letter brought a completely unexpected question: "Would she be willing to take the name Finestone?" She was shocked. "Marry a renegade! She, the daughter of Rabbi Levy Yitzchok! What a shame and disgrace that would be!"[7]

Her first inclination was to ignore his letter entirely, but she could not push him out of her thoughts. He had not mentioned Jesus in his letters, and that was a good sign. Besides that, her brother-in-law spoke very highly of him, and surely she would be able to win him back to the faith of their fathers. She wrote back, agreeing to come to Constantinople with her mother to marry him, only to hear back from him that the marriage would have to be postponed due to his failed business venture. But Esther was not easily dissuaded. She finalized her travel plans and sent word ahead that she was coming despite his financial problems. So they married. Esther kept her Jewish faith, and Julius held to his belief in Jesus—and it seemed to work out.[8]

The incident that changed Esther's heart was the conversion of Enoch, an Orthodox Jew who had studied in Jerusalem. When Enoch began working with Julius, she was hopeful that he would bring him back to the Jewish faith. But the exact opposite occurred. Julius convinced Enoch that Jesus was the Messiah.[9]

Esther was so distraught that she could not sleep that night. Could it possibly be true that Jesus is the Messiah? "All night this thought revolved in her mind. The next day when she was alone, she locked her door, and for the first time in her nineteen years knelt down to pray...." She asked God to give her the truth. Then she went to the workroom where Julius was working on his lathe and asked if he would take the time to read some Scriptures to her.... He turned to Isaiah 53, and read:

He was wounded for our transgressions,
He was bruised for our iniquities:
The chastisement of our peace was upon Him;
and with His stripes we are healed.

Upon hearing those words, Esther knew in her heart that she had found the truth. Jesus was the one of whom Isaiah wrote.[10]

Not long after her conversion, Esther and Julius, with their baby boy, moved back to Odessa, where they became actively involved in Jewish evangelism. Among the converts were Esther's nieces and years later her sister. During that time, Julius served as a representative for the Mildmay Mission to the Jews with headquarters in London. This activity brought persecution—sometimes physical attacks—but that ministry continued until a fateful workday afternoon. Julius, not yet forty years old, was working at the bench as usual when he suffered a heart attack. He died later that night.[11]

The next three years were very difficult for Esther, but eventually she married Wolfe Kendal. A Jewish Christian widower with no children, Wolfe had been a friend of Julius. In fact, his first wife had become a follower of Jesus through Esther's ministry. Two years after Wolfe and Esther married, they moved to London, where Esther bore two more children and served for seven years with the Mildmay Mission. In 1910 the Kendals moved to Toronto, where Esther continued her ministry to Jewish people for the next seventeen years. According to her biographer, she was committed to Jewish evangelism: "She was devoted to her own people, and was undaunted by their slowness of heart to believe, or by the most vigorous opposition. God rewarded her zeal and faith with a harvest of souls."[12]

Esther continued her ministry until her health began to fail in the 1940s. She died in 1950, leaving behind a remarkable legacy.

> Her eldest son Rev. Isaac Finestone became Director of the Messengers of the Covenant in Newark, N.J.... A young son Rev. Daniel Finestone worked in Philadelphia for 32 years and founded "The Presbyterian Hebrew Christian Congregation.... [Her] daughter Emma Kendal Glass is married to the Rev. Arthur E. Glass who...after pioneering a Hebrew Christian Congregation in Buenos Aires...returned to America [to]...work among Jewish people in Hot Springs, Arkansas. The youngest son Rev. Fred Kendal became founder and Director of Israel's Remnant.... A granddaughter is married to Rev. Albert Brickner...[who also served with] Israel's Remnant.[13]

The granddaughter mentioned is David's mother, Leah Brickner. David's father Avi Brickner, also a Jewish believer, was the first in his family to profess faith in Jesus as Messiah. He and Moishe became friends and colleagues in Jewish evangelism back in the 1960s, and Moishe has described him as "one of the bright lights in Jewish missions."

David grew up surrounded by Jewish people who believed in Jesus. In fact, he thought that all Jewish people believed in Jesus—until he started school: "Then I quickly found out it was otherwise."[14] His father served for a time as the director of Israel's Remnant, and today his parents live in Israel and continue to devote their lives to ministry to Jews.

Despite his upbringing, it was not until his teen years that David put his faith in Jesus. An encounter with Jews for Jesus set in motion a chain of events that led to his decision. They were distributing broadsides at Boston University, where David had enrolled in a music course.

David later recalled how he first came to know Christ:

> Being born in a Christian home didn't make me a Christian any more than being born in a bakery makes you a bagel.... I attended a Bible study offered by Jews for Jesus and was impressed with the

quality of their lives. I realized that, even though I'd been taught that Jesus was my Messiah, I'd never made a commitment to him.[15]

David had good reason to join the Jews for Jesus staff, having seen the fruit of this ministry in his own life. He graduated from Moody Bible Institute in 1981 with a diploma in Jewish Studies. He completed his bachelor's studies at Northern Illinois University in conjunction with Spertus College of Judaica, earning a B.A. in Judaica with a minor in music. He picked up his education the following decade, earning his master's degree in missiology at Fuller Seminary, School of World Missions, in Pasadena, California.

David joined the staff of Jews for Jesus in 1981 and completed many leadership assignments prior to becoming executive director in 1996. He led The Liberated Wailing Wall, the Chicago branch, and the flagship branch in New York. He served as minister at large and director of recruitment, and he gained international experience as portfolio holder and board member of Jews for Jesus South Africa.

However, no amount of experience can prepare a person to take over as the first successor to a founding executive director. For one thing, Moishe's leadership grew along with the ministry. He did not begin as a director of an international ministry; he began with a handful of hippies. But more important, he did not begin with a group of his contemporaries.

## A SELECTION PROCESS

Moishe knew that the organization's senior leaders would now have to submit to the authority of a peer. The next executive director would not be a father figure to them. Moishe removed himself from the selection process because he felt the choice should be theirs. They would have to commit themselves to following one of their own crowd—despite the fact that some who would not be chosen might feel just as qualified for the task. Nevertheless, Moishe did not hand down the rules as to who would choose his successor. Those procedures had been outlined in the ministry's bylaws long before Moishe ever dreamed of stepping down. According to those procedures, the nine council members entrusted with the task of nominating Moishe's successor had to reach a unanimous decision. As difficult a task as that may seem, it is even more remarkable in light of the fact that three of the voting members of the council were themselves slated as possible candidates. So in May 1996 in the upper room of the ministry's hospitality house, there was much prayer, much discussion, but a surprisingly brief period of voting before a new chapter of Jews for Jesus history began.

The Jews for Jesus Board of Directors unanimously accepted the council's choice—and David was elected. He was officially installed and stepped into the office in September 1996.

## CATCHING THE VISION

David has seized the vision of Jews for Jesus—a vision that has driven Moishe since 1973. Perhaps David's greatest challenge is to hold fast to the principles that have made Jews for Jesus what it is, while daring to step out and make changes he believes are necessary. To that end, David engaged the staff in the process of formulating a mission statement as well as a statement of core values. It was a way for the staff to reaffirm why the organization exists and what principles they hold dear, regardless of who the executive director is.

If David is successful in knowing what to keep and what to change, Jews for Jesus will remain a highly principled organization on the cutting edge of creative communications, whatever form that may take in the future. There will probably be a gradual shifting in roles and responsibilities between the older and younger leaders. But David and the rest of the staff want Jews for Jesus to be what it has always been: a group of adventurous and imaginative Jewish people who love Jesus and are called together to lift up his name so that others will be drawn to him.

The apostle Paul is often identified as the Apostle to the Gentiles, but Romans 1:16 captures his heartbeat: "to the Jew first and also to the Gentile." Jews for Jesus continues to reach out to the Jewish people first, but also makes a very conscious endeavor to reach non-Jews. Indeed, each year more Gentiles than Jews come to faith in the Messiah through this ministry. But as they evangelize, Jews for Jesus also challenges other Christians to support mission outreach to Jewish people. "The majority of evangelical believers and churches," David observes, "do not actively support missions to the Jews or specifically pray for the salvation of Jewish people. And even among those who do support Jewish missions, we find some who do so as more of an afterthought than a strategic commitment."[16]

In his book, *Mishpochah Matters,* David concludes with a powerful illustration of missions that demonstrates a biblical pattern for mission outreach:

> Hudson Taylor, who founded the China Inland Mission, had a tradition for starting each year. Every New Year's Day, he sent a check to the Mildmay Mission to the Jews in London. On each check he wrote, "To the Jew first."
>
> Simultaneously, John Wilkinson, leader of the Mildmay Mission, sent his personal check to the China Inland Mission with the notation, "And also to the Gentile."
>
> These two great nineteenth-century missionaries recognized something that today's church must remember. The Jewish people are still God's chosen people. They must be our starting point for fulfilling the Great Commission.[17]

# A VISION FOR THE TWENTY-FIRST CENTURY AND BEYOND

What does the future hold for Jews for Jesus? The ministry has changed considerably over its twenty-five-year history. It has evolved from a rag-tag group of hippies into a highly structured corporate mission organization. It is efficient, professional, polished, and disciplined, but is it positioned to move into the twenty-first century with the same effectiveness it had in the 1970s? Will the generation that grew up with Moishe be able to convey the vision to the younger generation? This is truly the most challenging test for any leader. Moishe passed that test in transferring the mantle to David. Will David and the rest of the Jews for Jesus leadership be able to meet the challenge of training a new generation of Jewish people with the message of Jesus?

I see Joshua Sofaer, a missionary in Los Angeles and one of the "next" generation of Jews for Jesus, as a promising answer to that question. I met Joshua when he was participating in the New York campaign as the leader of "Halutzim," a group of high school students from around the country. Josh is one of several newer staff members interested in possible changes to help Jews for Jesus reach the younger generation. How will those changes be met by long-term staff members?

As I write these words, leaders from around the country are flying to San Francisco for the August council meeting. They will have to answer these and other questions because issues regarding the future will be on the agenda. Several younger leaders will be present to give input, along with the senior leaders. The future is here, and Jews for Jesus must have a contemporary message for the millennium generation. If it should fail in this, the real history of the movement will end here—with twenty-five years.

—ɯ—

In many ways, Josh Sofaer represents the younger generation. He is twenty-eight, and one of the youngest leaders on the Jews for Jesus staff. As the founder and developer of *Halutzim,* the summer ministry team of Jewish high schoolers for Jesus, Joshua has a key role in charting the future of the movement. Jews for Jesus does not approach people under eighteen without parental consent, so most of these kids have Jewish Christian parents, but they are strongly influenced by their peers. Josh has found that an amazing amount of ministry takes place when young people are encouraged to share their experiences and spiritual insights.

Like many Jewish people of his generation, Joshua was born into a secular Jewish family. He describes his father as a psychologist and soccer coach and his mother as a feminist. Unlike many from the hippie generation who attended Hebrew school and grew up observing at least some Jewish traditions, Joshua was raised with no religion at all.

After high school, with no interest in college, Josh and a friend planned a trip around the world. Josh reached New Zealand without any money to continue the trip, so he took a job at an apple orchard. The owners turned out to be Christians who were lay evangelists as well as fruit farmers. When they asked Josh what he believed about God, he replied (despite his lack of religion), "I'm Jewish." They gave him a Bible, and Josh began reading the book of Ecclesiastes. He was amazed by how relevant it was, and he began attending a Bible study. Through further reading and study, he came to faith in Christ.

When Josh told his parents over the telephone about his new faith, his mother was displeased, and his father was furious. Soon after, they paid for a three-month educational trip to Israel so he could learn about Judaism. Josh did not even make it through the first day before being asked to leave. There was no place for an evangelical Christian in the program that had been designed to bring people back to their Jewish roots.

Unlike many of the Jews for Jesus staff, Joshua is not interested in becoming part of a messianic congregation—at least not at this point. He has no synagogue foundation upon which to look back, so it means little to him.

Besides, many of the messianic congregations are *Ashkenazic,* meaning their traditions are based on European Jewry Josh's family traces its roots to Iraq. They are *Sephardic,* and if Josh were to explore his Jewish roots, the traditions and forms of worship would be quite different from those practiced by Jewish people of European heritage.

Josh was a young believer when he came in contact with David Brickner, who recruited him for a short-term program in Israel called, Project Joshua. After that, Josh served as a volunteer and worked part time with the organization in New York City while completing his education at Brooklyn College. Since that time, he has served as a full-time missionary in Los Angeles and headed the *Halutzim.*

Joshua insists that the future of Jews for Jesus depends on an understanding of the Jewish community as it moves into the twenty-first century. He and many others believe that Jewish people today differ markedly from the Jewish people of their parents' generation—a generation bound together by their memories of the Holocaust, the establishment of the State of Israel, and widespread testimonies of anti-Semitism. For decades, American Jews were bound together by a political-cultural-social glue that superseded belief in God or religion. But many believe that is no longer the case.

"It was always the ethnic impulse that seemed to be a preserver of Jewish identity," says Leonard Fein, a leading Jewish writer and activist. "A generation back, no Jew had to apologize for being an agnostic or an atheist. Even the Jewish atheists knew what the God in which they did not believe expected of them."

But the bagels-and-Bloomingdale's brand of Judaism is disappearing almost as fast as Yiddish did in the last generation. To begin with, many of the key ingredients in the ethnic alchemy that produce the Jewish persona have been soaked up and absorbed by the larger culture. As a result, the secular Jewish world is losing its distinctiveness. Jewish humor, the Jewish perspective, and the Jewish sensibility are all being subtly blended into the American mainstream.[1]

Josh would agree that Jewish culture is changing. It is difficult to know which of his views may change with time; for that matter, it is difficult to know where Jewish culture is headed. In any case, Josh is excited about investing in the next generation of Jews for Jesus, realizing that they are the ones who will be using whatever means they can to keep on making the messiahship of Jesus an unavoidable issue to Jewish people worldwide. He also expects that the ministry will have to make changes in order to accomplish this.

Josh is not the only advocate for change. David gave the leadership of both the 1998 and the 1999 New York Summer witnessing campaigns into the hands of newer leaders. Both years saw innovations. The senior leaders regarded some of them as improvements, but felt that others were errors in judgment. It is difficult for the old guard to refrain from pointing out what they view as mistakes. Nevertheless, David is committed to allowing the leaders to make real choices, and thus to make real mistakes. So far, he believes that the newer leaders are learning from those mistakes and that they are rethinking innovations that did not prove beneficial either to the effectiveness or overall well-being of the campaigners.

Issues of change and new leadership are difficult to resolve. How does one discern which changes are merely for the sake of change—for the sake of ego or to build oneself up by criticizing the old ways? Such changes could prove detrimental to the quality of ministry. It's not always so easy to discern which changes fall into that category and which changes are healthy and even necessary for the organization. It is difficult enough for a person to measure his or her own motivation, much less to have that motivation evaluated by others. So David is endeavoring to maintain an atmosphere of trust. Yet there is inevitable tension as some want changes to come faster, while others who were once considered radical are now somewhat set in their ways. David has instituted some changes rapidly such as the addition of a multimedia department to help keep the ministry abreast of cutting-edge communication. Yet he is cautious about making substantial changes to structure, and he is proactive in seeking consensus among senior leaders. No one, least of all the old-timers, wants to see Jews for Jesus lose its edge, but they know that that is the natural way of things and that they will have to struggle to keep it from happening.

Are Jews for Jesus open to change? "If we were not," says Avi Snyder, who coordinates worldwide ministry to post-Soviet Jews from New York City, "I would still be in Russia. But I'm not there because we have raised up the younger generation. They are taking over, and they are doing some new things."[2]

When Moishe Rosen was asked "What does the future hold for Jews for Jesus?" he replied: "My dream is to see it dissolve—that it will be so successful that there won't be a need for it anymore—because all Jews will know about Jesus. But in the meantime? We'll build and keep on building as long as we're needed."[3]

Part of this building is using cutting-edge technology—especially the Internet—to communicate creatively. Moishe is fond of reflecting back on the days when he and his young associates were sending shock waves through the Jewish community:

> In our early days, one observer noted that Jews for Jesus was "on the cutting edge of evangelism." Our high profile created quite a stir in the Jewish community. In a warning to its readers, the *Jewish Press* of Brooklyn reported that Rosen was just a front man, and it was obvious that he had Madison Avenue backing. Of course we didn't have such resources, but our message was reaching many. Whether or not people liked what we were saying, they could no longer ignore us. That was 25 years ago, when we only had the simplest tools of communication. Now we have greater access than ever to the public through all communications media.[4]

Moishe credits David Brickner for bringing Jews for Jesus into the era of high-tech.

David has been particularly interested in reaching this group of young people who are in their teens and twenties. They grew up knowing and using computers, and the Internet has become one of the chief tools by which to reach them. It is a viable means of communicating with thousands of people.... To this end, Jews for Jesus was one of the first Christian organizations to have a web page on the Internet. Within months, we received the "Top Five Percent Award" for our Internet presentation.[5]

Web sites, chat rooms, bulletin boards—all these are proving effective means of ministry. On the fourth floor of the New York office, the younger generation is actively reaching out on the information highway, contacting Jewish people who might never be reached through broadsiding.

David is very serious about seeing Jews for Jesus keep abreast of cutting-edge communications to meet the needs of each new generation, but Moishe's underlying philosophy on ministry has remained the same: "We take God seriously, but not ourselves. We've got something to say and we are being heard."6

Whereas Moishe began without a clue as to how far-reaching the ministry of Jews for Jesus would become, David has inherited the leadership of an international mission. No one on staff claims to know exactly how far God intends the ministry of Jews for Jesus to go. David has vision and will continue pushing to bring the gospel to every city in the world where there are significant Jewish populations. But in order to meet that destiny, he faces complex challenges.

Today's Jews for Jesus is not only a multicultural and multilingual organization; it is an intergenerational family venture. The success of this journey depends on trust. First and foremost Jews for Jesus needs to trust in God, but they also need to trust one another. The younger generation will need to trust some of the insights and judgments that only age and experience can offer. The older generation will need to trust the excitement and vision that comes with youth. Together, sharing a vision of mission, by God's grace they will prevail.

# MY VISION FOR
# JEWS FOR JESUS

AN ADDRESS BY DAVID BRICKNER, EXECUTIVE DIRECTOR
*Given to staff and supporters following his election in 1996*

T he Lord did not provide me with foreknowledge that I would be the next executive director of Jews for Jesus. Nevertheless, I have dreamed of what could be. And I do believe that God led the council in our prayerful deliberations. The process was a profoundly moving and humbling experience. Through it, many of us, myself included, came to love and appreciate our fellow workers more deeply. The gracious way in which the senior staff united to show their support went beyond our usual camaraderie. It demonstrated once again that the people on our staff are a rich treasure and the main asset of Jews for Jesus. That meeting impressed upon me a sense of duty to fellow staff, to our donors, and to the community who needs the message of the Messiah. Most of all I am conscious of my duty to the Lord as he leads us Jews for Jesus into a new era.

The words of Haggai the prophet have taken on special meaning to me in recent days. "'But now take courage,' declares the LORD...and work; for I am with you,' declares the LORD of hosts" (Haggai 2:4). Haggai was speaking to a group of people who had shared some amazing history together. After a generation of exile, the Lord had stretched out his hand to deliver our people out of captivity and back into his land of promise. That generation had much for which to be thankful. They saw God perform mighty acts of deliverance and restoration. Yet they became complacent. They failed to see that God wanted to accomplish much, much more. God wanted them to build his Temple.

Haggai's job was to stir them from their complacency, to challenge them to get to work, and to remind them that the Lord would be with them as they moved ahead. Some elders who remembered the previous temple were skeptical.

The glory days of the past were a precious memory, but for some who cherished those memories, the promise of the future paled in comparison to that glorious past. It was for these skeptics that the word of the Lord came:

"'Once more in a little while I am going to shake the heavens and the earth, the sea also and the dry land.... The latter glory of this house will be greater than the former,' says the LORD of hosts, 'and in this place I will give peace,' declares the LORD of hosts" (Haggai 2:6–9).

Jews for Jesus has made some truly remarkable history over the last twenty-three years, and you who have been supporting us have had a crucial part in that.

Under the leadership of Moishe Rosen, we have seen the growth and expansion of this ministry around the world. We have changed the shape of Jewish missions forever. Never again will Jewish evangelism be viewed as a futile enterprise.

We have changed the climate of opinion in the Jewish community over the past two decades. No longer can Jewish leaders make an incontrovertible statement: "Jews don't believe in Jesus." We have led the charge against that lie by declaring, "We are Jews for Jesus; now reckon with us." Has there ever been such a professional approach and such high ethical standards applied to missionary endeavor in our field?

I know of no other Jewish mission where such levels of creativity in music, drama, the arts, literature, and use of secular media have been fostered and applied so effectively. We have set the highest standards for effective evangelism, creative communication, integrity of approach, ethics in fund-raising, and responsibility in reporting. This is the enormous legacy we have received from the Lord through Moishe Rosen, and I for one am deeply, deeply grateful.

It would be all too easy for some of us to be like those in the days of Haggai. We could either become complacent with the present or skeptical regarding God's prospects for the future.

But I am confident that the best is yet ahead. I believe that the latter glory will be greater than the former. It will be greater because "We all, with unveiled face, beholding as in a mirror the glory of the Lord, are being transformed into the same image from glory to glory" (2 Corinthians 3:18). The transforming work of the Spirit of God in our own lives and in this ministry is essential to our future. It will be greater because God has a commitment to our success. He promised to equip us for every good work and Jews for Jesus is a good work. Indeed, the future must be greater because we are facing many challenges.

I am confident that with God's enabling, the wisdom of our board of directors, and the strength of the Jews for Jesus staff, these challenges will be springboards to growth. They will be opportunities to amplify the message of the gospel around the world to his greater glory. Let me outline some of the challenges I see becoming opportunities for growth.

## PRIORITY

We've established principles, policies, and procedures that have stood us in good stead. I am charged with the responsibility to preserve and protect the integrity and reputation of Jews for Jesus. I must insist we maintain those principles that are the very heart and soul of what has made Jews for Jesus who we are today. That means keeping our priorities straight.

I want to underscore that our priority was, is, and will remain direct evangelism. I intend to continue and strengthen the legacy of Jews for Jesus by maintaining that focus. We must evaluate each opportunity and even each challenge by answering the question, "How can we use this to accomplish our goal of bringing the gospel to our Jewish people?"

What you know and love about Jews for Jesus will remain the same: Count on us to speak to as many unsaved Jewish people about Jesus as we possibly can. That is my commitment in leading this ministry into the future.

We must not compromise our quality of commitment or lower our standards for ministry and accountability. We must not allow ourselves to be shaped by the weaknesses of the flesh or the standards of the world. We must be clay in the hands of the master potter who will glaze us in the kiln of fiery adversity so that we resist being shaped by the forces of society.

## PEOPLE

One serious challenge for the future is recruiting the right people. I was director of recruitment before I moved to New York City. That position made me painfully aware of the significance of Jesus' words, "The harvest is plentiful, but the workers are few. Therefore, beseech the Lord of the harvest to send out workers into His harvest" (Matthew 9:37–38). We need to be proactive in praying and aggressively recruiting more staff. We need to raise up more leaders from our existing staff so that we can take advantage of opportunities and face challenges as they present themselves.

Jews for Jesus is a place where people can grow and accomplish things for God. We are a tough, highly structured, and well-organized group. However, we also have a great deal of room for individuality, for people with fresh ideas. I believe that Jews for Jesus has always been the best possible place for those with initiative and creativity. We can offer such people a place on a team that especially values their gifts.

We have plenty of room at the top for women and men who aspire to leadership, who desire opportunities to grow, and who are willing to exert the effort to meet those opportunities. We do have structure and we must work hard. Some Christians want to invest themselves in a ministry like ours—one that is not always convenient and comfortable—when they see that they can achieve more through sacrificing convenience and comfort.

We are seeking people with godly ambitions. We are seeking those with special gifts and abilities—especially to help us explore some of the areas that we want to be moving into in the next few years. Jews for Jesus is a place where people can belong, where they can take personal ownership of the vision that is our lifeblood.

Last August I spoke to the council about developing a "come and see" model of ministry relationships. When two disciples of John the Baptist came to Jesus and asked where he was staying, he responded, "Come and see." We need to invite people to come and see where we live and work. Sometimes our commitment to professionalism has closed out non-professionals from taking part in ministry. This must change.

That change has already begun in some areas of the world where we employ outreach workers. The category of outreach worker enables people who might not meet all our criteria to nevertheless serve with us because they have a unique strength or have demonstrated a gift in ministry. Avi Snyder has found this most effective in the CIS. He has the freedom to hire as many quality outreach workers as he can afford to pay, and they are a tremendous help in the ministry there. I would like to expand this model to all of the branches in Jews for Jesus—not to replace, but to augment our regular missionary staff.

As part of this, I envision an internship program for new believers. We may call it a school of discipleship. We will bring promising young believers alongside our regular missionary staff in mentoring relationships. They will have ministry responsibilities and will raise support, but they will also learn and grow in their faith and in knowledge of Scripture and Christian doctrine. Young believers may be invited to live in the homes of missionaries who are mentoring them.

Again, our most precious resource is our staff. In order to recruit the brightest and best, we must continue to provide the best that we can for those who serve with us. We must commit ourselves to providing our workers and their families with ongoing opportunities for educational and spiritual enrichment. I am eager to continue our master's program, whereby many of our career missionaries have utilized their summers to gain a degree in missiology.

We recognize that cultivating godly living is the responsibility of each individual on our staff, but I will also look for ways to encourage our staff as they pursue godly living. The ministry-wide day of prayer was so helpful that I want to incorporate it as a quarterly exercise in our ministry. Therefore, three times a year, at the discretion of leadership, each station and headquarters will set aside a half day of prayer for the work of the ministry and a full day once a year.

We must continue to strengthen both the chaplaincy and the ombudsman program. Ours is a necessarily difficult and demanding work, and we must provide our people with the best nurture and encouragement we can.

## PROGRAMS

Over the years we have said, and I believe it to be true, that Jews for Jesus is on the "cutting edge of evangelism." Our pioneering use of the secular media, the development of Jewish Gospel music, our extensive broadside ministry, as well as our other publications have demonstrated this. However, as we approach the twenty-first century, dramatic changes in communications technology have called into question our claim to cutting-edge evangelism. We have some catching up to do—especially in the area of multimedia—if we are to be pacesetters. We need to develop new ways to communicate the Gospel via secular radio and television. We need to develop evangelistic commercials, "infomercials," animation shorts, instructional videos, and the like.

We have hesitated to move aggressively into these areas because we lack expertise, and there is so much at stake in terms of the cost. We need to address the questions of access and funding. Do I know how we should move ahead in this area? I do not. I do know that the opportunities are enormous, and therefore I am committed to developing a multimedia communications department.

We have begun to work in this area through the Internet. Rich Robinson has done an excellent job of getting us started. Already his work in this field has gotten us listed in the top ten religious web sites in Mark Kellner's new book, *God on the Internet.* Eleven hundred or more people visit our web site each week. In a recent one-month period we had a minimum of 4,400 different people visit our site as well as many repeat visitors. We are merely scratching the surface of what will certainly be one of the most important tools for communicating the gospel in the next century.

We will need to raise funds, assemble a staff, and learn how to gain access to the major media markets in order to communicate the gospel more effectively. We've utilized media campaigns as one of our most effective tools for outreach, but we have no comprehensive media strategy at this time. We are exploring the possibility of utilizing billboards and bus stop ads as well as advertisements on subway cars to proclaim our message this summer.

I would also like us to expand our publications. This is an area where our founder, Moishe Rosen, will be very much involved. I believe that there are several books he has yet to write, books that we must publish in the next couple of years. The most important is a book for Christians on how to witness to Jews. Moishe is already working on this. Another book Moishe needs to write is on ministry and missionary ethics.

We also need to publish a definitive discipleship guide for new Jewish believers. We have the "Growth Book," which is a very simple manual, but we need to expand it. I envision a guide that will utilize some of the best structure for teaching, such as the Navigators employ in their "Growing in Christ" booklet, but it will be geared specifically for Jews. I also would like to see us develop evangelistic booklets in a similar workbook format with text based on the Gospel of John, messianic prophecy, and apologetics. We can and should produce these tools. If we publish the high quality resources I want us to use in our own mission, we will also be making a widespread contribution to the church.

I also envision a language department as part of our publications. We need people to oversee the translating of evangelistic materials into Russian, Spanish, Hebrew, and French. I would like eventually to translate our newsletters and other materials for Christians into German, Korean, Chinese, and other languages. Many of these brothers and sisters are eager to share our burden for Jewish evangelism, and we've got to be able to communicate with them.

We need to produce more music to evangelize the lost and to edify the church. We need to encourage members of our staff who are musically gifted to exercise their gifts. I have asked Stephen Katz, our new music director, to submit a proposal for a new children's album.

I believe that the best songs have yet to be recorded, the best books have yet to be written, the best literature has yet to be developed, and the best methods of outreach have yet to be employed in proclaiming the gospel. We will initiate programs that begin to move us in these directions. But they will all need funding. We will continue the "pay as you go" approach that has kept us debt free over the past twenty-three years. Do I know how to get funding for these programs? Not yet, but, I believe that it is possible and we will find a way.

We have constantly been amazed at how God's people have gotten behind different ideas for outreach that we have presented to them. The first time we presented the opportunity for secular media campaigns, we were overwhelmed by the response. I believe that we will see God's people get behind these new programs as well.

## PROCESS

All of these ideas create another challenge in the area of management. When I start thinking along these lines, I begin to feel overwhelmed with the scope of my responsibilities. On one hand I take great comfort in the fact that Moishe was my age when he began the ministry of Jews for Jesus. Moishe's ability to manage the process of growth in Jews for Jesus required tremendous growth on his part. On the other hand, I recognize that Jews for Jesus was very different back then from what it is now. In a sense, Moishe grew along with the ministry. Well, I have not instantly gained the degree of wisdom and oversight that Moishe has developed over the last twenty-three years. In short, the ministry is bigger than my present ability to manage, as I believe it would be for any successor.

Therefore, it may be necessary for me to develop some different structures to oversee the growth of the ministry. I believe that our overall structure is sound. The board documents and the worker's covenant provide the proper framework for oversight in the ministry. The position of executive director carries a necessary degree of authority and responsibility. Nevertheless, the responsibilities that I decide to delegate will be crucial in overseeing growth. The leaders in this ministry have been my peers, and I will need to rely much more on their input than did my predecessor. The buck will stop with me, but I will need help before it gets there.

I envision a directorate of leaders who will serve as a cabinet of advisors to me. I will delegate broad areas of responsibility and authority to these cabinet members, and they will be accountable to me. The people in this directorate will oversee the work in wider geographic locations as well as programmatic areas. I will work very closely with them. This is an important managerial change that I am prayerfully considering. I believe it will greatly enhance the process of growth for the future.

## PLACES

A fifth challenge for this new chapter concerns the places where we will focus our efforts. Our ministry has been undergoing a process of internationalization since our first overseas branch opened in 1989. This has been tremendously exciting. It also has created unique challenges that we are still struggling to overcome. As we continue this internationalization process, we must recognize the need for changes in our outlook.

We have become a global ministry. Our roots, our heritage, and our history will always be in North America, but the face of Jews for Jesus is changing. Opportunities for growth in Europe require us to strengthen our European board and provide more interfacing between European, Canadian, South African, and United States boards. In the next century, it may very well be that a large share of our staffing will come from Europe. We must be prepared to fund, train, and direct the Jews for Jesus missionaries indigenously.

Another area I wish to explore is the future of our ministry in Israel. There used to be more Jews in the New York City area than anywhere else in the world. Today 4.4 million Jews live in Israel and the population is growing. We must move aggressively and strategically into this new frontier of ministry. Tuvya Zaretsky, our Israel portfolio holder, has eloquently stated in a recent *Christianity Today* article that Israelis will be best reached by other Israelis. I believe Tuvya is right. We must be prepared to cultivate and train Israelis to reach their own. We have moved slowly and deliberately, but now is the time for new energy to be applied to our work in Israel.

It may just be that Russians will contribute more to ministry in Israel and other areas of Jewish evangelism than English speaking missionaries. We need to get up to speed in our ability to train and deploy this new generation of Russian Jews for Jesus.

We have begun to make forays into Australia, and that part of the world promises great opportunities for Jewish evangelism. Australia is also significant because of its proximity to the Far Eastern nations, where we need to develop relationships with the church. One of the keys to funding will be the generation of new support. I believe that the Korean and Chinese churches are ready to hear how they can have a part in an effective ministry such as ours.

Having said all of this, I want to reiterate my commitment to New York City as our flagship branch. Historically this has been a fundamental commitment of Jews for Jesus. Moishe moved to San Francisco in order to reach New York City. I believe it must remain our major focus here in North America. It is still the crossroads of the world, the capital from which our best efforts must go forth.

If there is one regret I have in assuming my new responsibilities, it is leaving the work in New York City. In a sense though, I think I can see the hand of God in sending me to New York in advance of this election. Never before have I been so keenly aware of the need to reinvigorate that work. But this will require tremendous effort on our part and a certain amount of investment and allocation of resources. It will require more from the staff and more from the organization in general.

We need a team of some of our brightest and best missionaries in New York. I've learned the importance of making certain that we remain centered in Manhattan, and that presents a problem: adequate, affordable housing.

I propose that we purchase a brownstone in the Murray Hill district, which is in the same area as our Manhattan office. The facility should be large enough to house several families and singles. I have spoken on a preliminary basis with a member of our board about this idea, and we need to be prepared to move ahead with the board's help. I would like to ask the chairman of the board to reconstitute the properties committee of the board in order that we might expedite this process.

There is another committee that I would like to ask the chairman to reconstitute, which is our relocation committee. It was some ten years ago or so that the board looked into the feasibility of other locations for our headquarters. I do not want to move too quickly in this area, but I think that we need to be open to considering the relocation of our headquarters.

Back in 1973 none of us could have imagined the variety of places God had in mind for Jews for Jesus. It will help us to remember that wherever he might move us, each place is only a temporary dwelling, a way station on the road to our final destination. We should all be excited about where the Lord is taking us on this earth at this time.

## CONCLUSION

I hope you agree with me that this is an expansive and exciting vision. I will need the strength of the staff, the wisdom of the board, the prayers and support of all our friends, and the grace of our great God to move ahead. I covet your prayers for me, for Patti, and the children as we move back to San Francisco.

When Haggai spoke to the people of his day and promised that the glory of the latter would be greater than the former, it was hard for many of his contemporaries to believe. The challenges were so big. The resources were so limited. How could they compete with "the good old days?" Those people needed the eyes of faith and the strength of the Spirit. The glory of the latter would indeed be greater than the former. Haggai's words were fulfilled and the Lord Jesus himself walked in that second temple they were starting to build. The people of Haggai's day did not live to see the fulfillment of that promise, but it was true nonetheless.

I believe that God has a great and glorious future for Jews for Jesus, but the glory of our future will be greater only insofar as Y'shua walks in our midst to make it great. More than anything in the world, I long for the presence and power of the living God to fill our lives, to direct our thoughts, and to bring his plans and purpose to fruition in our midst. May our commitment and obedience to him grow ever greater, so that all the greater glory goes only to him.

# QUESTIONS AND ANSWERS ON JEWS, JEWISHNESS, AND JEWS FOR JESUS

Yesterday *Yonat Shimron of the* Raleigh News and Observer *called to ask me questions about messianic Jews for a story she is writing. A good friend of mine who knew of my research for this book had put her in touch with me. Yonat was born in Israel and has strong ties with the Jewish community, though she is not particularly observant when it comes to religion. I explained to her that I was writing the history of Jews for Jesus and that messianic congregations, the focus of her story, were not my specialty. Still, she was eager to talk. We went right to the heart of the matter: the claim that one cannot be Jewish and a Christian at the same time and that you cannot mix the two.*

*"Says who?" I asked rhetorically. Christianity is a "mix" of Old Testament Judaism and the teachings of the New Covenant. For a Jew to become a Christian yet remain Jewish is not, as so many protest, a matter of mixing religions because they have already been "mixed." It is a mixing of one's culture and heritage with a faith that began in one's own backyard, so to speak. Christianity began in a Jewish culture. The mixing occurred as Jewish missionaries like Paul and Barnabas encouraged Gentiles to adopt the faith. Two thousand years later, the Jewish roots of Christianity are all but forgotten by those whose ancestors first practiced it.*

*Questions like Yonat's and other arguments lead to hot debates in the arena of Jewish-Christian relations, particularly concerning those who identify as messianic Jews. I find these questions fascinating, although I am in many cases still uncertain about the answers. In the pages that follow, I present questions and answers, points and counterpoints. In some cases I present answers from Jewish rabbis and make no response to their statements. I include them to demonstrate the force of their arguments and to show you, my readers, the types of issues that are on the minds of serious thinkers on both sides of the debate.*

—m—

**Q: Is it wrong to "mix religions" like Christianity and Judaism?**

**A:** One statement often repeated about messianic Jews is that they mix Christianity and Judaism into a hybrid religion that is not considered authentic by adherents to either religion. Bernie Farber, former director of research for the Canadian Jewish Congress, says, "It is the bastardization of Jewish traditions and rituals...that antagonizes Jews." He goes on to say that the "mixing and matching" debases both Christianity and Judaism.[1]

Arguments could be made against mixing and matching contemporary Jewish doctrines with Christianity, but to claim that it is wrong to blend Christianity and those Jewish beliefs or traditions that do not contradict the New Testament defies history and logic. Christianity began as a Jewish sect. Messianic Jews who go back to their roots follow the path of first-century Jews who followed Jesus, and they should not be viewed as bastardizing a religion any more than other religious movements that have taken traditions and rituals from the religions from which they developed.

**Q: Did Jesus and Paul begin an entirely new religion?**

**A:** Most Jewish people view Christianity as an entirely separate religion from Judaism. Many believe that Jesus founded this "new religion" and that Paul and others further developed it. They would say that Jesus and Paul clearly separated themselves from Judaism and the Old Testament law. A more contemporary and perhaps more popular variation is that Jesus never intended to create a new religion, but that Paul twisted his teachings to make them acceptable to non-Jewish masses.

Neil Altman, a messianic Jew from Philadelphia and an expert on the Dead Sea Scrolls offers a counterpoint:

Though Jesus decried religious hypocrisy, He never preached against Judaism, but against sin—the failure to keep God's standards. Jesus said He did not come to destroy the [Mosaic] Law but to fulfill it. Neither Jesus nor the apostle Paul tried to create a new religion.[2]

Writer Lloyd Gaston noted in an article titled "Paul and the Torah" that the apostle "took for granted that the Law of Moses was still binding on Jewish believers...."[3] Paul's responsibility was to teach the Gentiles which of the laws of Torah (the first five books of the Bible) applied to them, such as the moral and ethical laws and which did not, such as the ceremonial laws (keeping kosher, circumcision, sabbaths, etc.)[4]

**Q: How do Jewish people view their history in light of Christianity?**

**A:** Emil Fackenheim, a renowned Jewish philosopher of the late twentieth century, sums up what many Jewish people have learned from their childhood:

> The Holocaust was the culmination of a 2,000-year campaign by the Christian world against the Jews. It began early on with them telling us, "You cannot live here as Jews." And in country after country, they forced us to convert. Later the message became, "You cannot live here." And in country after country, they forced us to leave. Hitler's message was, "You cannot live." And they exterminated one third of our people."[5]

**Q: Who is a Jew?**

**A:** The question of Jewish identity is hotly debated within the Jewish community; Jewish people have differing views of who is a Jew and who is not. Yet, according to Dov Aharoni, an Orthodox rabbi, the issue becomes complicated only when dealing with non-Jews who wish to convert. But when it comes to anyone who was born Jewish, the matter is simple.

> I do not understand why the subject of "Who Is a Jew" must be debated in an atmosphere so filled with hyperbole and even mendacity—and so bereft of simple facts.

No Orthodox rabbi would even contemplate reading out of Judaism those of our people who are non-observant. Reform Jews, Conservative Jews, Reconstructionist Jews, Humanistic Jews, atheistic Jews, homosexual Jews, Hare Krishna Jews, Moonie Jews, and Jews for Jesus—all these—are every bit as Jewish as are Orthodox rabbis. In taking such a position, Orthodox rabbis are not being "lenient" or "nice guys"; rather, they are consistent with the fundamental Halachic creed that a Jew even though he has transgressed Torah law, remains a Jew. Even if he wants out.

The Jew who intermarries, then, is a Jew, and we Orthodox believe that he will be so all his life. If he "converts" to his spouse's faith system, we maintain that his conversion is null and void, despite what he may think. The poor fellow is stuck. If, later in his life, he wishes to teshuvah—to return—he need not convert. He never left.... These are the facts, plain and simple. No Jew can ever be legislated out of Judaism.[6]

**Q: Does the Bible say it is possible to lose one's Jewishness?**

**A:** Rabbi BenTzion Kravitz says yes. He points to a passage in the Old Testament, from which he infers his answer, though many Christians, including Jews for Jesus, would argue that the passage does not support his conclusion regarding Jews who believe in Jesus.

So-called "Hebrew-Christians" argue that a person who is born Jewish can never lose his birthright or heritage. However, the Bible teaches that your beliefs do influence your Jewish status and that a person who was born a Jew can at some point temporarily cease to be called a Jew.

We learn this from the biblical story in First Kings 18, where Elijah the prophet is sent to rebuke Jews who were worshipping a foreign god called Baal. Elijah says to him, "How long will you waver between two opinions? If the Lord is G-d, follow Him: but if Baal follow him." You are either a Jew or a worshipper of Baal; you can't be both.

We see from the end of this story that a Jew does remain Jewish to the point that he retains a spiritual obligation to live a Jewish life and must repent and return to Judaism if he has gone away. But as long as his beliefs are idolatrous and foreign to Judaism, he can't call himself a Jew. Obviously a non-practicing Jew is different from a Jew who has chosen to follow a foreign path.[7]

**Q: Who and what do Jewish people say the Messiah is?**

**A:** While through the centuries a significant minority of Jews have accepted Christ, the majority of Jewish people have rejected the claim that Jesus is the Messiah. The issue is not simply a matter of *who* is or is not the Messiah; it is also a matter of *what*. *What* is the Messiah? Jewish views on this vary, but each Jewish expert presumes to represent all of Jewry in this regard, as in the case of Professor Lawrence Schiffman of New York University:

> Jews have always believed in the notion of an end of days in which religious and even temporal life would far surpass that which we experience in our own time. These ideas are rooted in the Bible and are traceable in a number of sources. In Second Temple times they were articulated in a variety of texts as what we know as the messianic concept. This belief expects that a human leader of great proportions, the messiah, will lead the people of Israel in a religious and national revival and reestablishment of old glories of the Davidic era.
>
> This messiah in Jewish tradition has no divine nature nor does he have the power to abrogate or modify our obligation to observe the laws of the Torah. His coming will only be recognized when, under his leadership, the Jewish people realize their dreams and aspirations for the perfect society in the land of Israel and the surrounding world. The belief in a messiah or a messianic era of this kind has become normative in the Jewish community for two millennia.[8]

**Q: Why didn't most first-century Jews accept Jesus and his teaching?**

**A:** Rabbi Jacob Neusner offers a thoughtful response to this question in his book *A Rabbi Talks with Jesus*. Here he seeks to put himself back in the first century and explain why he could not accept the teachings of Jesus. He argues that although Jesus insisted he did not come to "abolish the Torah and the prophets...but to fulfill them," he did abolish them through his seeming indifference to the Law. Neusner points not only to the Sabbath, but also to laws of ritual purity. "What bothers me in Jesus' harsh judgments about the scribes and Pharisees," says Neusner, "is that I'm one of those people who do the things that the scribes and Pharisees observe." How can Jesus reinterpret the Torah? What right does he have to do that? Neusner would ask him, "Who do you think you are—God?"9

But it is not merely Jesus' radical claim of divine authority that bothers Neusner, nor his call to radical discipleship which seems to conflict with the responsibilities of hearth and home. No, something more troubles him. Jesus' message does not appear to be directed primarily at the Jewish people as a whole, to eternal Israel, which, for Neusner, is the core of rabbinic Judaism: the covenant between God and the Chosen People....

What counts for Jesus is moral righteousness, the Christian will argue, the goodness within the human heart. Jesus demands a righteousness "that exceeds that of the scribes and Pharisees." Anything that gets in the way of this interior moral righteousness for example, laws that demand adulteresses to be stoned or prohibits pious Jews from eating with prostitutes and tax-collectors—Jesus opposes.

For Neusner, however, as for other Jews, morality is not the only thing that counts. Holiness, being set apart as a chosen people among the nations, is also important, and the laws for ritual purity that Jesus ignores or deems less important are, he says, very important. The Jews are to be holy because God, in the Torah, commands them to be holy.10

**Q: How do some Jewish people respond to the idea of a crucified Messiah?**

**A:** According to Rabbi Fuchs, it is the doctrine of the crucifixion that says more about the character of God than of Jesus. Fuchs refers back to the Genesis account of how Abraham took Isaac to Mount Moriah to sacrifice his son, Isaac. But God stopped him. "The lesson is that no true religion requires human sacrifice in its name.... Human sacrifice is abhorrent to the God we

worship." From this story of Abraham, Fuchs moves to the idea of the crucifixion: "It is an abhorrent, unforgivable act to God. The gospel idea that
God would sacrifice his son is antithetical to Jewish teaching from that day
to this."[11]

**Q. How do Jewish leaders respond to the Old Testament prophecies?**

**A:** Many passages in the New Testament point to Old Testament prophesies
as fulfilled in Jesus. Rabbi Stephen Fuchs argues that the later developments
in the New Testament are anything but a fulfillment of biblical prophecies.
His is a typical Jewish response that maintains that the New Testament was
written purposely to "fulfill" Old Testament prophecies. He offers an illustration:

> Once there was a man riding through the countryside in his wagon.
> He came upon a long barn, and on the side of the barn were several
> targets. Right smack in the middle of the bull's eye in each and every
> target was an arrow.
>
> The man stopped his carriage and said, "I must meet this
> person who shoots so perfectly every time." So he stopped his car-
> riage and found the owner of the barn. He asked him, "How is it
> that you never miss hitting the dead center of the bull's eye every
> time you shoot your arrow?"
>
> It's quite easy," the man answered. "You see, first I shoot the
> arrow into the barn, and then I draw the target around it."
>
> How do New Testament writings show that Jesus life and
> actions comply with predictions in Hebrew scriptures? It's easy. New
> Testament writers wrote their stories so that their accounts of Jesus'
> life would match the prophetic passages which they knew so well
> from Hebrew scriptures."[12]

**Q: Is the term "Jew for Jesus" a contradiction?**

**A:** Rabbi Stephen Fuchs backs his point of view by quoting an interchange
from a radio call-in show. Don Finto, a Christian minister, was on the program. Fuchs says:

For me, the highlight of the evening occurred when [a woman] called to ask Dr. Finto, "When a Christian gives up Jesus to convert to Judaism, is he still a Christian?" "No" was his answer, and "Bingo!" was my unspoken response. That's the point. A Jew for Jesus is every bit as much a contradiction in terms as a Christian Not for Christ."[13]

If a Christian renouncing Christ no longer is a Christian, the rabbi says, a Jewish person embracing Christ is no longer a Jew. He makes a tremendous leap in logic to connect the two. In one instance you have a logical conclusion that a person cannot be a Christian if he or she turns away from Christ. By definition, a Christian is a follower of Christ. In order to make his point, the rabbi would have to say that a Jew, by definition, is one who does not follow Christ. But most Jewish people would not agree that the definition of a Jew is based on a particular religious belief. The rabbi in this story uses the terms *Judaism* and *Jew* interchangeably, but surely he knows better. To be a true believer in the religion of Judaism would exclude the belief in Jesus as Messiah, whereas the definition of "Christian" relates precisely to belief. The definition of Jew or Jewish does not pertain only to religion. In fact, the Jewish community contains people who embrace a wide array of religious beliefs, including agnosticism and even atheism.

**Q: Why do many Jewish people feel threatened by Jews for Jesus?**

**A:** Rabbi Stephen Fuchs responds:

People ask me, "Why do Jews for Jesus campaigns cause you such pain? Why do you feel a need to respond so forcefully?" My answer is that I have learned the lessons of history.... In country after country after country, Christians have lovingly expressed their concern for our salvation and invited us to accept Jesus. Over and over and over again, when we refused that invitation, that love has turned to venom and hatred. Often it has led to expulsion and death....

If one wishes to be a Christian, I hope that path brings him or her spiritual fulfillment. But he or she cannot be a Jew at the same time. So if the campaign to bring Jews to Jesus meets with its ultimate success, if it reaches its ultimate goal and every Jew becomes Christian, then the end result will indeed be as if Hitler had won the war. There will be no more Jews. That, in a nutshell, is why these campaigns cause such pain.[14]

Most literature seems to indicate that the Jewish community is less concerned about losing members to atheism than to belief in Jesus. Perhaps part of the answer can also be found in the fact that many studies indicate that the messianic movement is growing while Judaism itself is declining in numbers.

**Q: Are messianic Jews traitors?**

**A:** This is a common accusation against Jews for Jesus and other Jewish people who believe Jesus is the Messiah. Some go so far as to say that the evangelistic ministry of these Jewish Christians is equivalent to another inquisition or Holocaust. They say that these believers are despicable. Yet, as Neil Altman points out, some of the most loyal and "patriotic" Jewish people are those who wholeheartedly believe the Scriptures—both Old and New Testaments:

> Messianic Jews recognize that God gave the land of Israel to Abraham, Isaac, and Jacob and their descendants for an inheritance forever. A divine mandate accompanied this: God would bless those that blessed Israel and the Jewish people, and curse all those that were against them. Accordingly Jewish believers see that it is imperative for America to aid Israel in order to sustain the blessing. History is littered with great nations that disregarded the divine curse by going against Israel or the Jewish people.[15]

**Q: Are messianic Jews deceptive?**

**A:** Some Jewish observers say yes, but where there is a difference of opinion perhaps it would be more logical for Jews who do not believe in Jesus to say that those who do are simply wrong. While many attribute motives like deception, others do not. In describing a messianic congregation in Israel, Michele Chabin writes. "Anyone happening upon the congregation for the first time would think, at least initially, that they were attending some sort of Jewish service or sing-along." But she goes on to admit: "In truth, there is nothing really hidden or closeted about Kehilat Brit Yerushalayim. Anyone who knows Hebrew or takes the time to read the brochures will figure it out at a glance."[18]

**Q: Is it wrong for Christians to tell Jewish people they need Jesus?**

**A:** Rabbi Stephen Fuchs, from Congregation Ohabal Shalom in Nashville, argues that Jewish people are excluded from the Great Commission.

> Unfortunately, from my perspective, fundamentalist Christians talk of their unavoidable claim to follow the "Great Commission" of the 28th chapter of the book of Matthew and other passages in the New Testament to bring the word of Jesus to all the nations. But, according to my friend and my teacher, Prof. A. J. Levine, who has been a frequent speaker at this Temple, the "Gentile nations" is the reference in Matthew 28. The Greek word often translated as "nations" has a similar connotation to the Hebrew word *goyim,* which means all the nations except the nation and the people of Israel.[17]

A woman once wrote, "Rabbi, how can we not proclaim Jesus to you? If you had cancer, and I had the cure for cancer, would it not be an act of friendship and love for me to share my cure with you?" His answer was that his faith was complete and he had "no need of any cure or any outside savior." He then went on to offer a response based on his biblical beliefs:

> If I wanted to put the argument in biblical terms, I would do it this way. Did God make a covenant with Abraham? Of course, God did. God promised the Jewish people protection, progeny, permanence as a people, and property, the Land of Israel. In return, God stipulated that we, the children of Israel, had to be a blessing in their lives (Genesis 12:2). We have to walk in God's ways and be worthy

(Genesis 17:1). We have to be teachers and examples of justice and righteousness (Genesis 18:19). Those are the terms of the covenant in the book of Genesis that God established with Abraham and us, Abraham's descendants. Is that covenant irrevocable? Of course it is. Christian scripture says it over and over again. Is God a liar? Of course not. So I say to any Christians who would be my friend: We have our covenant with God. It is complete. It is irrevocable. God is not a liar. We have no need for Jesus.[18]

### Q: Why do some Christians say that Jewish people do not need Jesus?

A: After thirteen years of service, Rev. George J. Sheridan was dismissed from his position as director of the interfaith witness department of the Southern Baptist Home Mission Board over this issue. He accused the church of being guilty of the Marcion heresy—that the God of the Old Testament is different than the God of the New Testament.

> If God's covenant has been broken with the Jews, it's reasonable that other covenantal relationships might also be broken. Therefore, we in the church would be an endangered species.
>
> My point is that the covenant with the Jews was not abrogated.... I believe in Jesus Christ, that Jesus Christ is God, but for me to believe that the God of Jesus Christ is not the God of Jews rooted in their Scripture is the heresy of two different Gods.... I believe that the Jews of today, as ever, receive salvation through their having been chosen by God in covenant with Abraham, Moses and the prophets.
>
> The election of the church is prefigured in this election of Israel, and if the election of one is subject to cancellation, so, too, is the election of the other.[19]

### Q: What is two-covenant theology?

A: Two-covenant theology, as it has come to be known, suggests that God has two separate covenants—one for Jews and one for Christians. Jews for Jesus argue that this is heresy because it teaches there are two ways to be saved and because Jesus said "I am the way, the truth, and the life. No one comes to the Father except through me" (John 14:6). Why would God say the gospel is for the "Jew first" (Romans 1:16), if the Jewish people have no need of the gospel?[20]

In addressing the issue of the two-convenant theory, it is crucial to remember that the covenants God made with the Jewish people did not deal with forgiveness of sin or reconciliation with God. They dealt with promises regarding a land, a people, and a Messiah. Atonement, or forgiveness of sin, was not a covenantal issue. God had set up a system of atonement through substitutionary sacrifices as a means of reconciliation. Jewish believers in Jesus do not believe that God has turned away from his covenant with the Jewish people. In fact they believe that the Jewish religion has turned away from God's provision of atonement, a provision that reached its fulfillment with Jesus.

**Q: What about efforts at dialogue between Jews and Christians?**

**A:** Rabbi Mark Greenspan, the leader of Beth El Temple in Harrisburg, Pennsylvania, believes that interfaith discussions are very helpful. However, like most Jewish people interested in dialogue, he excludes Jews who believe in Jesus:

> We are fortunate to have developed a climate of openness and dialogue between Jews and Christians in the religious community of the United States. Today, groups like the Jews for Jesus are the single greatest impediment to such open dialogue between communities who respect one another's differences.[21]

Jews for Jesus reject the idea that the dialogue is honest if it will not take seriously Jews who believe in Jesus. The charge that they are an impediment to interfaith dialogue is challenged by the organization. A former staff member wrote:

> Ecumenical dialogue is a waste of time unless the issue of Jesus' messiahship is brought to the surface. It's just one religious body stroking another. That doesn't mean we shouldn't get along and try

to understand each other. I respect the next one's right to believe whatever they want to believe.... But unless the issue of Jesus is brought out, then it's really not true dialogue.... it should be called "ecumenical stroking."[22]

**Q: What is replacement theology and why do Jews for Jesus oppose it?**

**A:** Timothy Weber touched on this theology in a 1998 cover story in *Christianity Today* entitled "How Evangelicals Became Israel's Best Friend."

In the nineteenth century, most British and American evangelicals did not believe in the restoration of the Jews. They believed that God is essentially finished with the Jews as a people. According to this "replacement theology," because Jews had rejected Jesus, God had rejected them and had transferred divine favor to the church. The church has become the New Israel and has received all the Old Israel's promises and prophecies.[23]

Jews for Jesus oppose replacement theology because they believe that God has a continuing plan and purpose for Jewish people as a nation.

**Q: Do Jewish people bear a "terrible responsibility" for "killing Jesus"?**

**A:** Many Christians might view this as a strange question because they have never heard anyone in their churches or religious education classes allude to Jewish guilt. Nevertheless, some contemporary scholars have answered this question in the affirmative, and many Jewish people believe that such statements reflect the belief of many—if not most—Christians. One scholar who made such a remark in a radio address in 1978 was Dr. Harold Ockenga, president of Gordon Conwell Theological Seminary. There was an immediate outcry from Jewish groups in response to his statement that "There is a terrible responsibility that Israel has in the killing of Jesus."[24]

Though Ockenga argued that the newspaper accounts were unfair and that this particular statement was taken out of context, most Christian scholars and lay people would insist there is *no* context within which such a statement is applicable. One of the seminary students interviewed said that she did not regard the news accounts as unfair and that many of the students she had talked with were "upset" and "would not agree with the basic theological stance in the talk."[25]

**Q: Must the church repent for sins of anti-Semitism?**

**A:** Most Christians would agree that people are obligated to repent for those of their own sins and not for those of all of Christendom over the ages. Pastor Don Finto, however, believes this is a necessary step in reconciliation with Jewish people. In a sermon in 1997 he spoke of various endeavors that were aimed at bringing Christians closer together with Jews and Muslims.

> Part of what is happening in the Reconciliation Walk, The Crusader Walk [which retraces the Crusaders' route from Spain and Germany to Jerusalem], is that believers are going into mosques and synagogues through Eastern Europe and the Mideast confessing the sins of former generations.
>
> "Have mercy on us! Forgive our ancestry for the horrible things we did 900 years ago when the Crusaders went across these lands."
>
> Next March a group of us will go to the sites of the Inquisition—Jew and Gentile together, confessing the sins of our generations. Let us encourage Gentile Christians, as individual believers and as churches, to recognize and grieve over the church's sins against Jews. Let us repent for all forms of replacement teaching that treated the first covenant as obsolete and discarded, believing that the church has now taken the place of the Jews.[26]

**Q: Is it appropriate to refer to messianic Jews as "completed" Jews?**

**A:** Stephen Katz, minister at large of Jews for Jesus, recently responded to this question in a conversation with the author:

> If Jewish believers in Jesus want to describe themselves as completed Jews, that's fine. It's certainly their right to do so, but it's not a term I use myself.
>
> It's true that our hope has been fulfilled in Jesus and the prophe-

cies have been fulfilled in Jesus, but the phrase "completed Jew" tends to imply that Jews who don't believe in Jesus are incomplete. While that is true from a faith standpoint, Jews who don't believe in Jesus are no less complete than Gentiles who don't believe in him. I prefer to think of my fellow Jews as complete people who have yet to discover the true hope of the Jewish prophets.

Rabbi Barry Weinstein, a vocal critic of Jews for Jesus, accuses messianic Jews of being deceptive and misleading when they use that term.

It misleads people into thinking that in order to be a "completed Jew" one must accept Jesus. That's simply untrue. Judaism exists and has existed for over 4,000 years as a bona fide, integral authentic religion.[27]

**Q: Is it correct to speak of Jewish people who believe in Jesus as "converted Jews"?**

**A:** Most Jews who believe in Jesus would say no. Mitch Glaser spoke to this issue in an interview in 1982. The fact that he regards himself as a Christian does not mean that he is no longer Jewish, and like most Jewish believers in Jesus, he rejects the term "converted Jew" because it implies a loss of Jewish identity.

I'm indeed a follower of the Messiah. I'm just a Jewish follower of the Messiah. Converting means to change and the only thing I changed from is sin, not from being a Jew.... Being a Jew is just as important to me as being a human being. But following Jesus is the most important thing in my life.[28]

He and his family celebrated Jewish holidays: Passover, Hanukkah, and Yom Kippur. Although many messianic Jews celebrate both Jewish and Christian holidays, the Glaser family does not. "The celebration of Christmas and Easter are not in the Bible and it's not part of my culture, though I can appreciate my Gentile brothers doing so."[29]

**Q: What do you call a Jew who believes in Christ?**

**A:** There are many terms to choose from: Jewish Christian, Christian Jew, messianic Jew, Hebrew Christian, completed Jew, born-again Jew. Some of these labels rub certain people the wrong way. For example, "Jew for Jesus" or "Hebrew Christian" are not acceptable to those who avoid the anglicized name "Jesus Christ" in favor of *Yeshua*. "In fact, some believing Jews avoid using 'Christian' altogether, because the Jewish community traditionally interprets the term as synonymous with 'Gentile,' thus excluding all Jewishness."[30] The label that most irritates the Jewish community is "completed Jew," a term that implies the incompleteness of Judaism as a religion.

> Not surprisingly, the Bible reveals what labels described believers in Jesus in the early church. At that time, Gentile believers were called "Christians" (Acts 11:26). Jewish believers, considered a sect within Judaism, were known as "Nazarenes" (Acts 24:5).[31]

**Q: Should Jews who believe in Jesus behave like other Christians?**

**A:** Most Jewish leaders would insist they should. They should join a regular church and worship like other Christians because to continue with Jewish customs and rituals is deceptive. However, Don Finto, minister of Belmont Church in Nashville, insists that their "Jewish" form of worship is right and natural:

> I recently visited the Dallas, Texas, messianic congregation led by the president of the Union of Messianic Jewish Congregations. We sang Jewish songs, recited the Sh'ma, read from the handwritten Torah scroll (words being read in Jewish synagogues throughout the world). There were prayer shawls and yarmulkes. We met on the Sabbath. These were Jews, worshipping as Jews. Many of them had never been to a church.
>
> Our Gentile customs, if we go back far enough, have their origin in pagan customs. We took the celebration of the Spring Goddess and turned it into Easter. We take the celebration of when the sun starts coming in and when the Norwegians brought in their trees, and we celebrate Jesus' birthday.

The Jewish holidays all have their origin in God. Gentile Christians, for centuries, told Jewish believers who began to believe in Jesus that they needed to give up their Jewishness. Today a group of Jews have arisen who are saying, "We are Jews and we are believers in Yeshua (Jesus)." They do not intend to come to our churches. They do not see themselves as having "converted." They have simply accepted their own Messiah. They circumcise and bar-mitzvah their sons. Many eat kosher. They use God's calendar, not the calendar of the western Gentile Christians.

This is exactly what was happening to the apostle Paul, the Jewish apostle to the Gentiles. He was accused of having forsaken the Torah (Acts 20). To show that he still observed the law (which he saw as fulfilled) he took a vow and went into the temple. Gentiles were not called to observe the law (Acts 15), but Jews never forsook it....

When Israel took Jerusalem again in 1967, something happened in the heavens prophetically. Jews began to come to Messiah. Messianic synagogues began to form around the world. There is now another form of Judaism in our day: Jews who believe in Jesus.[32]

**Q: Are Jews for Jesus the most prominent Jewish Christians?**

**A:** Jews for Jesus may be the largest and most recognized mission agency to the Jews, but many prominent Jewish Christian leaders are also in the public eye. One of the most noted of these is Archbishop Msgr. Jean-Marie Lustiger who heads the Paris See. He was born in Paris, the son of nonreligious Polish-Jews, and was baptized into the Catholic church at age fourteen, despite his parents' disapproval.

Speaking of his heritage, Lustiger wrote that "I always continued to feel Jewish. How can it be otherwise for the son of poor immigrants? I was also reminded of my Jewish belonging by some of my schoolmates to whom I had not tried to hide my Jewishness."[33]

His Jewish roots are indeed strong. His mother died at Auschwitz in 1943. And while many would argue that he cannot believe in Jesus and be a Jew, he insists that his conversion was not a "renunciation but...an affirmation of my

Jewish identity which I assumed within Christianity." He has refused to accept the effort some have made to deny him the very essence of who he is. "I was born a Jew and I shall remain one...even if the rabbis do not agree to this."[34]

**Q: Why is it so difficult for Jewish people to accept the gospel?**

**A:** Perhaps in part it is because Christians of past generations have made it difficult to recognize either Jesus or his teachings as being in any way Jewish. Moishe Rosen responded to this issue by using Leonardo Da Vinci as an illustration, as reported by a California newspaper:

> In Da Vinci's painting of the Last Supper, all but two of Jesus' apostles are portrayed as northern European stereotypes, Rosen claims. Jesus himself is blue-eyed and of light complexion.
>
> Instead of lamb—which Jesus and his apostles would have eaten at the Last Supper, a Passover meal—fish is the main course. To further alienate the Jew, leavened rather than unleavened bread is pictured.
>
> The problem for Jews is Christianity has become "gentilized," or adapted to whatever culture it has been immersed in.
>
> "I'm just using this as an illustration. I could give you a thousand illustrations," he asserts. "The Jewishness of Jesus and the Jewishness of the New Testament was obscured. The way that Christians were presenting Christ to the Jews, the Jews couldn't see him as Israel's Messiah."[35]

**Q: Why do Jews for Jesus use a forceful style of evangelizing? Is it biblical? Is it necessary?**

**A:** Avi Snyder, who has served with Jews for Jesus in Los Angeles and the former Soviet Union, responds:

> Whether in America or in the former U.S.S.R., most of us would much rather temper our beliefs and accommodate our action in order to avoid the unpleasant result of incurring disfavor. Yet the

gospel leaves little room for navigating on the sea of accommodation. Either Jesus is the Messiah or He is not. Either the gospel is true or it is a lie. Either the tomb was empty or it was not. Both points of view cannot be correct.

And if Y'shua is not the Messiah, then no one should believe in Him or follow Him. If He was merely a man, then to worship Him in the manner He requires amounts to an act of idolatry for both Jews and Gentiles.

But if Y'shua is the Messiah, then we all must believe and obey. Y'shua said to those who would rather not choose, "He who is not with Me is against Me, and he who does not gather with Me scatters" (Luke 11:23).[36]

Steve Cohen, who served as the Canadian director of Jews for Jesus in the late 1980s, responded to similar questions in a magazine editorial:

Our evangelism methods are patterned after the prophets. They called out to an Israel that wasn't listening to God. Most Jewish people still are not listening. We aim to capture the people's attention and proclaim that Y'shua...is the promised Messiah of Israel!

Most people we meet are spiritually indifferent. Some choose to take offense to the message; but...we reach out to many that a few might be won.[37]

**Q: Is there one standard Jewish response to Jews for Jesus?**

**A:** No, there is not. The most publicized responses (whether by Jewish community leaders or countermissionary groups like Jews for Judaism) do not account for all the thoughts or feelings of every individual within the Jewish community. A significant minority of Jewish people want to hear the message of Jews for Jesus, either because they are already interested in Jesus, or because they are spiritually seeking and unwilling to discount anything without investigating it for themselves. But those who oppose Jews for Jesus are not necessarily united in their response, either. While some feel duty-bound to fight what they view as the missionary threat, this response has its critics, including Rabbi Chaim Seidler-Feller: "It's not that Jews for Jesus needs to be combatted. Jews for Nothing needs to be combatted. We want to make them irrelevant; we don't want to fight them because they thrive on publicity of a fight."[38]

# NOTES

INTRODUCTION

1. Moishe Rosen with William Proctor, *Jews for Jesus* (Old Tappan, N.J.: Revell, 1974), 36–7.

2. A. W. Tozer, *Wingspread: A. B. Simpson: A Study in Spiritual Altitude* (Harrisburg: Christian Publications, 1943), 71.

3. Ann Landers, *San Francisco Examiner,* 1 January 1984.

CHAPTER 1

1. Catherine Damato, "The Man Behind the Jews for Jesus," *Power for Living,* 2 September 1979, 2.

2. Ibid.

3. "A Message from Squares," unpublished tract, Moishe Rosen papers, n.d.

4. Moishe Rosen, interview with author.

5. Ceil Rosen, "It Started with a Song…" in *Testimonies of Jews Who Believe in Jesus,* edited by Ruth Rosen (San Francisco: Purple Pomegranate Productions, 1987), 3.

6. Ibid., 4.

7. Ibid., 5.

8. Ibid.

9. Ibid., 7.

10. Ibid., 8.

11. Ibid., 11.

12. Moishe Rosen with William Proctor, *Jews for Jesus* (Old Tappan, N.J.: Revell, 1974), 27–8.

13. Ibid., 42.

14. Ibid., 43.

15. Ibid., 45.

16. Ibid., 45–6.

17. Ibid., 48.

18. Ibid., 55–8.

19. Ibid., 63.

20. Moishe Rosen, interview with author.

21.Robert T. Coote, "How Kosher Can Christianity Get?" *Eternity,* September 1975, 25.

22.Gary Clayton, "The Jews, Jesus and 'Jewishness,'" *Prophecy Today,* July/August 1995, 30.

23.Ibid.

24.William Willoughby, "Moishe Rosen Stays in the Spotlight," *Washington Times,* 5 August 1983.

25."Jews for Jesus Founder Due," *Argus* 18 (28 January 1988).

26.Alexandra J. Wall, "Jews Who Choose the Pews," *New Voices,* September/October 1994, 10.

27.Wanda Adams, "A Dichotomy of Faith?" *Everett Washington Herald,* 27 March 1982, 9A.

28.*Jews For Jesus Newsletter* 8:5757 ( June 1997): 3.

29.Ibid., 2.

30.Ibid.

31.Ibid.

CHAPTER 2

1.John G. Taylor, "Jews for Jesus Founder," *Houston Post,* 29 October 1994.

2.Ben Witherington, III, *The Jesus Quest: The Third Search for the Jew of Nazareth* (Downers Grove, Ill.: InterVarsity Press, 1997), 16.

3.Ibid., 40.

4.Jacob Gartenhaus, *Famous Hebrew Christians* (Chattanooga: International Board of Jewish Missions, 1979), 21.

5.James G. D. Dunn, "The First Christians," *U.S. News & World Report,* 20 April 1992, 61–2.

6.Hugh J. Schonfield, *The History of Jewish Christianity* (London: Duckworth, 1936), 23.

7.N. T. Wright, *What Saint Paul Really Said* (Grand Rapids: Eerdmans, 1997), 34–5.

8.Ibid., 37.

9.Schonfield, 27–8.

10.Ibid., 28.

11.Robert T. Coote, "How Kosher Can Christianity Get?" *Eternity,* September 1975, 17.

12.Dunn, 70.

13.Quoted in Schonfield, 25.

14. John Foxe, *Foxe's Christian Martyrs of the World* (Chicago: Moody Press, 1990), 51.

15. Quoted in Gartenhaus, 22.

16. F. F. Bruce, *The Spreading Flame* (Grand Rapids: Eerdmans, 1979), 263–4.

17. Philip Yancey, *The Jesus I Never Knew* (Grand Rapids: Zondervan, 1995), 50.

18. Rabbi Larry Gevirtz, *The New Style Missionaries,* Cheshvan/Kislev, October/November 1982, 10.

19. John G. Gager, *The Origins of Anti-Semitism: Attitudes toward Judaism in Pagan and Christian Antiquity* (New York: Oxford University Press, 1983), 8–9.

20. Ibid.

21. Ibid., 118–20.

22. Ibid., 133.

23. Jean-Marc Heimerdinger, "Advertising Jesus the Jew," *Third Way,* October 1993, 26.

24. Schonfield, 98.

25. Ibid., 100.

26. Ibid.

27. Ibid., 107.

28. V. Raymond Edman, *The Light in Dark Ages* (Wheaton: Van Kampan Press, 1949), 267–8.

29. Philip Schaff, *History of the Christian Church,* V (Grand Rapids: Eerdmans, 1979), 94–5.

30. Quoted in Schonfield, 155–6.

31. Edman, 270.

32. Ibid.

33. Ibid., 274.

34. Schonfield, 175–6.

35. Ibid., 168.

36. Bruce A. Demarest, "Interpreting the Bible," in *Eerdmans' Handbook to the History of Christianity,* edited by Tim Dowley (Grand Rapids: Eerdmans, 1977), 286.

37. Roland H. Bainton, *Here I Stand: A Life of Martin Luther* (New York: Mentor Books, 1963), 297.

38. Ibid.

39. Eric W. Gritsch, "Was Luther Anti-Semitic?" *Christian History* 39 (n.d.): 38.

40. Ibid.

41. Wanda Adams, "A Dichotomy of Faith?" *Everett Washington Herald,* 27 March 1982, 9A.

42. Schonfield, 17–8.

CHAPTER 3

1. Jacob Gartenhaus, *Famous Hebrew Christians* (Chattanooga: International Board of Jewish Missions, 1979), 23.

2. A. E. Thompson, *A Century of Jewish Missions* (New York: Fleming H. Revell, 1902), 46.

3. Ibid.

4. Ruth Mason, "When Jews Convert," *Reform Judaism,* Fall 1991, 5.

5. Thompson, 47.

6. Ibid., 27.

7. Rabbi Larry Gevirtz, *The New Style Missionaries,* Cheshvan/Kislev, October/November 1982, 11.

8. Hillel Halkin, "Unraveling the Mystery of a Proud Christian's Jewishness," *Forward,* 20 December 1996, n.p.

9. Ibid.

10. Quoted in Gartenhaus, 73.

11. Ibid., 30.

12. Ibid., 33.

13. Ibid., 34.

14. Ibid.

15. Ibid., 35.

16. Ibid., 22.

17. Ibid., 135–6.

18. Ibid., 136.

19. Ibid., 138.

20. August Neander, *General History of the Christian Religion and Church* (Boston: Crocker & Brewster, 1850), 171.

21. Gartenhaus, 141.

22. Kai Kjaer-Hansen, *Joseph Rabinowitz and the Messianic Movement* (Grand Rapids: Eerdmans, 1995), 19.

23. Gartenhaus, 150.

24. Quoted in Kjaer-Hansen, 2–3.

25. Ibid.

CHAPTER 4

1. James Hefley, "Everyone's Talking about Those Jewish Christians," *Moody Monthly*, May 1973, 27.

2. Efraim Goldstein, interview with author.

3. Doug LeBlanc, "2 Views of Jews for Jesus," *Morning Advocate*, 4 May 1985, 12A.

4. Ibid., 68.

5. Moishe Rosen with William Proctor, *Jews for Jesus* (Old Tappan, N.J.: Revell, 1974), 77.

6. Moishe Rosen, "Letters," *Logas Journal*, May–June 1974, n.p.

7. Rosen and Proctor, 77.

8. Ibid., 78.

9. Ibid., 80.

10. Moishe Rosen, interview with author.

11. Ibid.

12. Ibid.

13. Ibid.

14. William Willoughby, "Moishe Rosen Stays in the Spotlight," *Washington Times*, 5 August 1983.

15. Shamai Kanter, "They're Playing Our Song," *Moment*, March 1984, n.p.

16. Ibid.

17. Ibid.

18. Ibid.

19. Karen Bossick, "Jew for Jesus," *Idaho Statesman*, 12 November 1983, 1.

20. Sue Perlman, "I Love You, Is That OK?" *Good News Broadcaster*, March 1977.

21. Lyn Rosen Bond, interview with author.

22. Juliene G. Lipson, *Jews for Jesus: An Anthropological Study* (San Franciso: University of California, 1990).

CHAPTER 5

1. Stanley N. Rosenbaum, "Jews for Jesus: Causes and Treatments," *Midstream*, December 1985, 11–2.

2. Sue Perlman, "Furor Over Jewish Evangelism," *Eternity*, April 1973.

3. Ibid.

4. Ibid.

5. Carl F. H. Henry, *Christianity Today*, March, 1973, 28.

6. Ibid.

7. Gary Rosenblatt, "Are 'Jews for Jesus' Coming to Baltimore?" *Baltimore Jewish Times,* 16 May 1980, n.p.

8. Roseann Nicodemo, "Jews for Jesus Incite Caf Riot," *Phoenix,* 13 October 1980, 1.

9. Dave Palermo, "Jews for Jesus Are Latest Target of Attacks by Anti-Semitic Vandals," Los Angeles *Herald Examiner,* 14 January 1981, n.p.

10. Quoted in Juliene G. Lipson, *Jews for Jesus: An Anthropological Study* (San Franciso: University of California, 1990), 73.

11. Moishe Rosen, interview with author.

12. "Looking Backward and Forward," *Jews for Jesus Newsletter* 2:5744 (1983).

13. Ted Ojarovsky, "Good News for Modern Jews," *Charisma,* September 1986, n.p.

14. Ibid.

15. Ibid.

16. Jan Hoffman, "Inside Jews for Jesus," New York, 29 April 1986, 47.

17. Elie Wiesel, "The Missionary Menace," in *Smashing the Idols,* edited by Gary D. Eisenberg (Northvale, N.J.: Jason Aronson, 1988), 161–3.

18. Ruth Mason, "When Jews Convert," *Reform Judaism,* Fall 1991, 5.

19. Ibid.

20. Ibid., 6.

21. Moise Rosen, interview with author.

22. Arlene G. Peck, "Jews for Jesus Ride Again," *Jewish Post and Opinion,* 25 April 1980, n.p.

23. Alan Edelstein, "Jews Who Choose," *Moment,* August 1994, 38.

24. George G. Higgins, "Proselytizing Condemned," *The Tidings,* 25 December 1987, 7.

25. Ibid.

26. Akiva Powers, "Jews Are United in Not Allowing Others to Define Who Is Jewish," *Patriot News,* 22 January 1988, n.p.

27. Walter Riggans, "Messianic Judaism: A Case of Identity Denied," *International Bulletin of Missionary Research,* July 1992, 130.

28. Ibid.

29. Moishe Rosen, "Rabbis Avoid the Real Issue over the Messiah," *Patriot News,* 22 January 1988, n.p.

CHAPTER 6

1. Philip Messing, "Crowd Sees Woman's Kidnap Terror," *New York Post,* 26 January 1983, n.p.; "Abducted N.Y.C. Woman Found in Palisades Park," *Record,* 26 January 1983, n.p.

2. Ken Levitt with Ceil Rosen, *Kidnapped for My Faith* (Van Nuys: Bible Voice, 1978), 59.

3. Ibid., 12.

4. Ellen Kamentsky, *Hawking God: A Young Jewish Woman's Ordeal in Jews for Jesus* (Medford, MA: Sapphire Press, 1992), 1–3.

5. Levitt, 14.

6. Ibid., 17–18.

7. Kamentsky, 27.

8. Ibid., 31.

9. Ibid., 58, 61–2.

10. Ibid., 92.

11. Randy Frame, "And Now—Deprogramming of Christians Is Taking Place," *Christianity Today,* 22 April 1983, n.p.

CHAPTER 7

1. "The Fred Wertheim Story," *ISSUES* 3: 1–2.

2. *Testimonies of Jews Who Believe in Jesus,* edited by Ruth Rosen (San Francisco: Purple Pomegranate Productions, 1987), 244.

3. "I Escaped From Hitler Twice," *ISSUES* 3: 1–2.

4. Ibid., 2–3.

5. Rosen, ed., 247.

6. Ibid., 249.

7. Ibid., 250.

8. Ibid., 250–1.

9. Ibid., 251.

10. John G. Taylor, "Jews for Jesus Founder," *Houston Post,* 29 October 1994, n.p.

CHAPTER 8

1. *Charisma,* October 1994, n.p.

2. William F. Willoughby, "Moishe Rosen Stays in the Spotlight," *Washington Times,* 5 August 1983, n.p.

3. "How to Use Broadsides," unpublished paper, Jews for Jesus, 1.

4. "How to Write a Broadside," unpublished paper, Jews for Jesus, 2.

5. Avi Synder, unpublished broadside, Jews for Jesus.

6. "How to Use Broadsides," 3–4.

7. Janice Gosnell Franzen, "All in a Woman's Day," *Christian Life,* July 1983, n.p.

8. Marjorie Hyer, "God and Mary Hartman," *Washington Post,* 17 April 1976, B3.

9. Adon Taft, "He Is Pen to Questions on 'Mary Hartman' Spoof," *Miami Herald,* 5 June 1976, 7B.

10. Hyer, B3.

11. *UCLA Daily Bruin,* 13 May 1976, 8.

12. Wesley Jackson, "Will Pac-Man vs. Jews for Jesus Be the Legal Battle of the Century?" *Times Picayune,* 17 July 1982, n.p.

13. "Griffin Suing Jews for Jesus," *Beacon Journal,* August 22, 1987, n.p.

14. Ibid.

15. Judith S. Antonelli, "Jews for Jesus Uses Bart Simpson in Its Pamphlets," *Jewish Advocate,* 1 March 1991; Garth Wolkoff, "Bart Simpson Is Converted," *Northern California Jewish Bulletin,* 13 September 1991, 4.

16. John MacDonald, "The New 'Broadside' Witness," *Eternity,* April 1973, 42.

17. Jay Alan Sekulow, "My Mother and MasterCard," *Jews for Jesus Newsletter* 8:5747 (1987): 5–6.

18. Moise Rosen, interview with author.

19. Faye Flore, "Jews for Jesus Wins Right to Hand out Tracts," *News Pilot,* 27 March 1986, n.p.

20. Ed Meza, "Jews for Jesus Charge Civil Rights Violations," *Pierce College Roundup,* 30 November 1988, n.p.

21. Al Martinez, "A Campus Mix of Jews, Jesus and Cows," *Los Angeles Times,* 18 December 1988, n.p.

CHAPTER 9

1. Joel Clemons, "Spreading the Gospel with Jews for Jesus," *Peninsula Times Tribune,* 5 November 1979, n.p.

2. Ibid.

3. William F. Willoughby, "Moishe Rosen Stays in the Spotlight," *Washington Times,* 5 August 1983, n.p.

4. Moishe Rosen with William Proctor, *Jews for Jesus* (Old Tappan, N.J.: Revell, 1974), 36–7.

5. Moishe Rosen, interview with author.

6. Unpublished Jews for Jesus training lecture.

7. Juliene G. Lipson, *Jews for Jesus: An Anthropological Study* (San Franciso: University of California, 1990).

8. Ruth Rosen, interview with author.

9. Lipson, 158–9.

10. "The Kosher Revolution," *Christianity Today,* 5 October 1979, 57.

11. "Jews for Jesus Group Revises Mission Effort," *Baton Rouge State-Times,* 8 September 1979, n.p.

12. Moishe Rosen, "More Thoughts on Deputation," *Eternity,* December 1979, n.p.

13. Moise Rosen, interview with author.

14. David Brickner, interview with author.

15. Moishe Rosen, "Christ in the Passover Presentation," unpublished paper, Moishe Rosen papers, n.d.

16. Jacqueline Swartz, "Jews for Jesus Crusaders Sport Jewish Symbols," *Now,* 28 May–3 June 1992, n.p.

CHAPTER 10

1. Moishe Rosen, "Jews for Jesus as Community," unpublished lecture, Moishe Rosen papers, n.d., passim.

2. Ibid., 32–3.

3. Moishe Rosen, "Etiquette," unpublished lecture, Moishe Rosen papers, n.d.

4. Ibid., 7–9.

5. Ibid., 18–20.

6. Ibid., 10–1.

7. Moishe Rosen, "Standards," unpublished lecture, Moishe Rosen papers, n.d., 15.

8. Rosen, "Etiquette," 13, 15, 25.

9. Moishe Rosen, "A List of Things That Moishe Rosen Will Say Over and Over Again," unpublished paper, n.d., 1.

CHAPTER 11

1. "Operation Birthday Cake," *Covenant Companion,* September 1976.

2. Hesh Morgan, "'Operation Birthday Cake' Mass Conversion Attempt," *Jewish Press,* 18 June 1976, 2.

3. Ibid.

4. Ibid.

5. Susan Perlman, "Witnessing Brings Trials to 'Jews for Jesus,'" *Lutheran Standard*, 7 September 1976, 23.

6. Ibid.

7. Susan Perlman, "Furor Over Jewish Evangelism," *Eternity* (April 1978), 21

8. Ibid., 20, 23.

9. Ibid.

10. Ibid., 20.

11. Joe Murchison, "Messianic Jews Lead Quiet Existence in Richmond Area," *Richmond News Leader,* 15 January 1983, n.p.

12. "Over 12,000 Respond to Jews for Jesus Ad Campaign," *Christian Courier,* June 1984, 4.

13. Steven Lawson, "Jews for Jesus Conduct National Campaign," *Charisma,* March 1985, 106.

14. "Leaders Slam 'Jews for Jesus,'" *Sunday Times,* 16 September 1984, n.p.

15. "Trouble Breaks Out at 'Jews for Jesus' Do," *The Citizen,* 12 September 1984, 12.

16. Don Albert, "Controversial, but Precise and to the Point," *The Star Tonight,* 13 September 1984, 7.

17. "Leaders Slam...."

18. Joel Kleinbaum, "Testimony," *Jews for Jesus Newsletter* 6:5742 (1982): n.p.

19. Ibid.

20. *Times of London,* 27 January 1992.

21. Sue Perlman, "I Love You, Is That OK?" *Good News Broadcaster,* March 1977.

22. *Jews for Jesus Newsletter* 2:5758, November 1997, n.p.

23. Steffi Geiser, "Music on Kibbutz Kfar Blum," *Jews for Jesus Newsletter* 9: 5735 (1975): n.p.

24. Michele Chabin, "True Believers?" *Jewish Week,* 20 October 1995, 26.

25. Ibid., 25.

26. Ibid.

27. Gary Clayton, "The Jews, Jesus and 'Jewishness,'" *Prophecy Today,* July/August 1995, 29.

28. Don Lattin, "Retiring Jews for Jesus Leader Nurtures a Growing Faith," *San Francisco Chronicle,* 15 June 1996, A15.

29. "250,000 Jews Now Are Jews for Jesus," *Post & Opinion,* 28 May 1997, n.p.

30. "Jews, Jesus and Jews for Jesus," ministry pamphlet, 10–11.

CHAPTER 12

1. David Rorden, "What's a Nice Jewish Boy Like Him Doing among Christians?" *Journal American,* 31 July 1982, n.p.

2. Ibid.

3. Judith S. Antonelli, "Jews for Jesus Uses Bart Simpson in Its Pamphlets," *Jewish Advocate,* 1 March 1991.

4. Ibid.

5. Ibid.

6. Avi Snyder, "From the Pacific Ocean to the Black Sea," unpublished manuscript, 1.

7. Ibid.

8. Ibid., 2.

9. Ibid., 3.

10. Ibid.

11. Avi Snyder, "A Passover in Russia," *Jews for Jesus Newsletter* 6:5757 (April 1997): n.p.

12. Avi Snyder, "To Remember, to Return," prayer letter, Fall 1991, 3.

13. Ibid.

14. Gary Clayton, "Home and Away," *Prophecy Today,* 1 October 1992, 2–3.

15. Rachel Katz, "Bringing Jews to Jesus in Russia," *Moment,* February 1997, 48.

16. Vera Kuschnir, *Only One Life: Biography of Leon Rosenberg* (Broken Arrow, Okla.: Slavic Christian Publishing, 1996), 187.

17. Ibid., 188, 202.

18. Ibid., passim.

19. Avi Snyder, interview with author.

20. Avi Snyder, "Jesus Loves Felix Melstein," *Jews for Jesus Newsletter* 6:5756 (March 1996): n.p.

21. Avi Snyder, interview with author.

22. Avi Snyder to Ruth A. Tucker, 16 July 1997.

CHAPTER 13

1. *Jews for Jesus Newsletter* 8:5745 (1985): n.p.

2. *Jews for Jesus Journal,* 2 (1995).

3. Jan Hoffman, "Inside Jews for Jesus," *New York,* 28 April 1986, 43–4.

CHAPTER 14

1. Quoted in Janice Gosnell Franzen, "All in a Woman's Day," *Christian Life,* July 1983, n.p.

2. Juliene G. Lipson, *Jews for Jesus: An Anthropological Study* (San Franciso: University of California, 1990), 96.

3. Quoted in Lipson.

4. Phyllis Hyman, "One Member: Being a Hebrew Christian Isn't Easy," *West County Journal,* 4 September 1987, 8A.

5. Ibid.

6. Susan Perlman, interview with author.

7. Moishe Rosen, interview with author.

8. Ibid.

9. Alexandra J. Wall, "Jews Who Choose the Pews," *New Voices,* September/October 1994, 10.

10. Mark MacNamera, "Evangelical Newcomer's Star Is Rising," *Marin Independent Journal,* 18 January 1987, A6.

11. Ibid.

12. Franzen.

13. Ibid.

14. Moishe Rosen with William Proctor, *Jews for Jesus* (Old Tappan, N.J.: Revell, 1974), 68.

15. Ibid., 71.

16. Ibid.

17. Neil Steinberg, "Jews for Jesus Say They Can Have It Both Ways," *Chicago Sun Times,* 8 August 1994, 13.

18. "A Testimony: Tuvya Zaretsky," *Jews for Jesus Newsletter* (1995): 8.

19. Ibid.

20. Ibid.

21. Tuvya Zaretsky, interview with author.

22. Ibid.

23. Ibid.

24. Tuvya Zaretsky, "You Never Know," *Jews for Jesus Newsletter* Classic Edition (1995): 8.

25. Tracy O'Shaughnessy, "A Foot in Two Faiths," *Potomac Almanac,* 9 October 1991, 11.

26. Ibid., 12.

27.Sharon Labi, "Meeting with Archbishop over Jews for Jesus," *Australian Jewish News,* 23 October 1998, n.p.

28.Ibid.

CHAPTER 15

1. David Brickner, *Mishpochah Matters: Speaking Frankly to God's Family* (San Francisco: Purple Pomegranate Productions, 1996), 35–8.

2. Robert J. Hutchinson, "What the Rabbi Taught Me about Jesus," *Christianity Today,* 13 September 1993, 28.

3. Ibid., 29.

4. Lyle Murphy, "Questions and Answers about Jews for Jesus," *Voice,* September/October 1977, n.p.

5. Ibid.

6. Wes French, "Work 'Touchy' for Jew for Jesus," *Rocky Mountain News,* 29 October 1982, n.p.

7. Elisabeth Hill, "A Woman's Place...", *ISSUES* 5: 3, 8.

8. Moishe Rosen, "Jewish Missions Then and Now," *Jews for Jesus Newsletter* 11:5758 (1998): 7.

9. Moishe Rosen with William Proctor, *Jews for Jesus* (Old Tappan, N.J.: Revell, 1974), 121.

10. Ted Ojarovsky, "Good News for Modern Jews," *Charisma,* September 1986, n.p.

11. French.

12.Alan M. Shore, "Is the Religious Right Good or Bad for the Jews?" *ISSUES* 11: 9, 2–3.

13.Susan Perlman, "So Where Do I Stand?" *ISSUES* 11: 9, 4–5.

14.David Brickner, "Jews for Jesus Core Values," *Jews for Jesus Newsletter* 6:5759 (1999): 1–2.

CHAPTER 16

1. David Brickner, "Our Jews for Jesus Destiny," *Jews for Jesus Journal* 3 (1997): 4.

2. Marcia Ford, "Jews for Jesus Appoints New Leader," *Charisma,* August 1996, 14.

3. Ibid.

4. Ibid., 14.

5. Brickner, 4.

6. Olive Deane Finestone, *The Romantic Career of a Twice-Born Jewess* (St. Petersburg, Fla.: Fred Kendal, n.d.), 23.

7. Ibid., 27–30.

8. Ibid., 30–42.

9. Ibid., 43.

10. Ibid., 44–5.

11. Ibid., 58.

12. Ibid., 62.

13. Ibid., 74–5.

14. "Jews for Jesus Chooses Successor to Rosen," *Southern California Christian Times* (Orange County), June 1996.

15. Karen Bossick, "Jews for Jesus," *Idaho Statesman,* 12 November 1983, 1.

16. David Brickner, *Mishpochah Matters: Speaking Frankly to God's Family* (San Francisco: Purple Pomegranate Productions, 1996), 157–8.

17. Ibid.

EPILOGUE

1. Craig Horowitz, "Are American Jews Disappearing?" *New York,* 14 July 1997, 33.

2. Avi Snyder, interview with author.

3. Moishe Rosen, interview with author.

4. Moishe Rosen, "Still on the Cutting Edge," *Jews for Jesus Newsletter* 8:5757 (June 1997): 1.

5. Ibid., 2.

6 Moishe Rosen, interview with author.

APPENDIX B

1. Michael McAteer, "A Missionary Jews for Jesus Out to Change Its Hard Image," *Toronto Star,* 6 August 1988, M10.

2. Neil Altman, "Jesus: The Hottest Issue in Judaism," *Philadelphia Tribune Review,* 25 December 1995, n.p.

3. Loyd Gaston, quoted in Altman, n.p.

4. Altman, n.p.

5. Quoted in Rabbi Stephen Fuchs, "Should Christians Convert Jews?" *Nashville Scene* (June 12, 1997), 33.

6. Rabbi Dov Aharoni, "Who Is a Jew?" *The Jewish Journal,* 25 November 1988, n.p.

7. Rabbi BenTzion Kravitz, "The Threat of the 'Jews for Jesus,'" *The Jewish Journal,* 18–26 December 1987, 15.

8. Lawrence H. Schiffman, "Hebrew Christians and the Jewish Community," *Jewish Tribune,* 23–29 June 1995, 2.

9. Robert J. Hutchinson, "What the Rabbi Taught Me about Jesus," *Christianity Today,* 13 September 1993, 28–29.

10. Ibid.

11. Fuchs, 36.

12. Ibid., 35.

13. Ibid.

14. Ibid., 33.

15. Altman, n.p.

16. Michele Chabin, "True Believers?" *Jewish Week,* 20 October 1995, 24.

17. Fuchs, 35.

18. Ibid.

19. George W. Cornell, "Ouster of Baptist Liaison Opens Old Wound," *Roanoke Times & World News,* 26 March 1988, n.p.

20. Fred Klett, "Consultation for Jewish Evangelism," *Messianic Jewish Center,* June 1988, n.p.

21. Mark B. Greenspan, "Jews for Jesus Put on Media Blitz," *Patriot News,* 18 December 1987, 8.

22. Doug LeBlanc, "2 Views of Jews for Jesus," *Morning Advocate,* 4 May 1985, 12A.

23. Timothy Weber, "How Evangelicals Became Israel's Best Friend," *Christianity Today,* 5 October 1998, 41.

24. Harold Okenga, "Seminary Officials Say Remarks Not Anti-Semitic," *Beverly Times,* 3 May 1978, n.p.

25. Ibid.

26. Don Finto, "The Rise of Messianic Judaism," *Nashville Scene,* 12 June 1997, 32.

27. LeBlanc.

28. Mitch Glaser, interview with author.

29. Doug Hoagland, "'Nice Jewish Boy' and Jesus," *Fresno Bee,* 27 March 1982, n.p.

30. Ted Ojarovsky, "What Do You Call a Jew Who Believes?" *Charisma,* September 1986, n.p.

31. Ibid.

32. Finto, 32.

33. Edwin Eytan, "Jewish-born Archbishop Still Considers Himself a Jew," *Sentinel,* 12 February 1981, n.p.

34. Ibid.

35. Alvaro Delgado, "Jews for Jesus Leader Unruffled by Controversy," *West County Times,* 18 September 1981, 4C.

36. Avi Snyder, "Impasses and Absolutes," *Jews for Jesus Newsletter* 10:5753 (1993): 5.

37. Steve Cohen, "Boldness in the '80s—Jews for Jesus," *Pentecostal Testimony,* November 1987, n.p.

38. Alexandra J. Wall, "Jews Who Choose the Pews," *New Voices,* September/October 1994, 23.

# INDEX